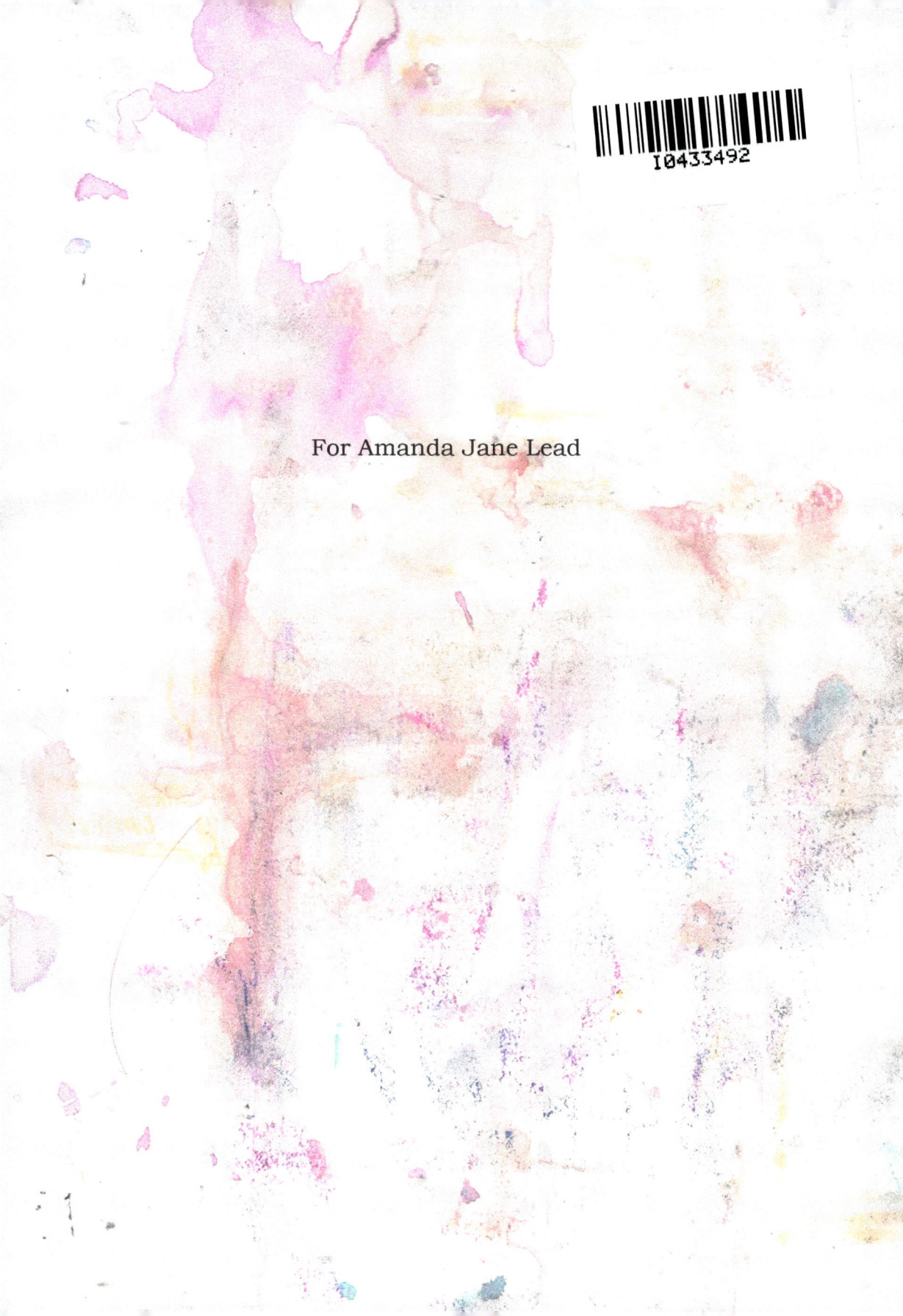

For Amanda Jane Lead

Aleister Crowley: Art Of The Waste ™ & © 2021 RH Stewart & Markosia Enterprises, Ltd. All Rights Reserved. Reproduction of any part of this work by any means without the written permission of the publisher is expressly forbidden. All names, characters and events in this publication are entirely fictional. Any resemblance to actual persons, living or dead is purely coincidental. Published by Markosia Enterprises, PO BOX 3477, Barnet, Hertfordshire, EN5 9HN. FIRST PRINTING, August 2021. Harry Markos, Director.

ISBN 978-1-914926-14-3

www.markosia.com

ALEISTER CROWLEY
ART OF THE WASTE

RHSTEWART

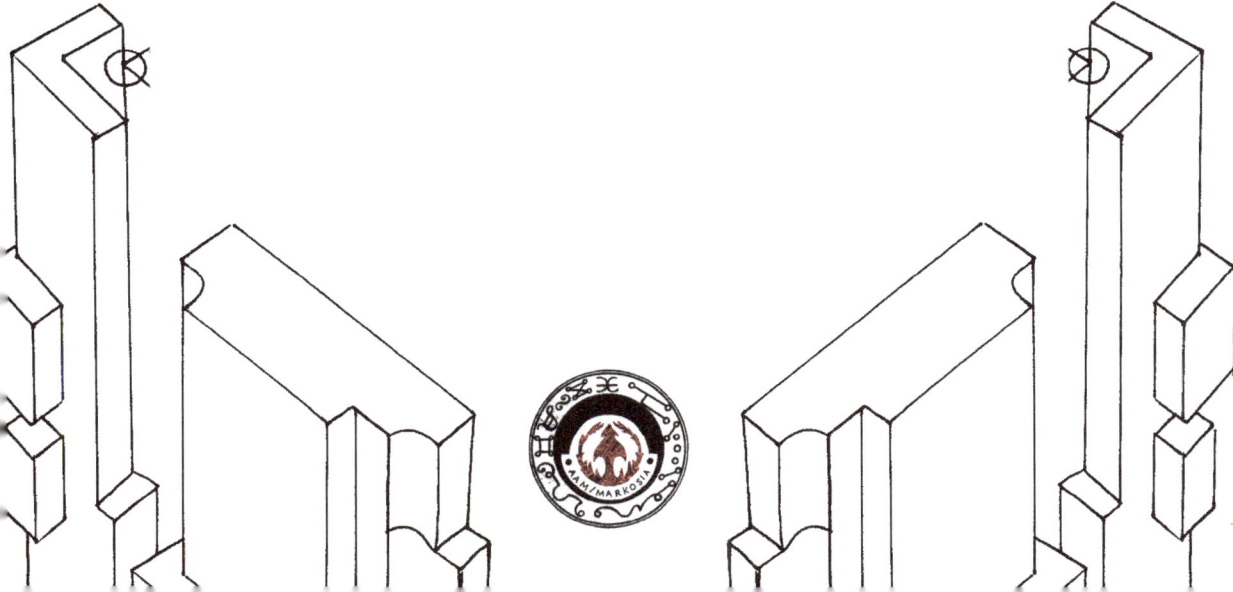

FOR **MARKOSIA ENTERPRISES** LTD

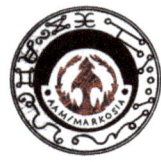

HARRY MARKOS
PUBLISHER & MANAGING PARTNER

GM JORDAN
SPECIAL PROJECTS CO-ORDINATOR

ANNIKA EADE
MEDIA MANAGER

ANDY BRIGGS
CREATIVE CONSULTANT

MEIRION JONES
MARKETING DIRECTOR

IAN SHARMAN
EDITOR IN CHIEF

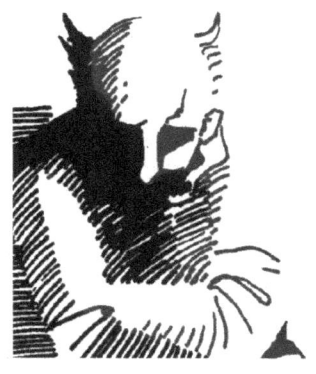

FOREWORD

I've just been checking back through my emails for the first contact between Roy and myself concerning the comic that would go on to become *Aleister Crowley: Wandering the Waste,* and I'm really quite appalled to find that said email was sent in the second half of 2009.

Christ almighty, where do all those years and months and moments go? The world is much changed as I write this, and our bodies further decayed, but what has not changed or decayed is the respect and admiration which I have for Roy's art. His art and, indeed, his artistic process.

For Roy immerses himself fully in the subject at hand. How else to explain the depth of feeling which his lines and textures convey? You don't just see it, you *feel* it. When Crowley cries as a child you can feel the intense loneliness and confusion eating away at the boy, and when he cries as an old man you can feel the abject waste of it all.

Here in this art book you will see Roy's Crowley work with fresh eyes. Small panels have been blown up to full-page size to show their detail, other pages are presented without their lettering layer, to allow the audience to soak in the skilfully executed line and collage work. Every image has some new detail which I'd missed in the original comic.

I was very fortunate to work with Roy on our Crowley comic, and I still greatly admire the varied styles and processes which he brought to his depictions of Crowley's world; the ice-encrusted Himalayas, the stilted Victorian households, the angels and gods and demons, even the observable manifestation of the universe itself. But above all those things, I admire his ability to covey the immense and overwhelming power of simple humanity. A baby wailing. An old man sobbing. And everything inbetween.

Martin Hayes
Locked down in Arklow, 2021

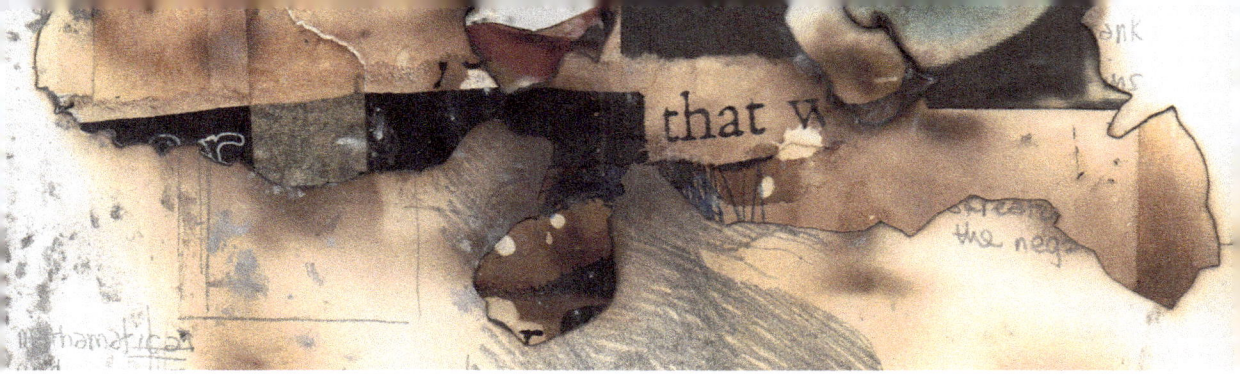

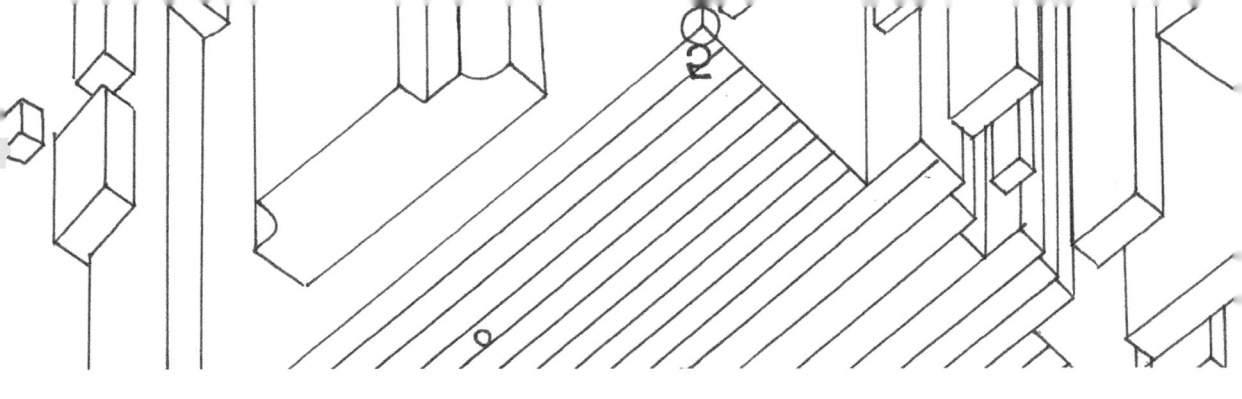

"Enough…the angels say enough…only three days left."
Lisa Smart, Words at the threshold.

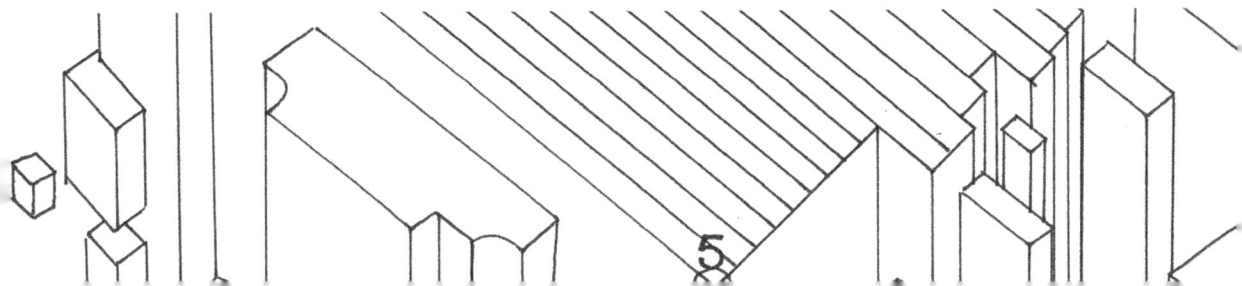

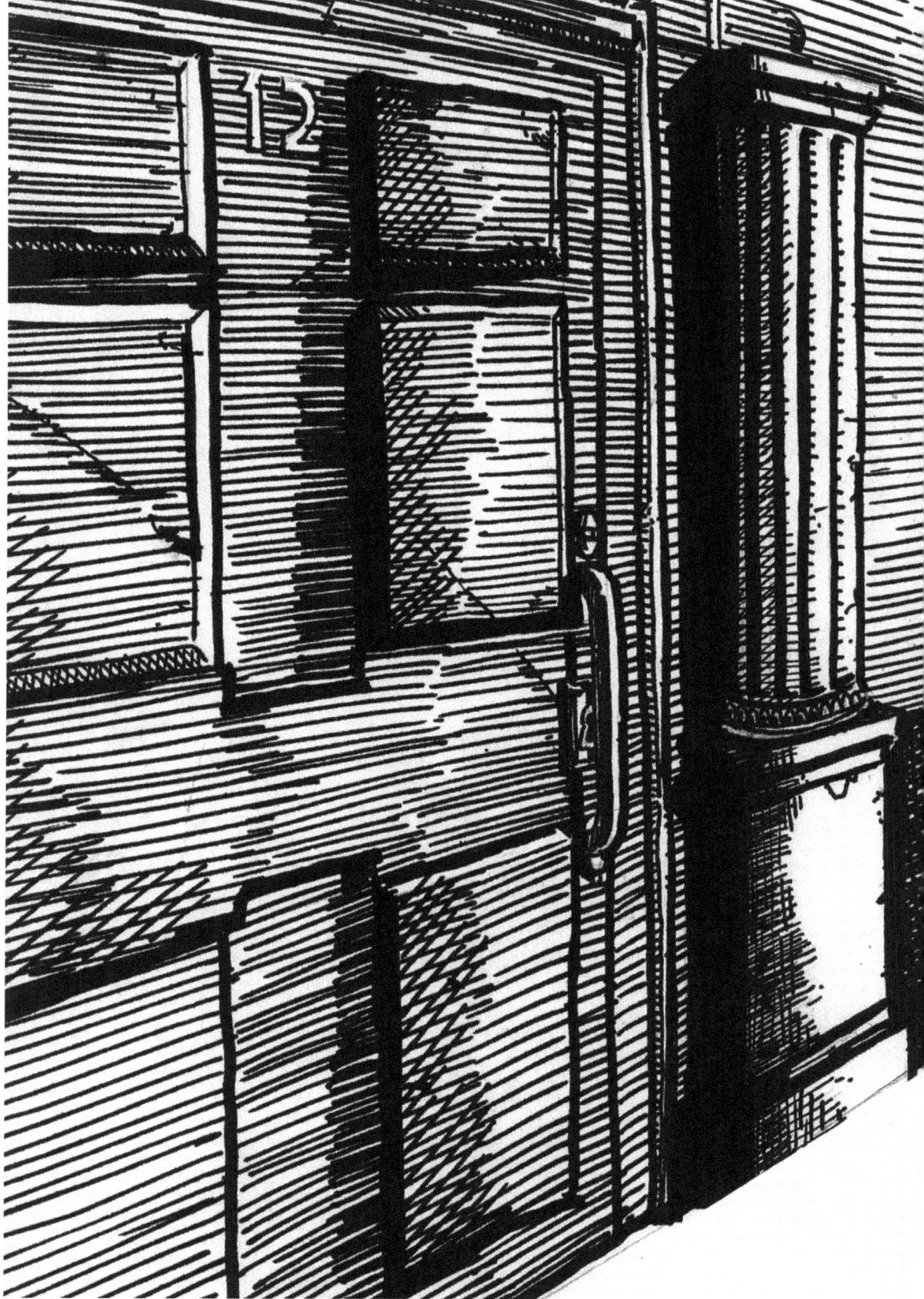

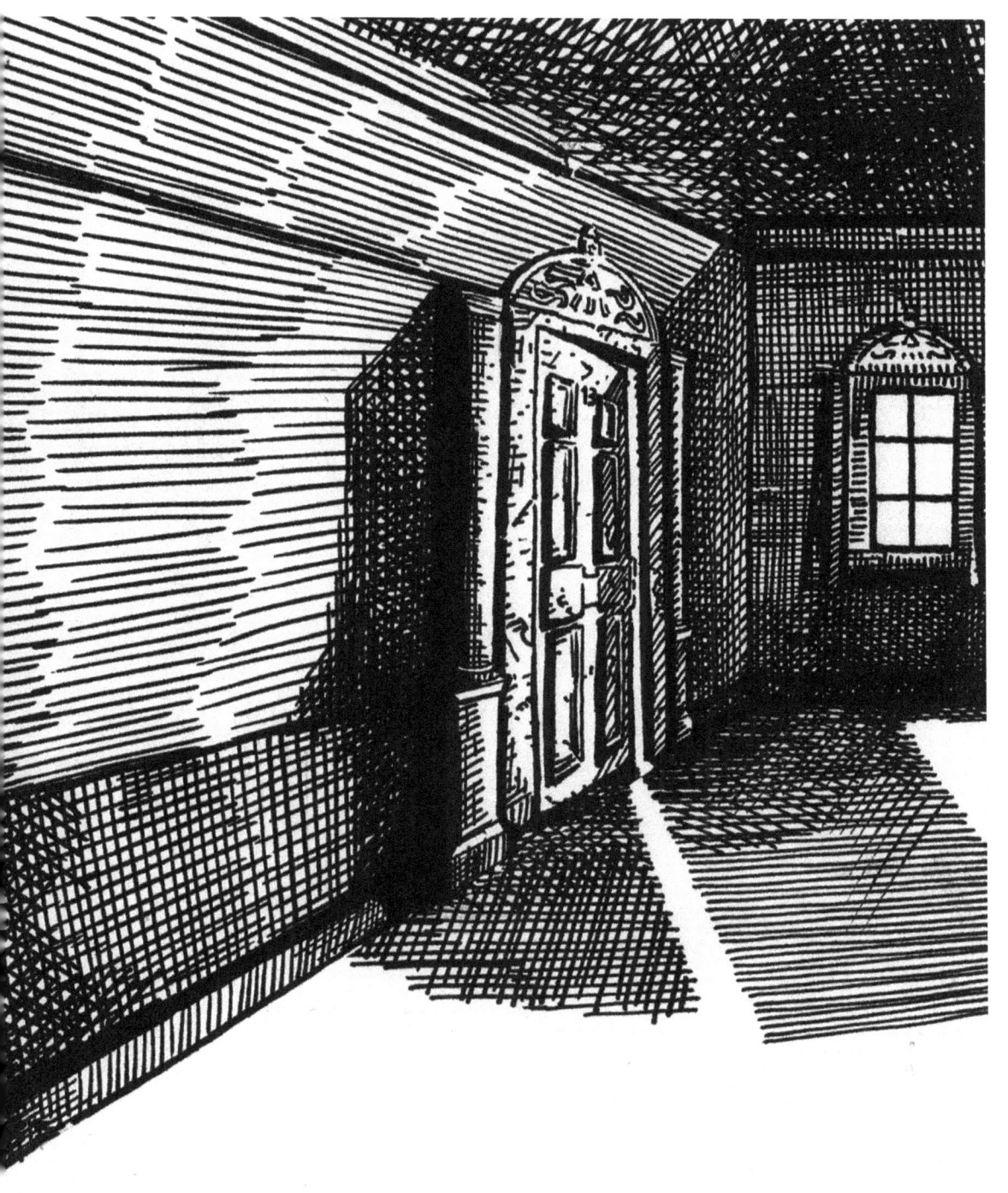

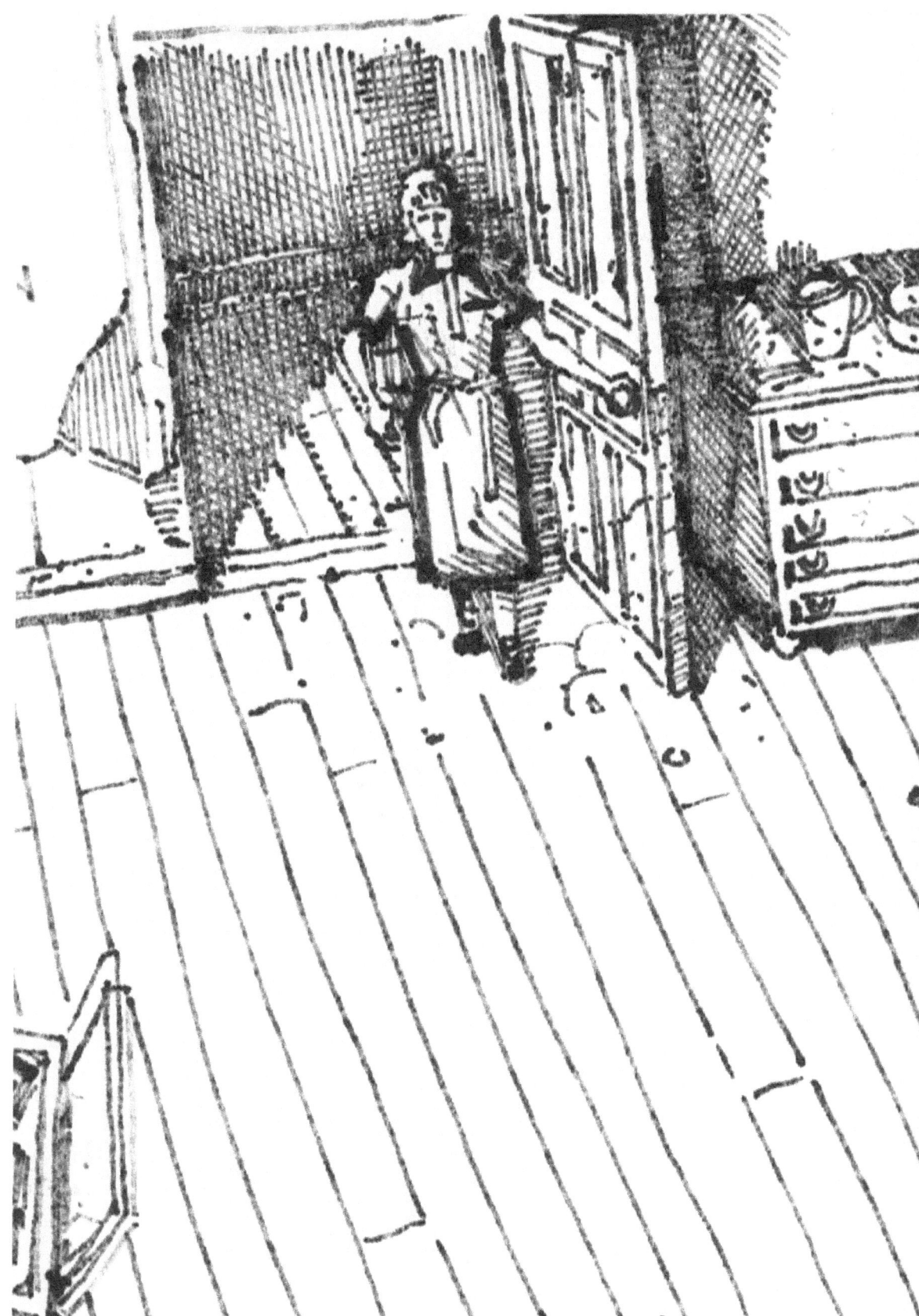

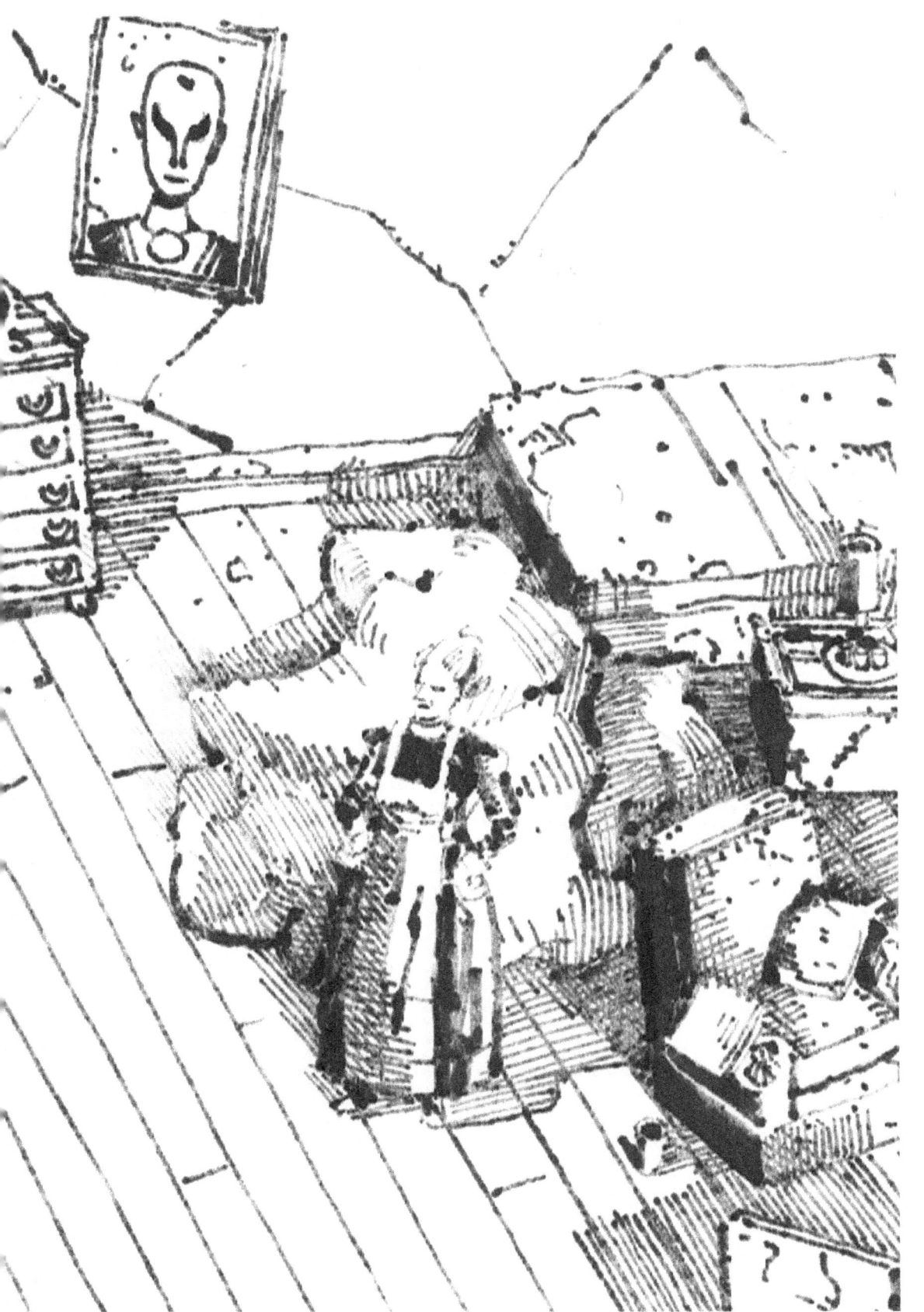

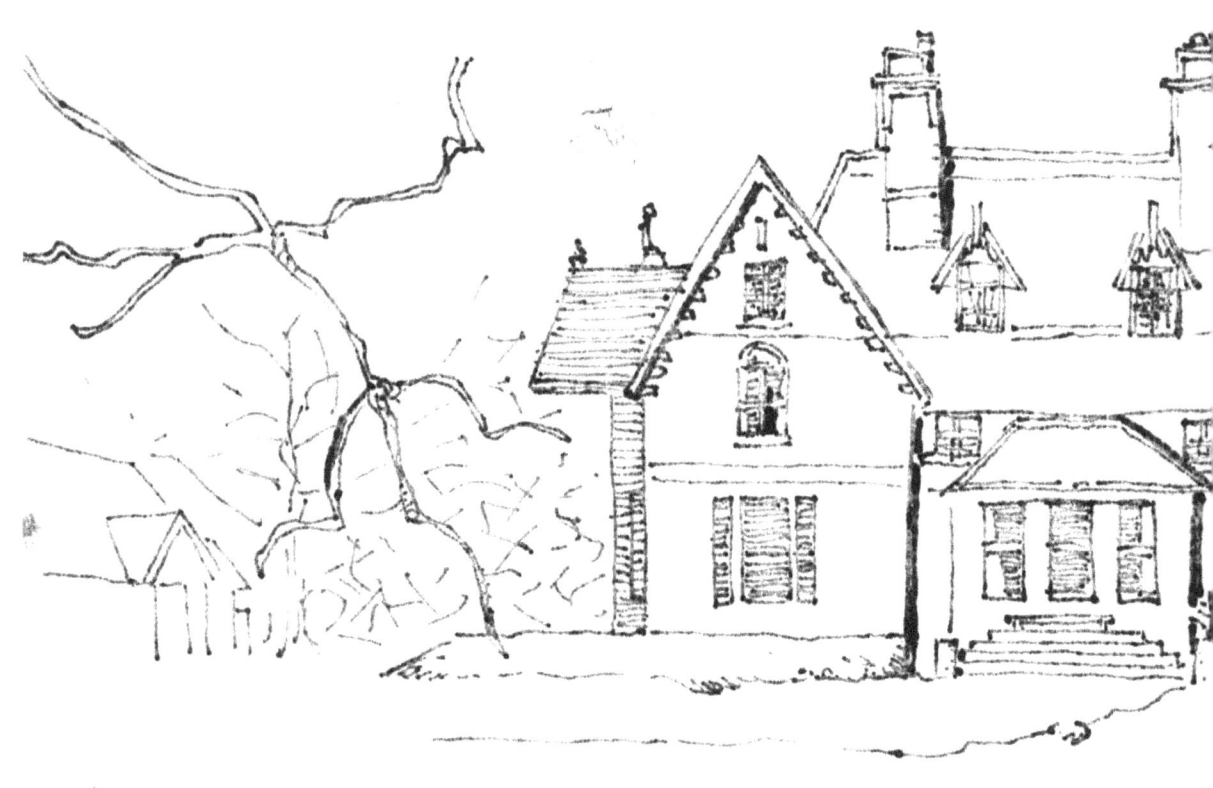

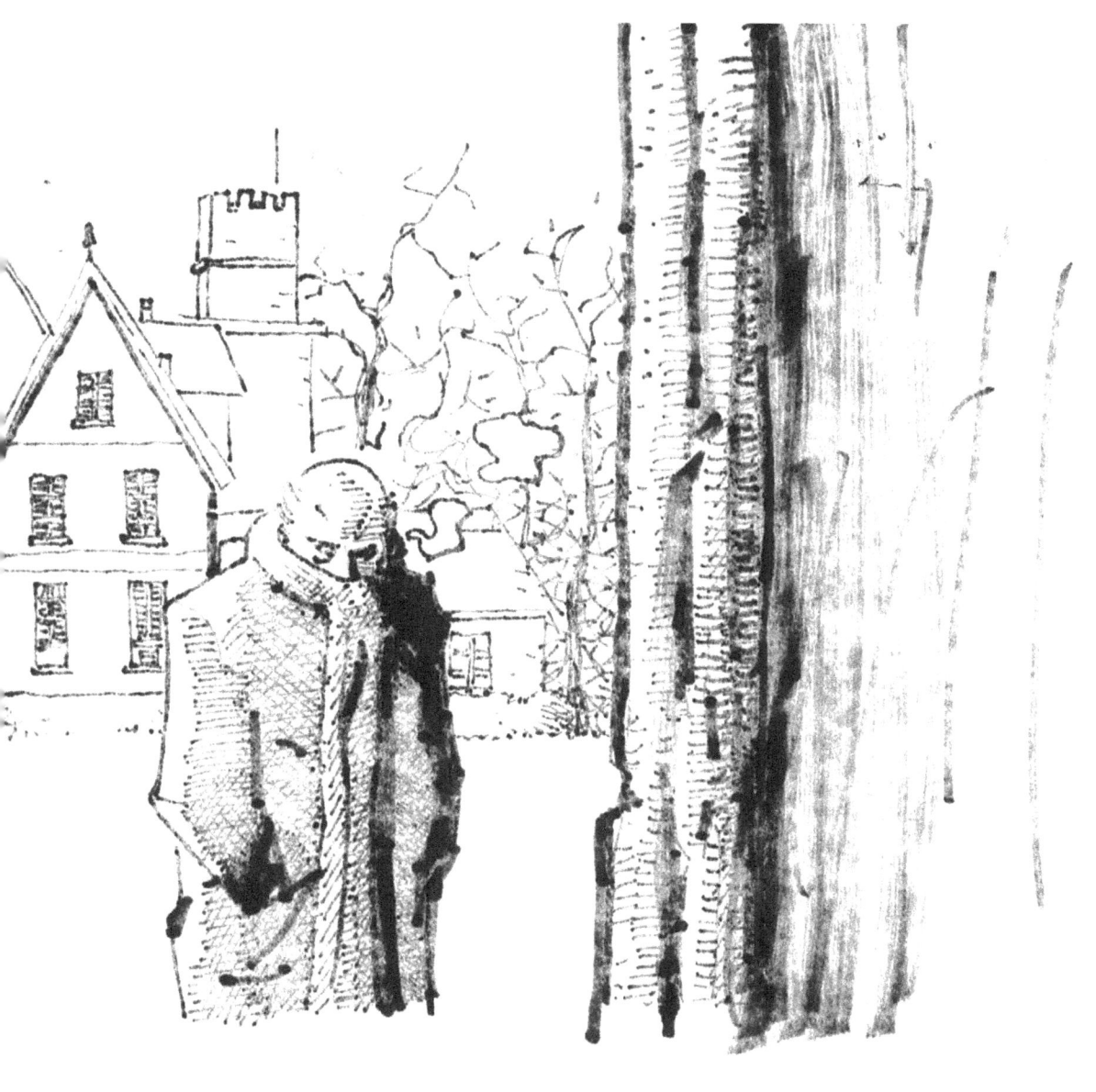

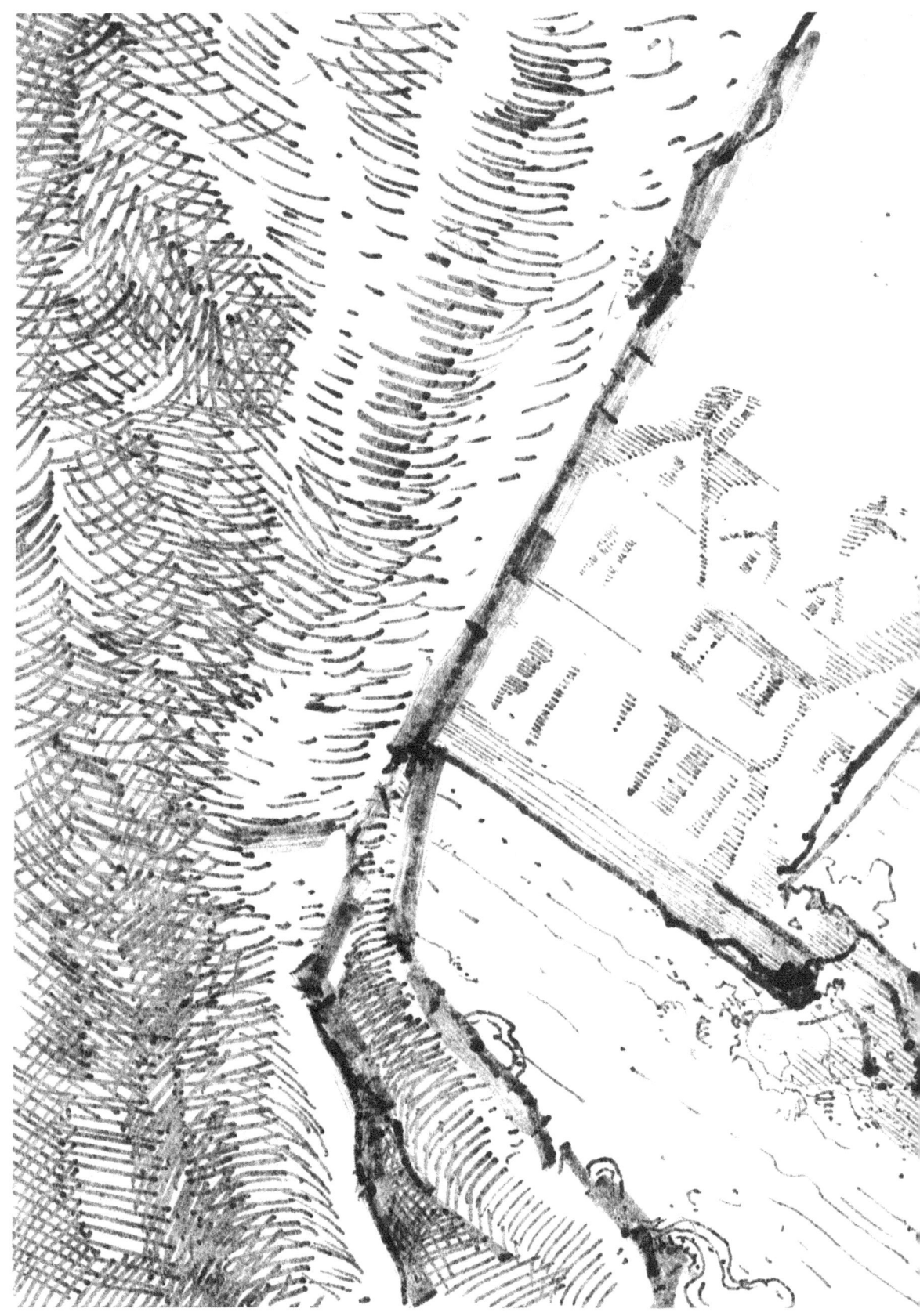

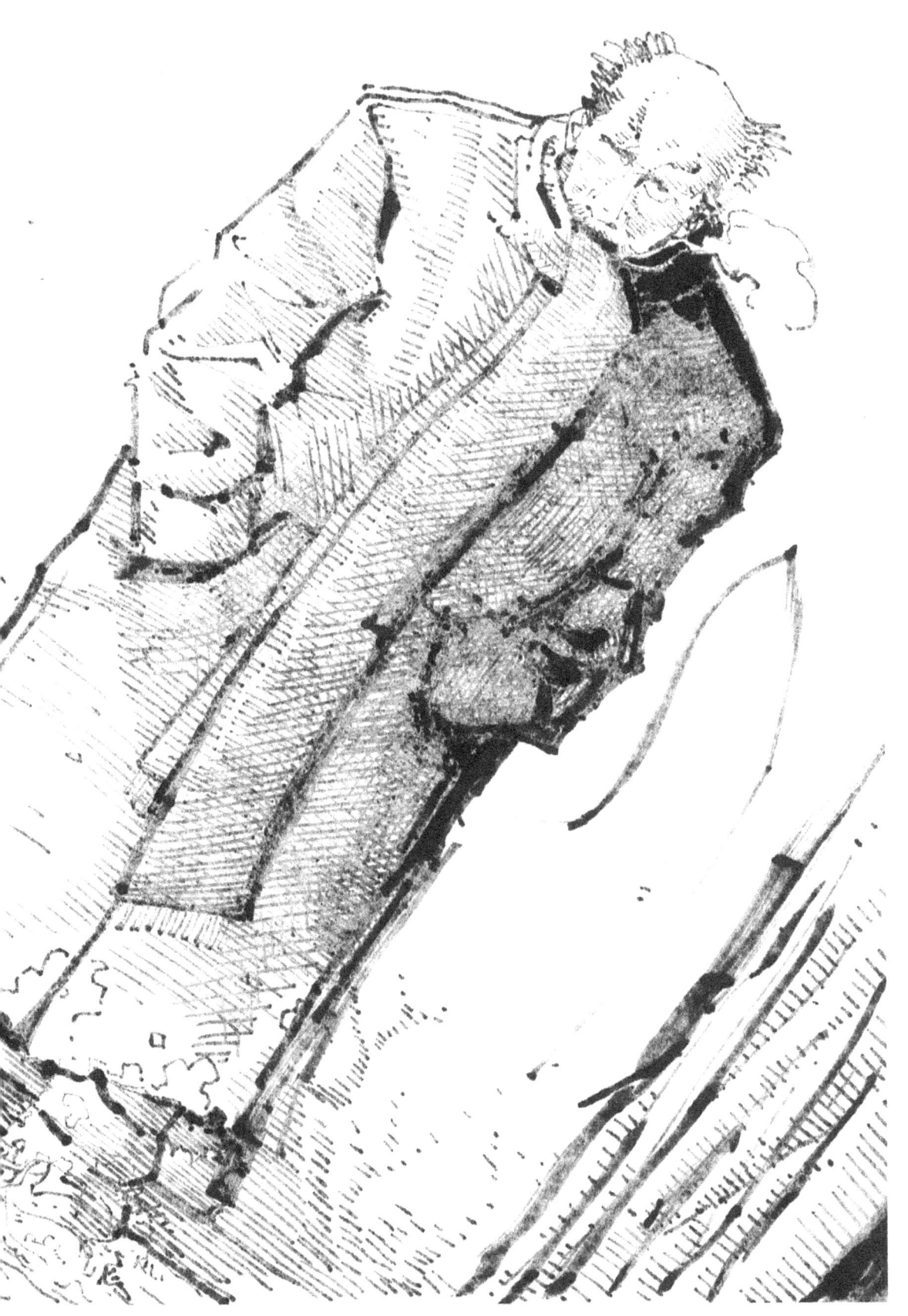

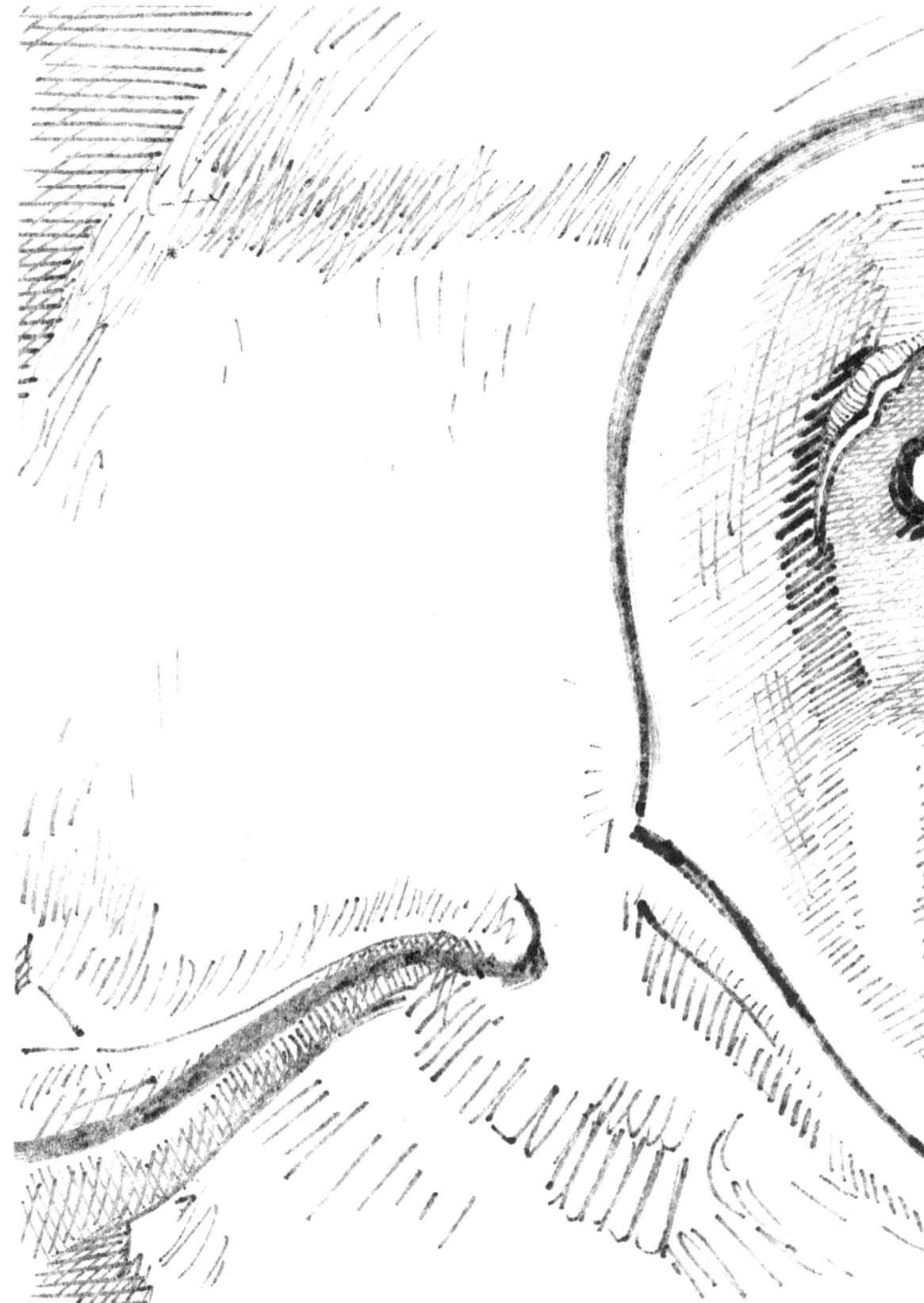

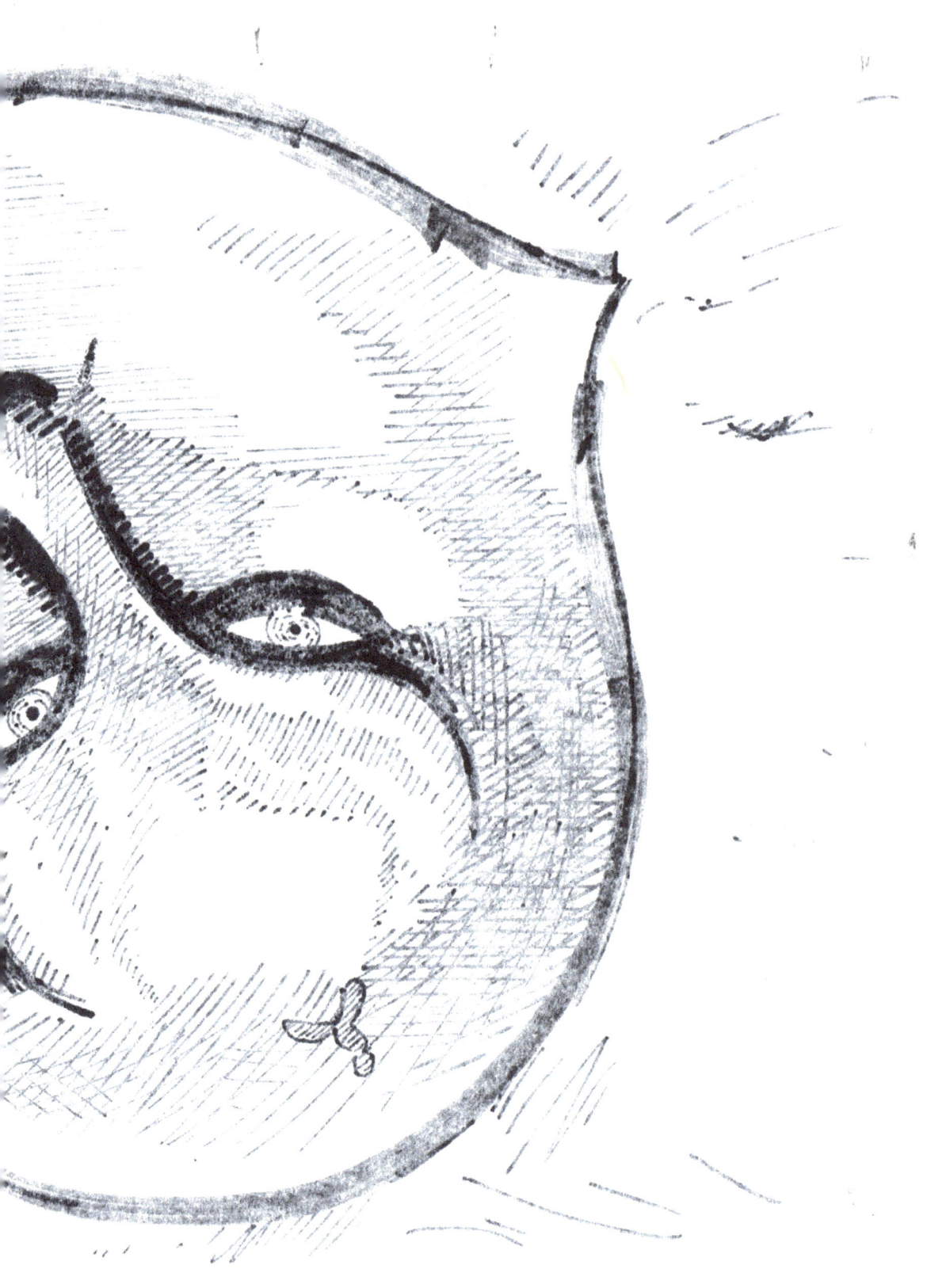

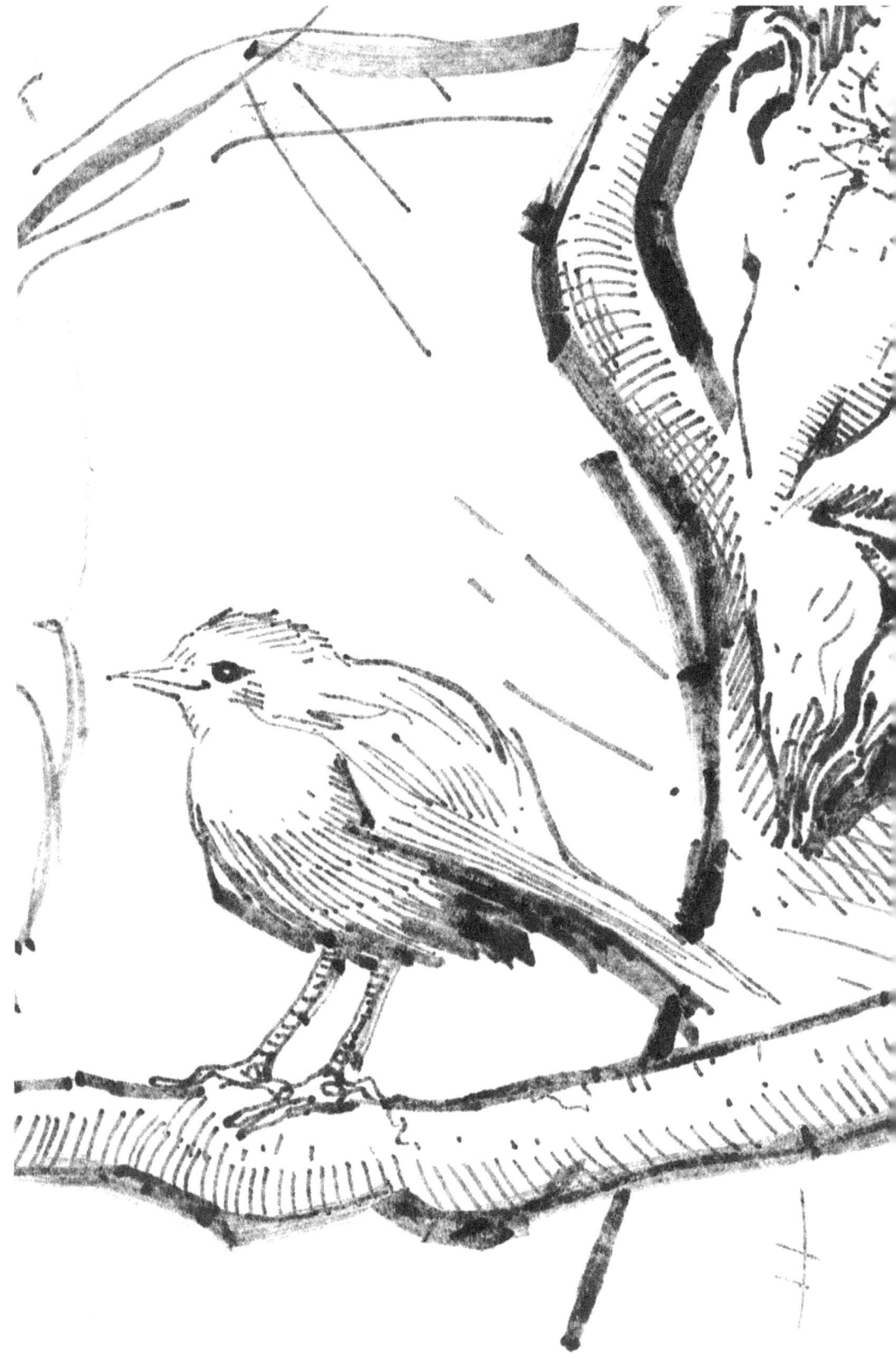

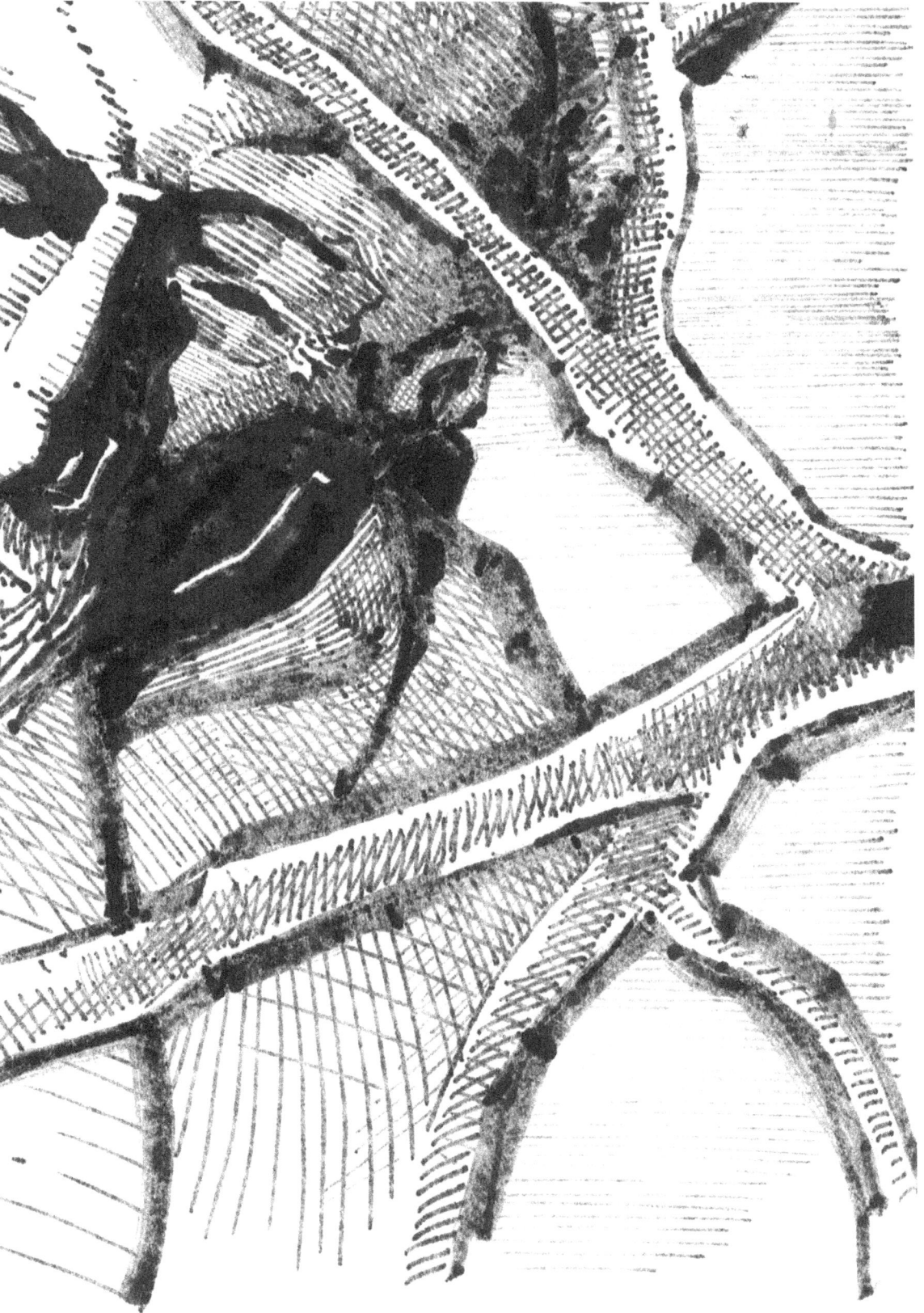

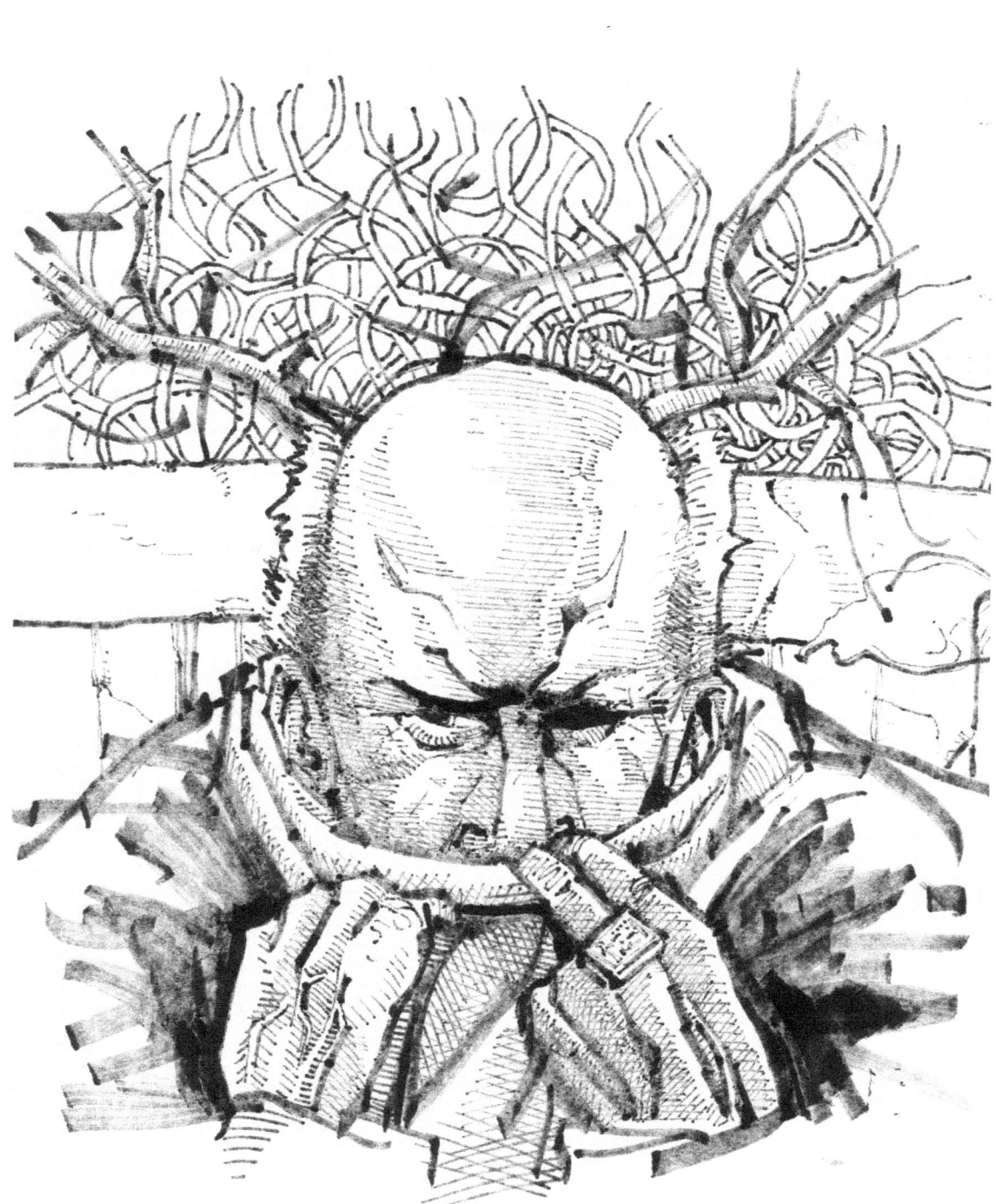

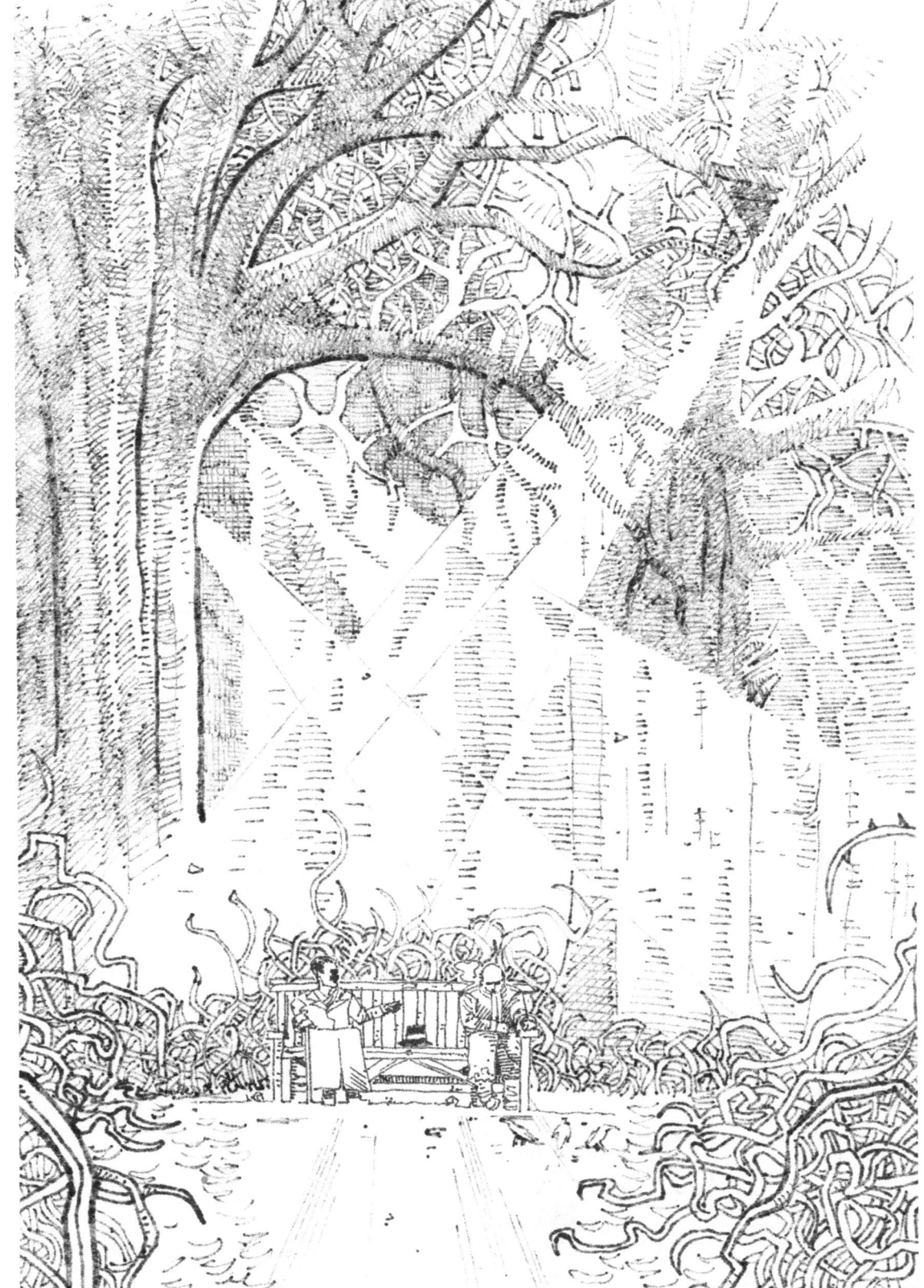

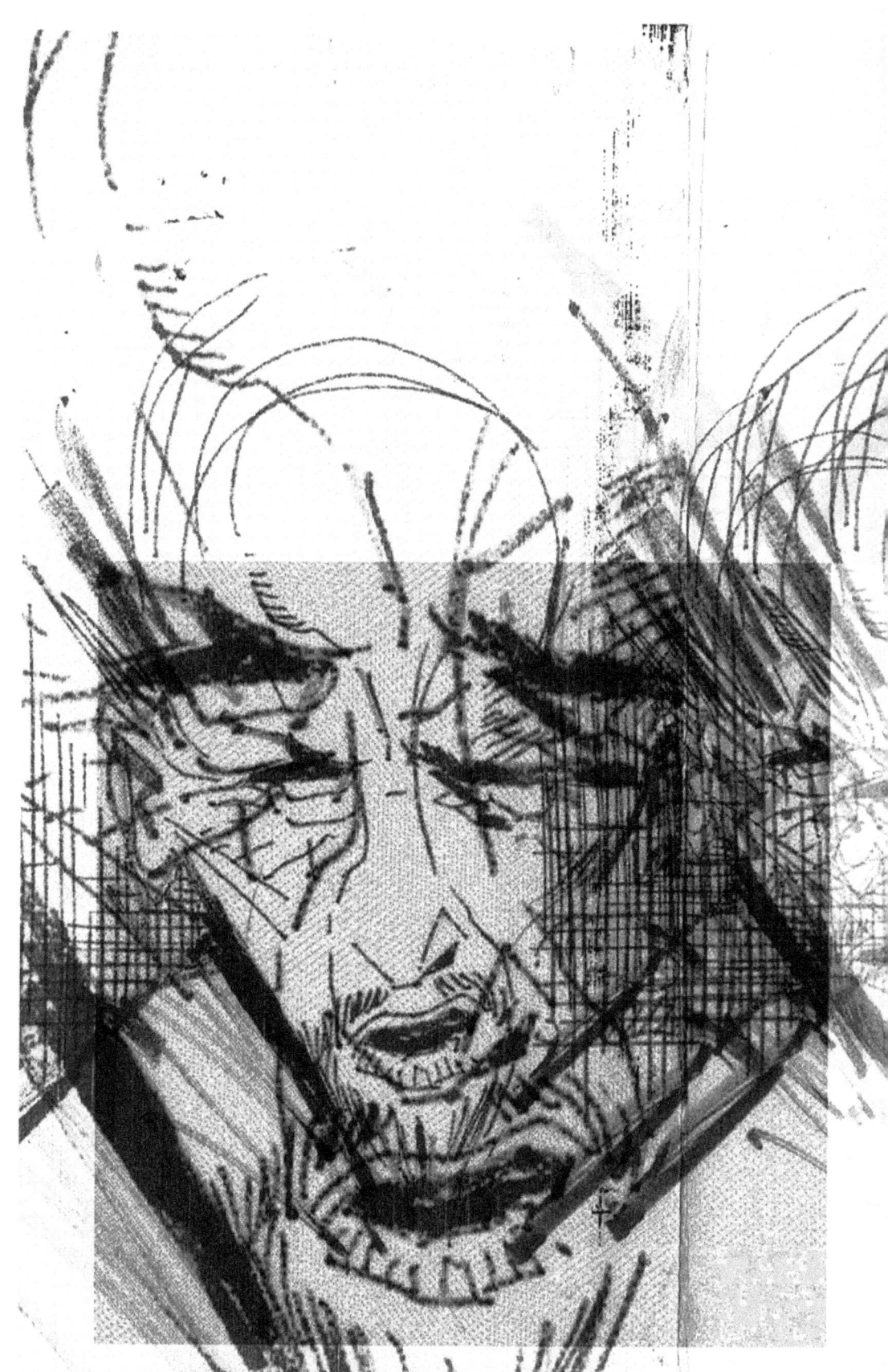

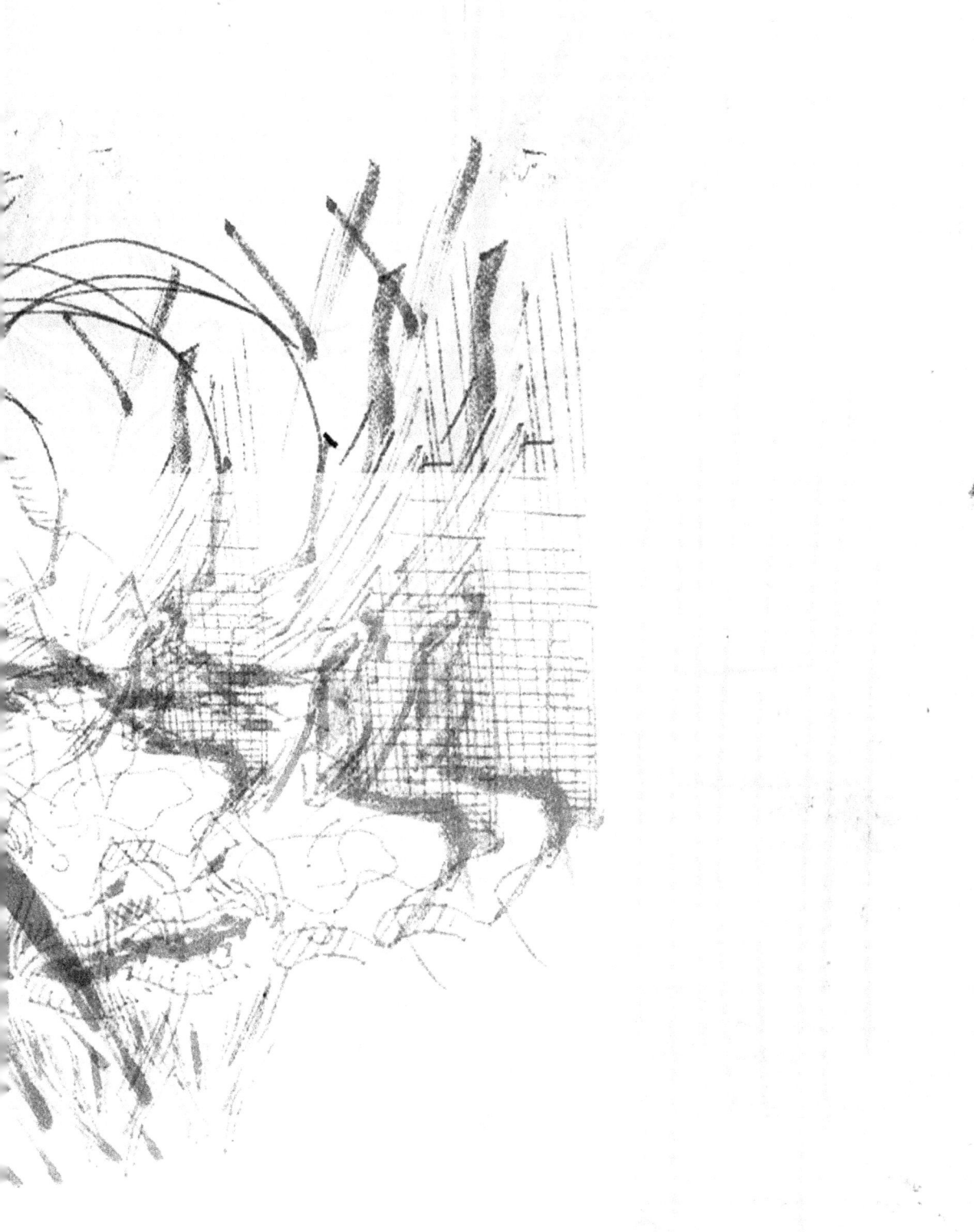

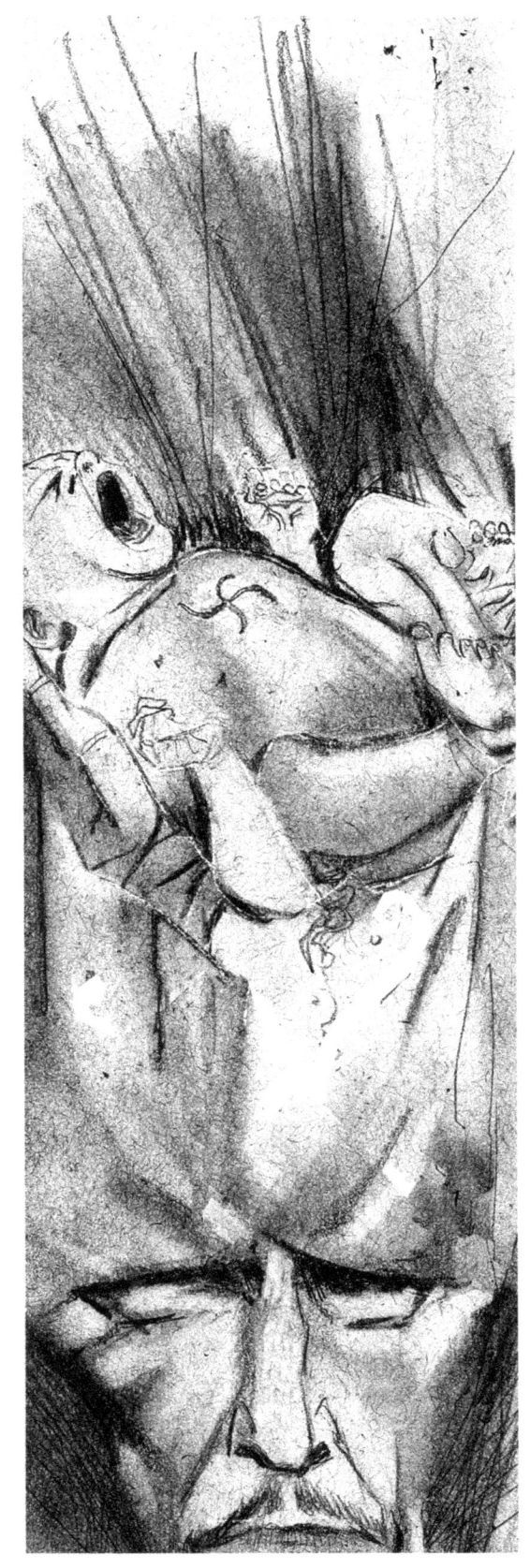

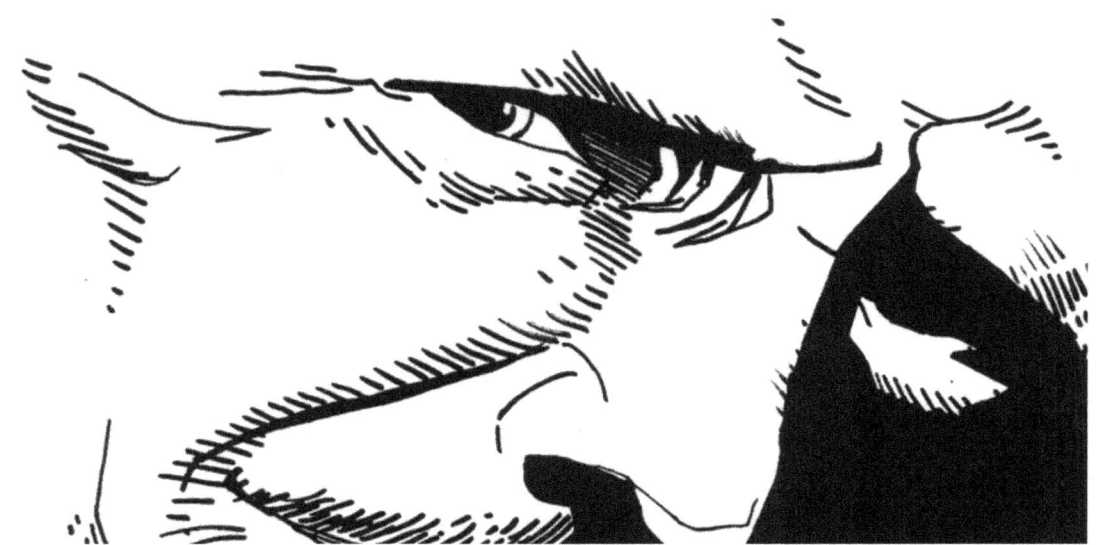

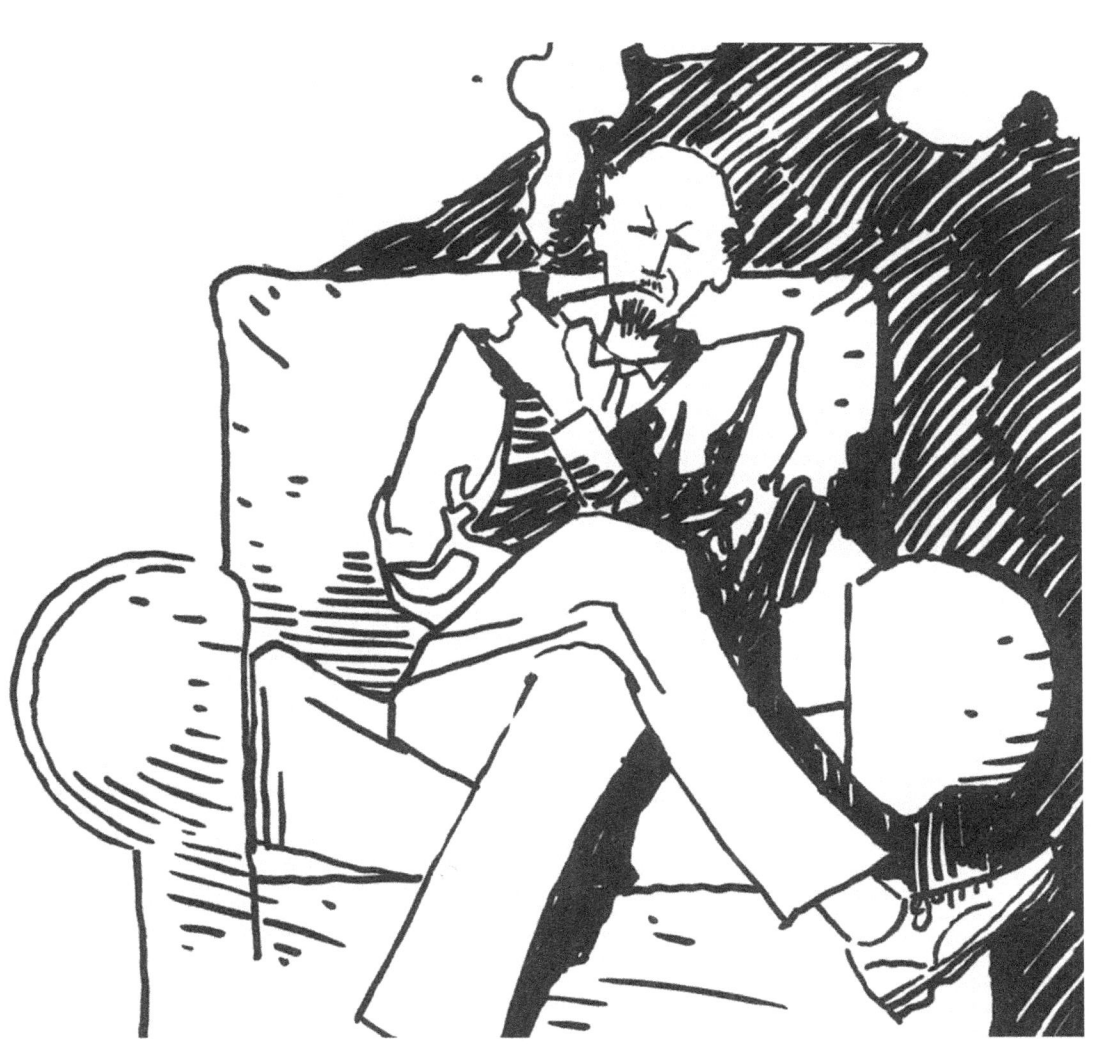

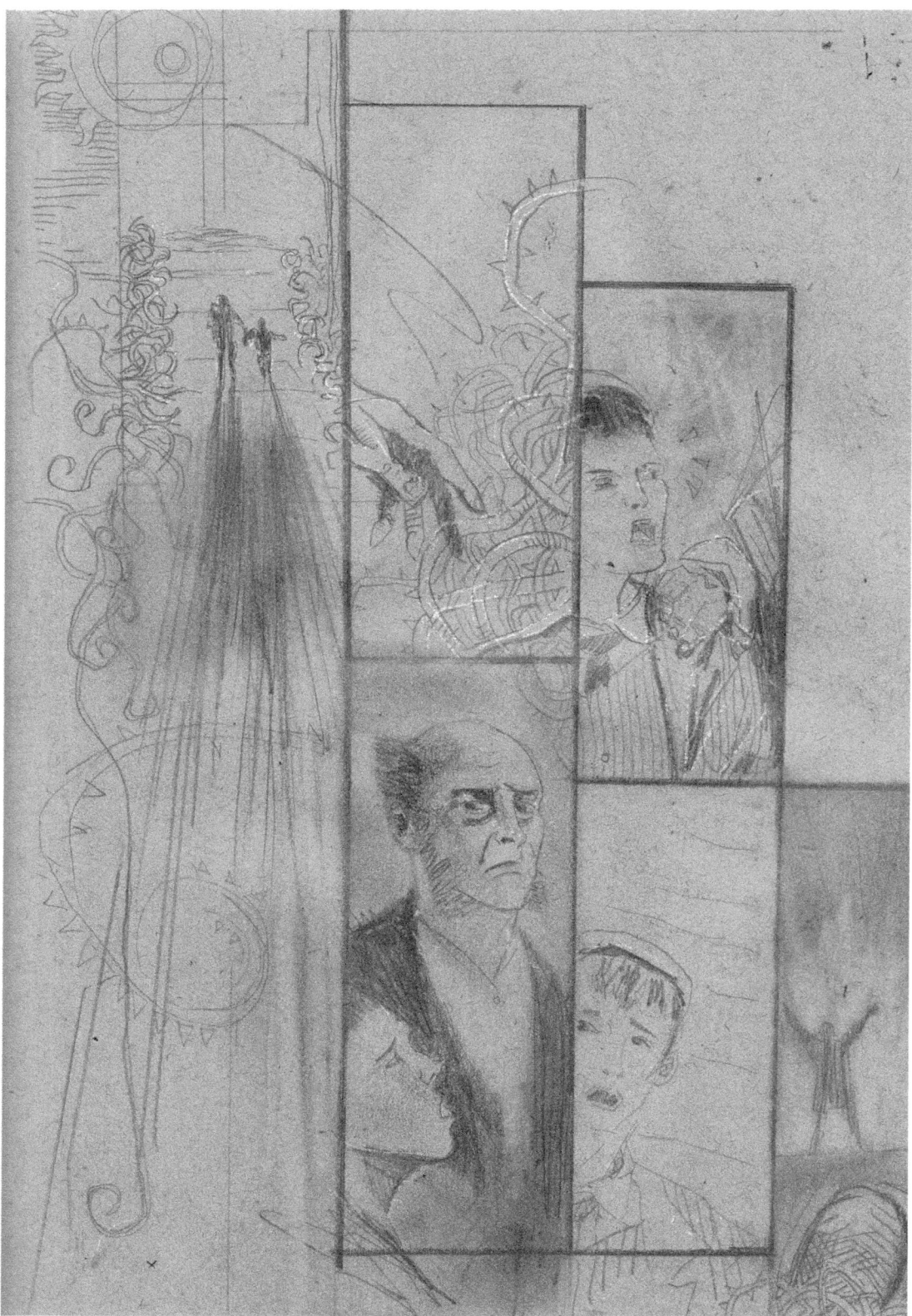

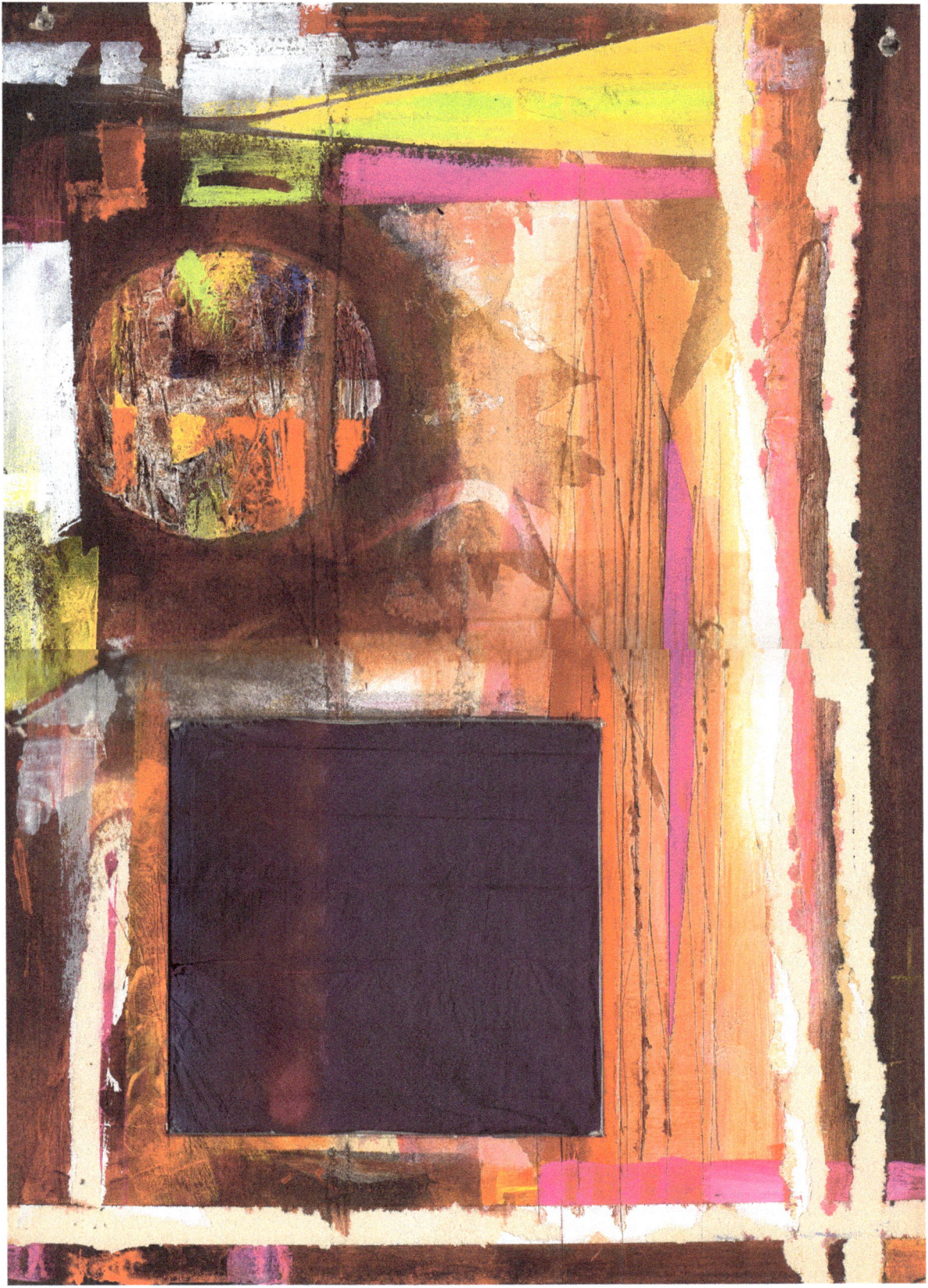

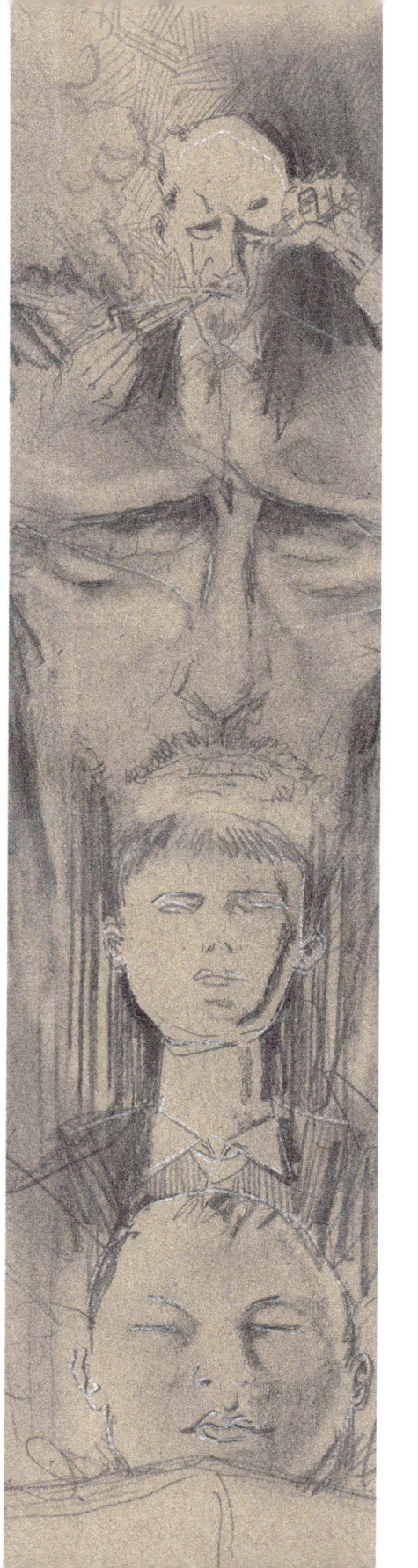

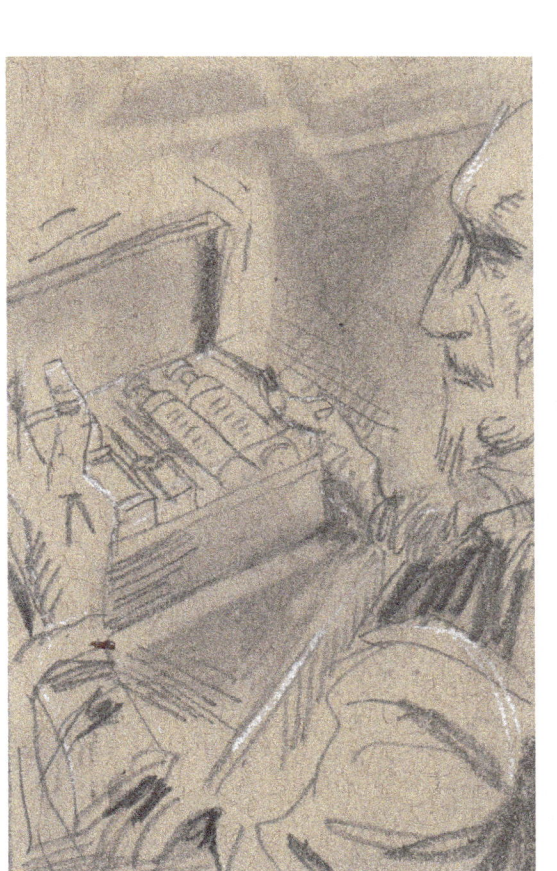 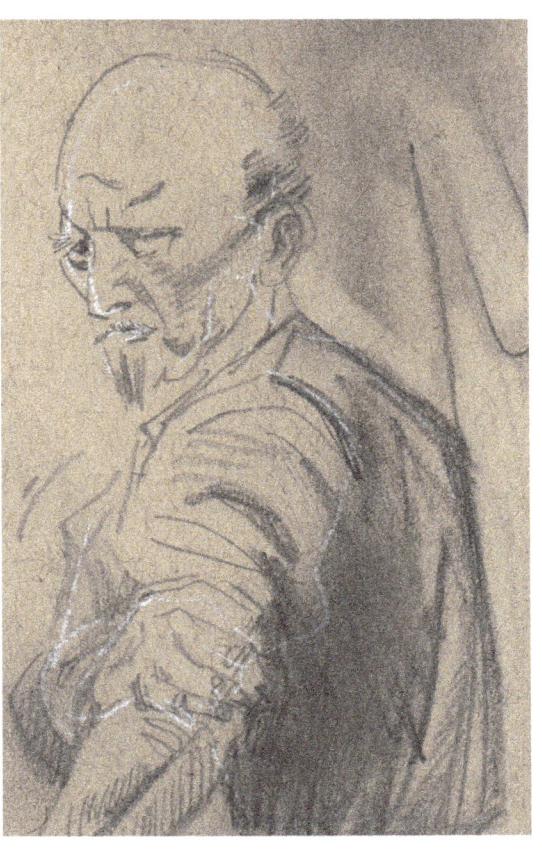

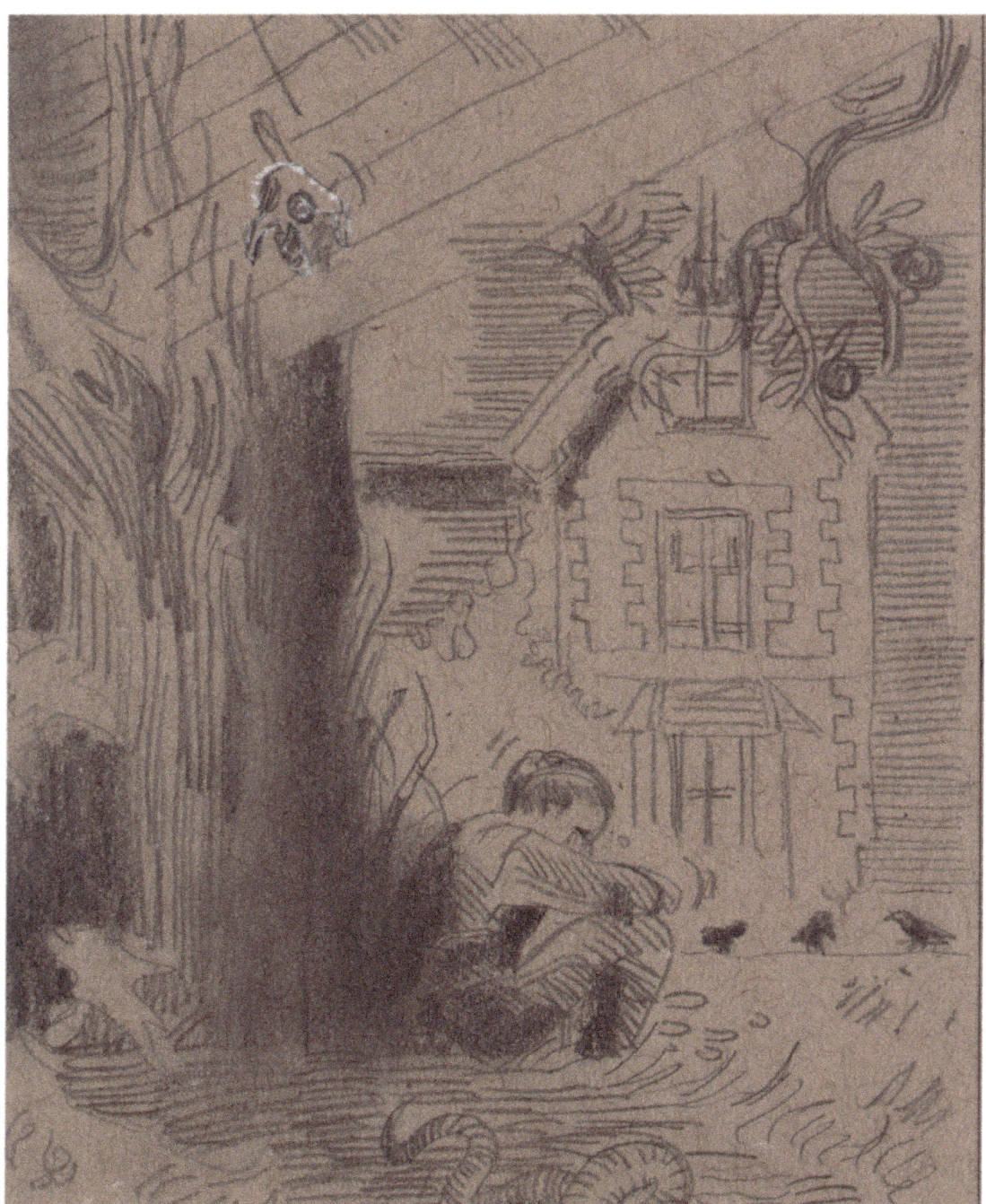

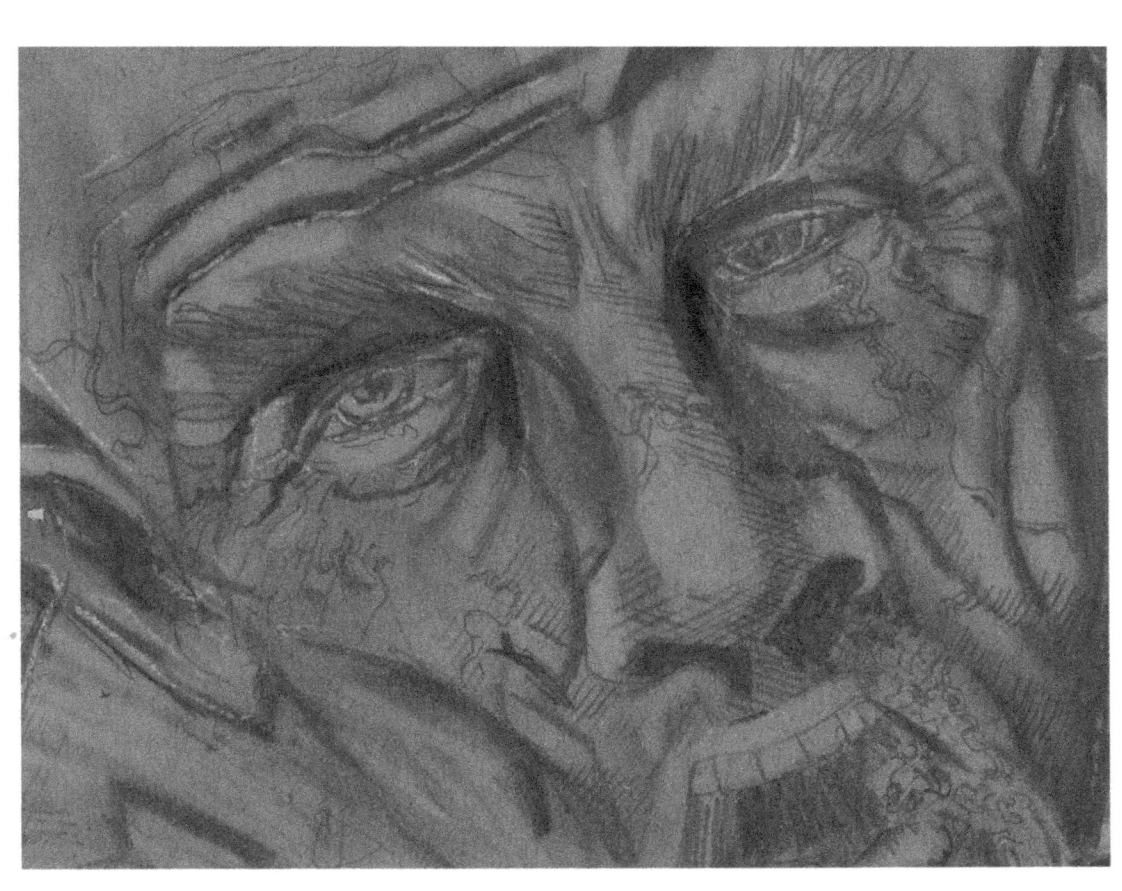

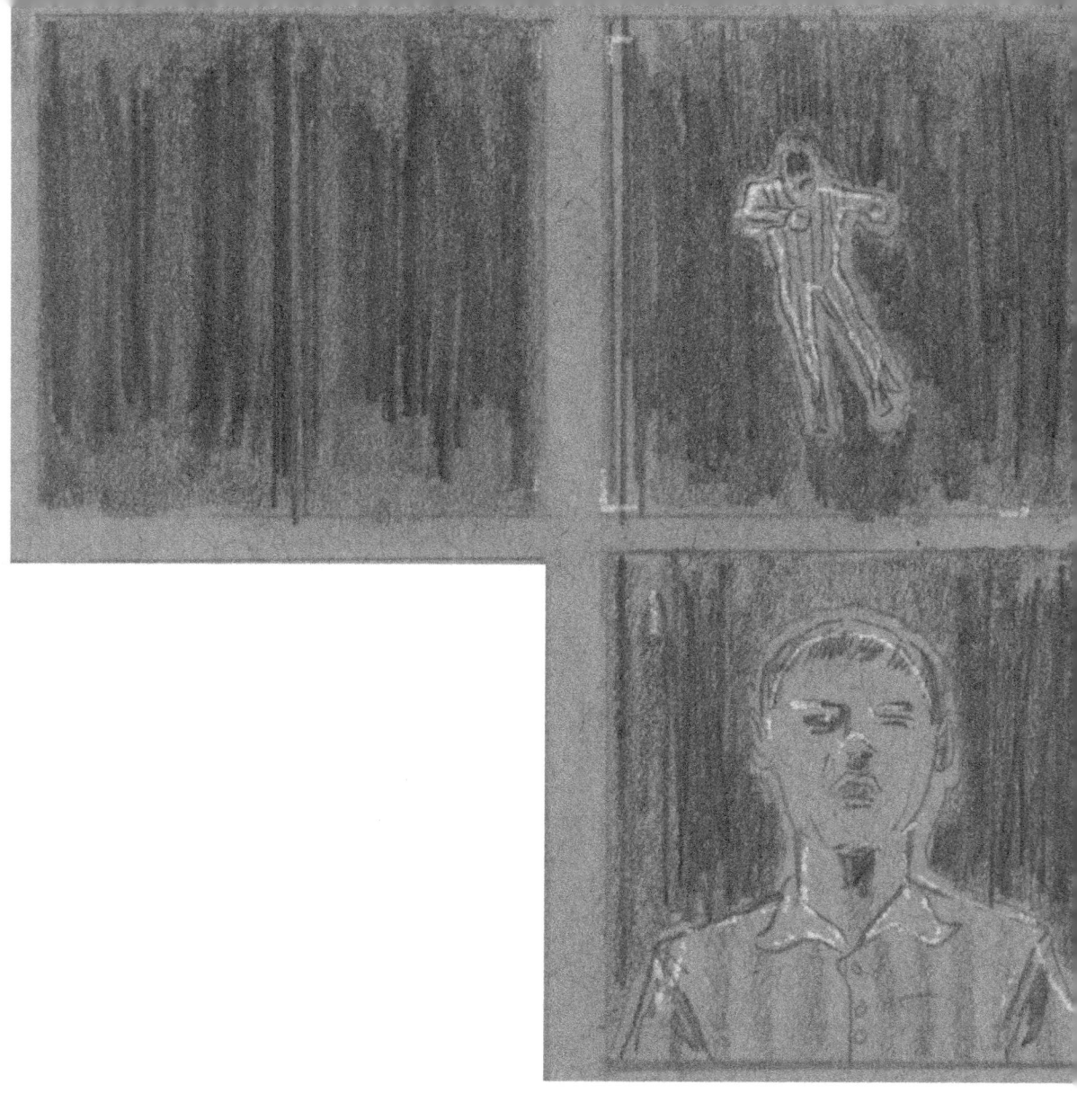

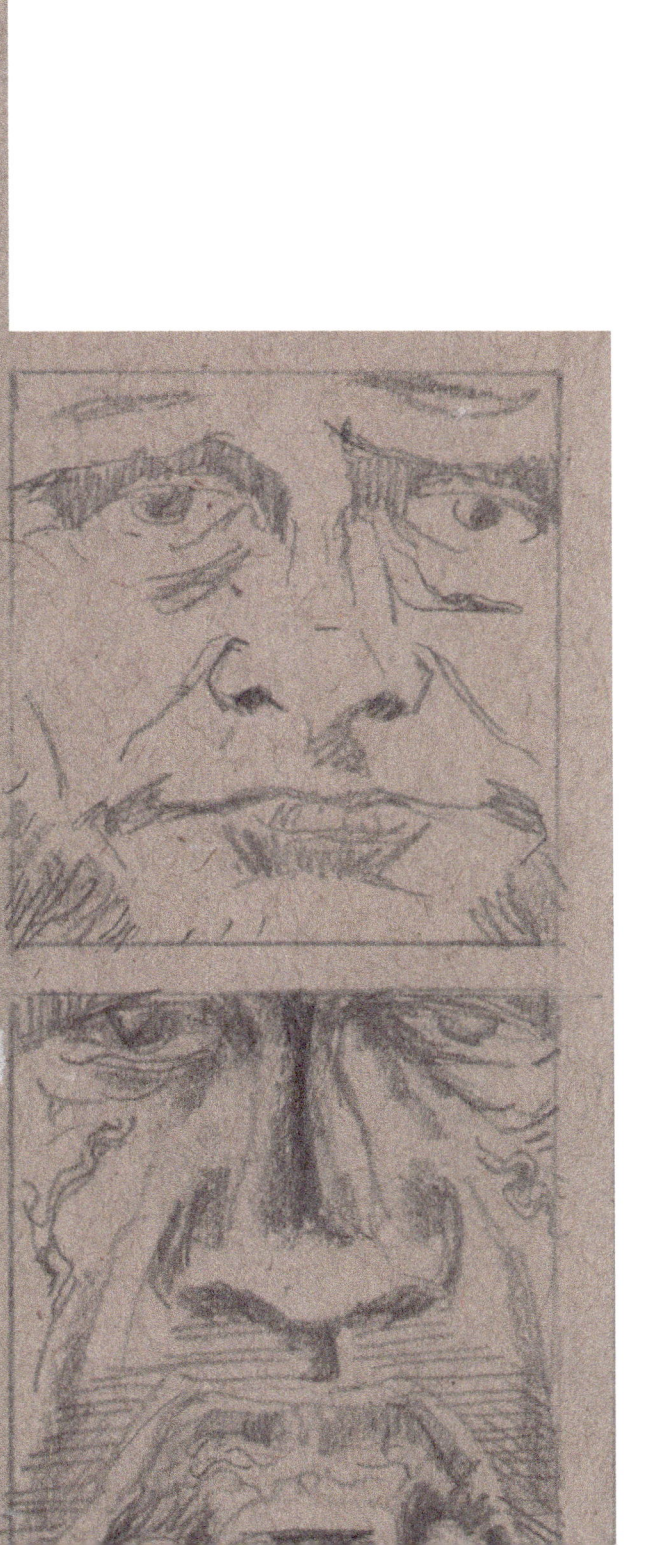

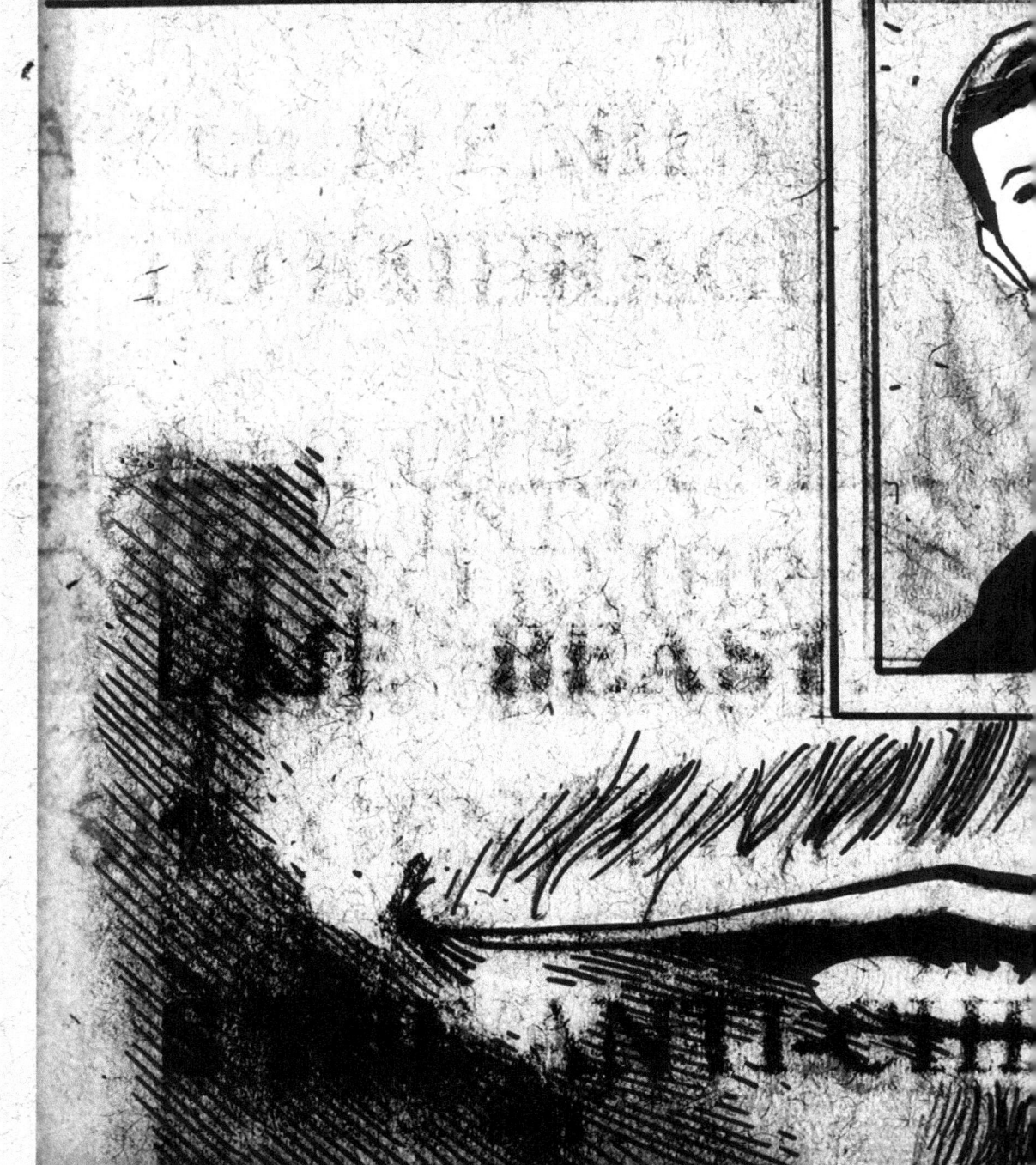

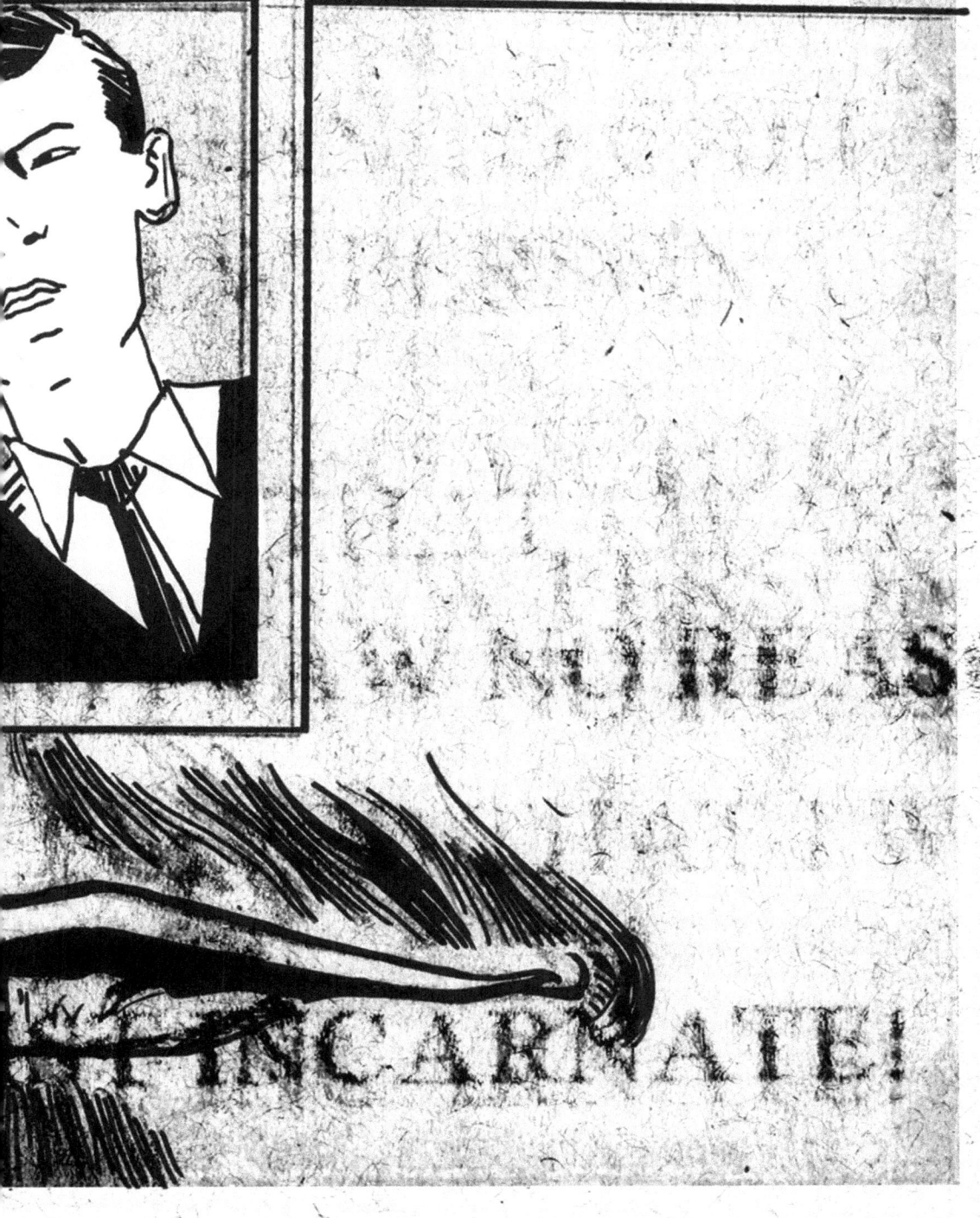

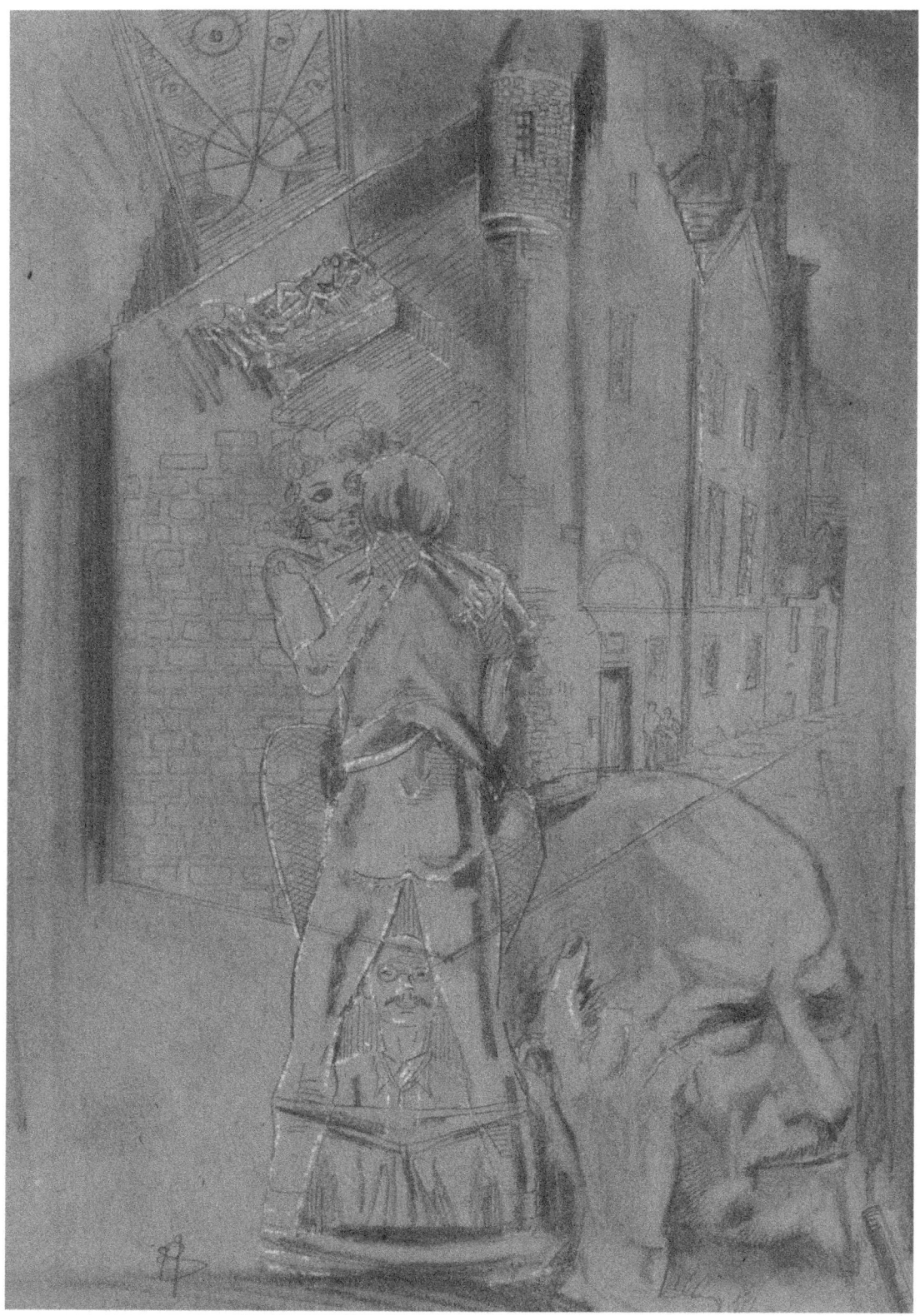

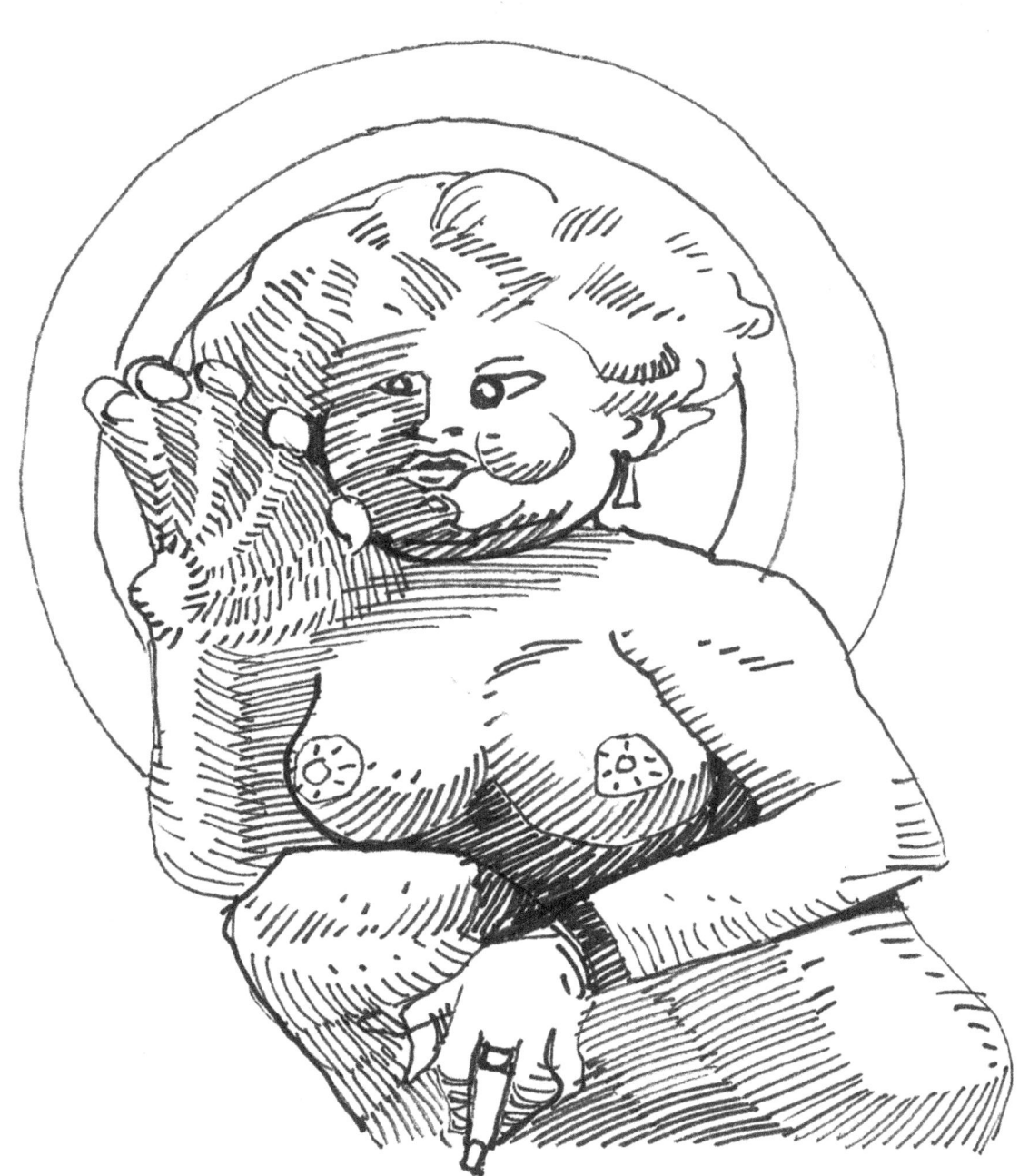

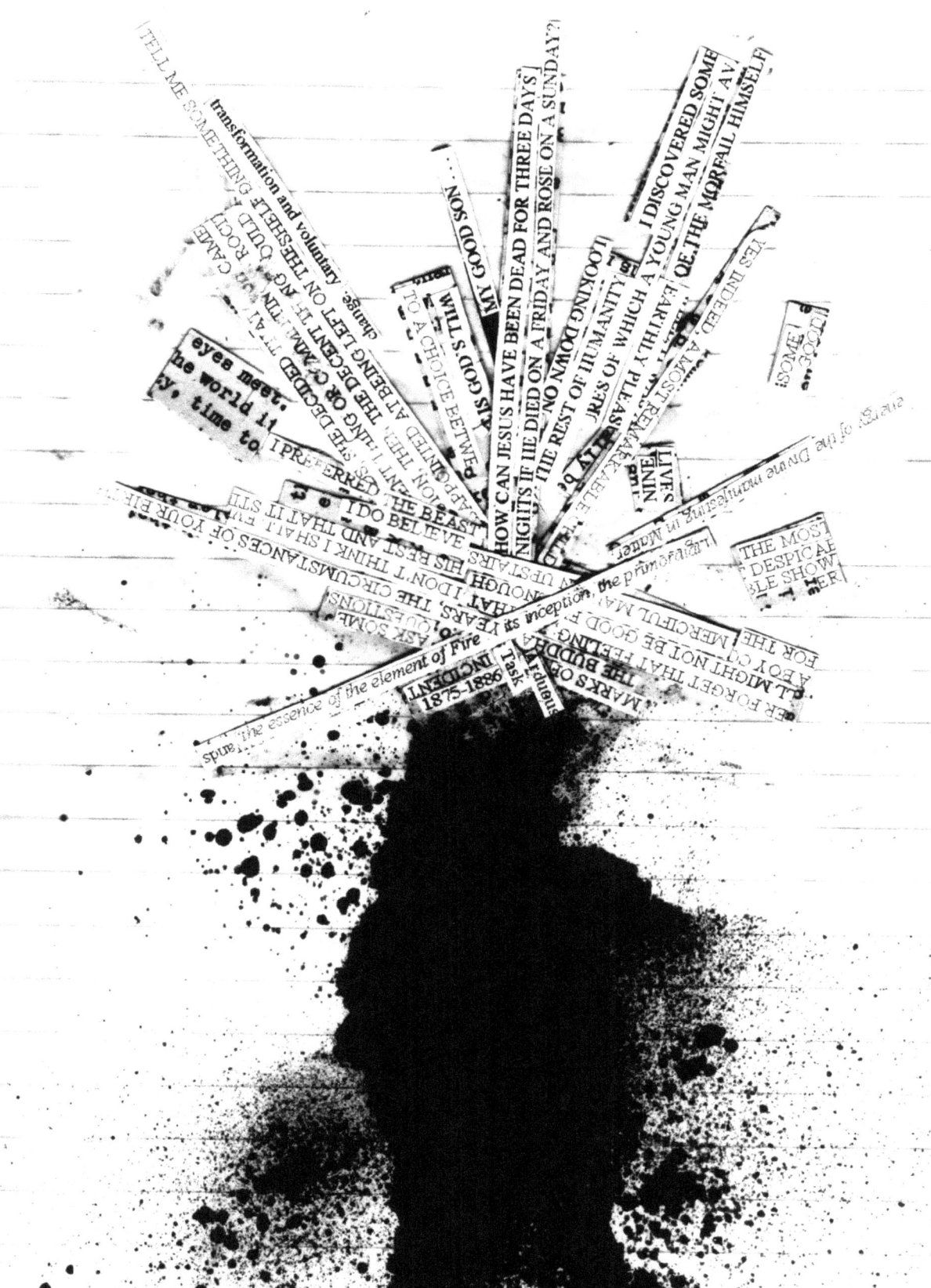

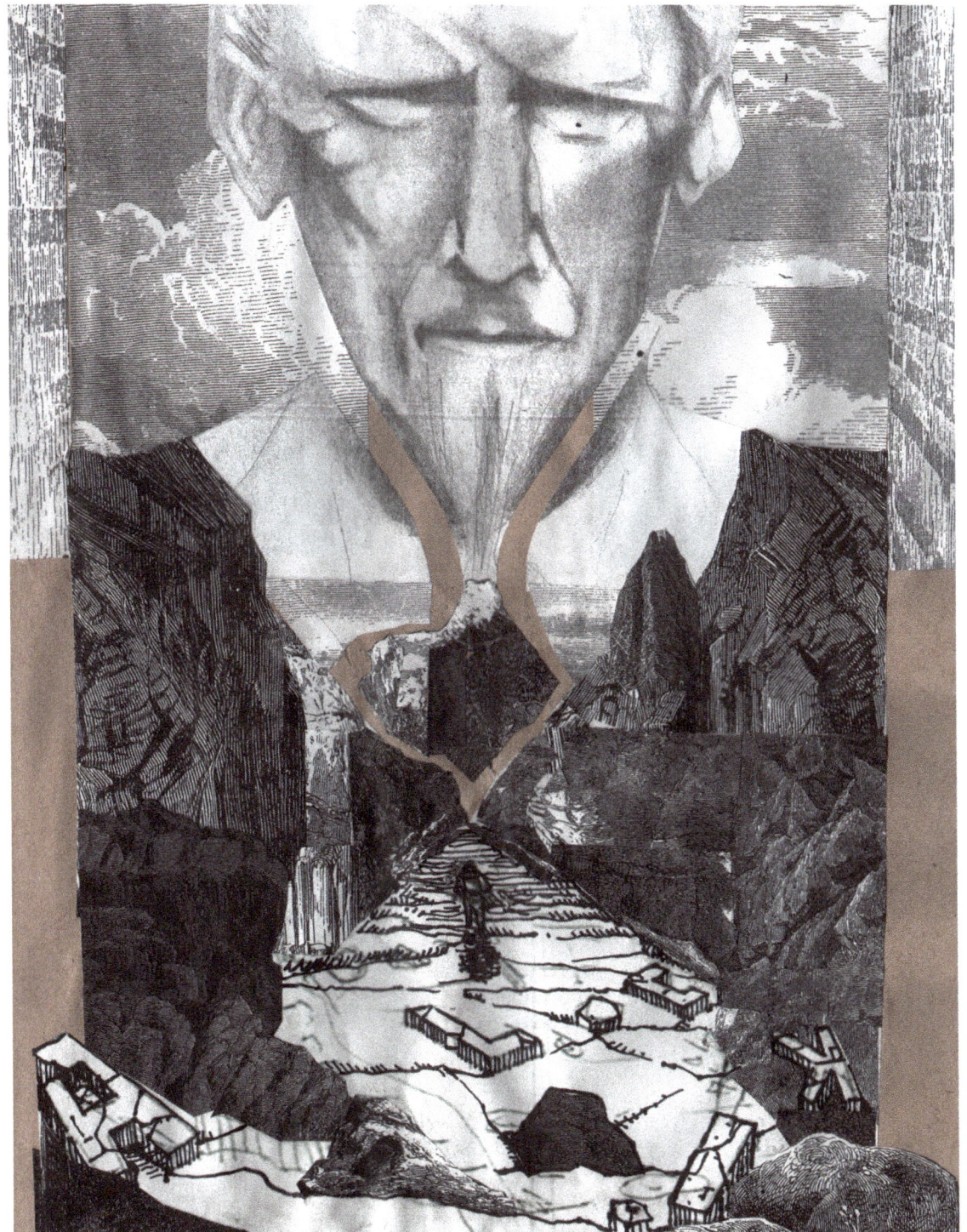

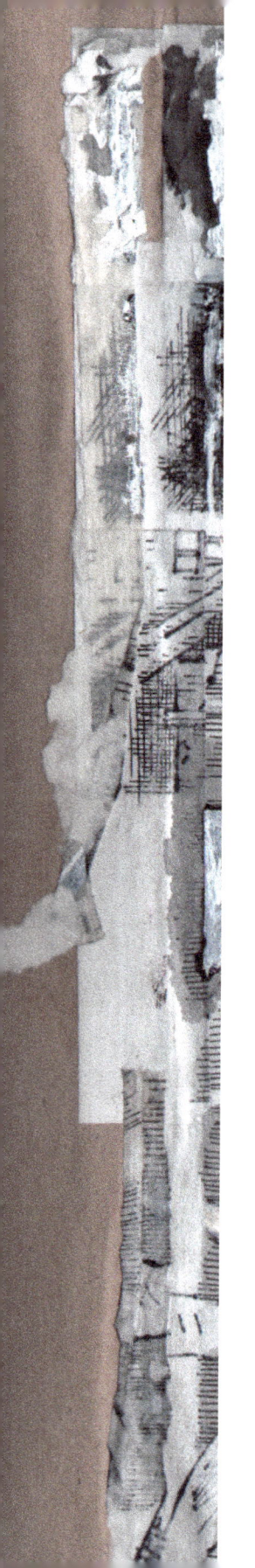

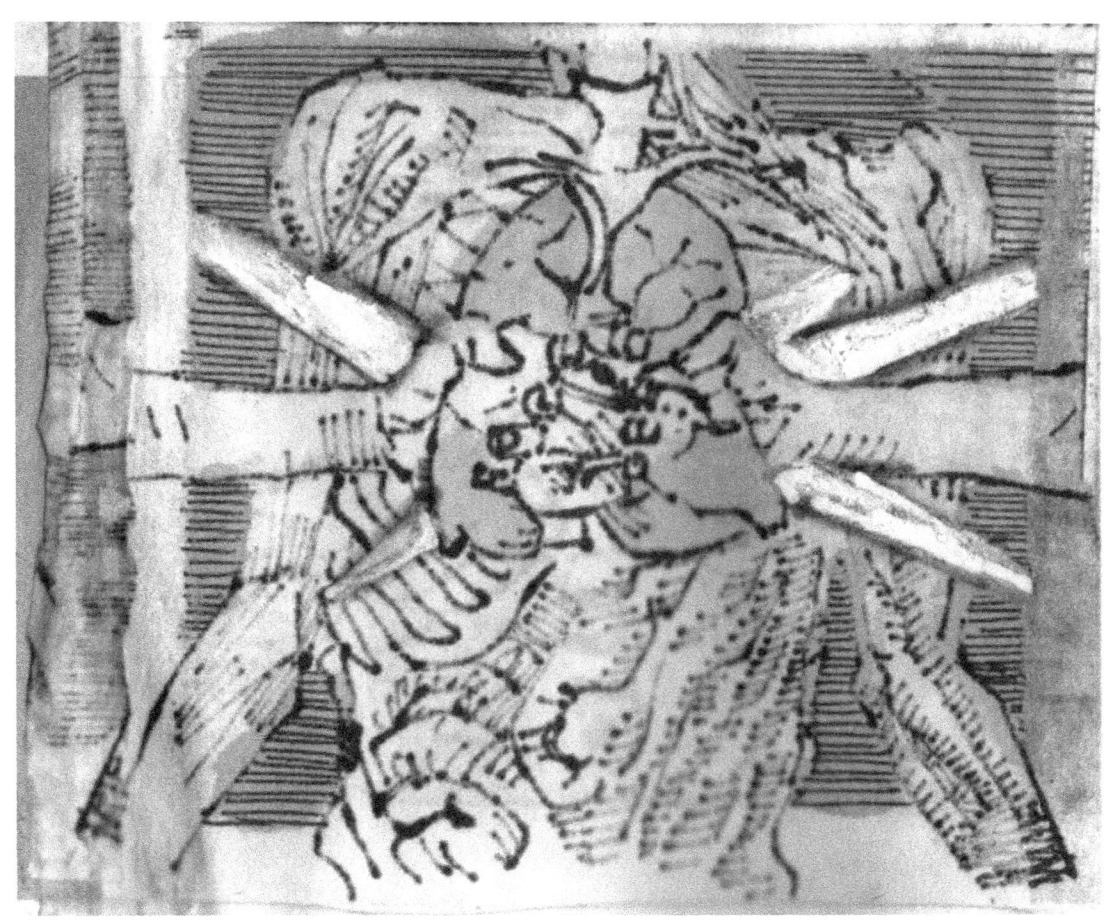

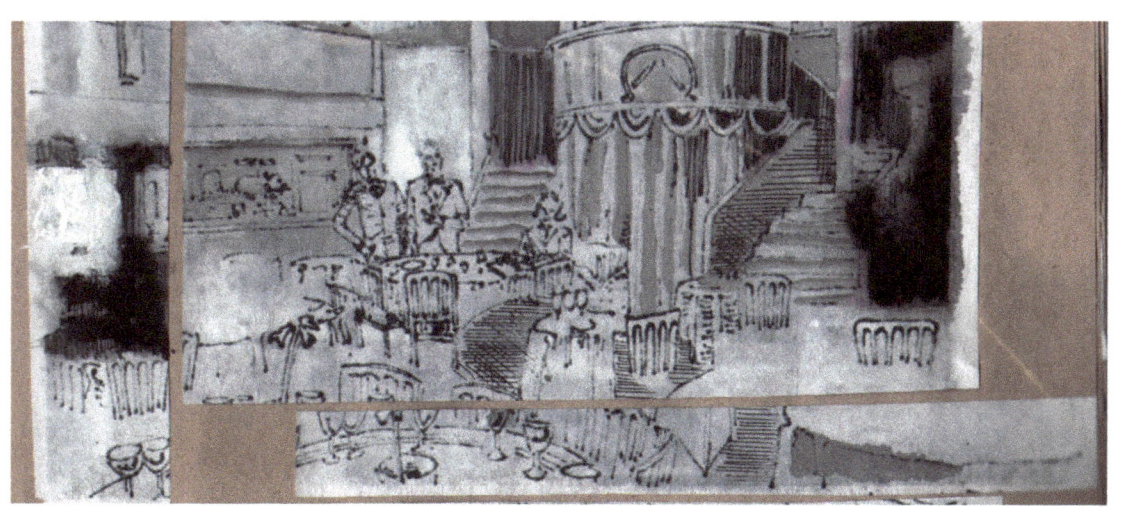

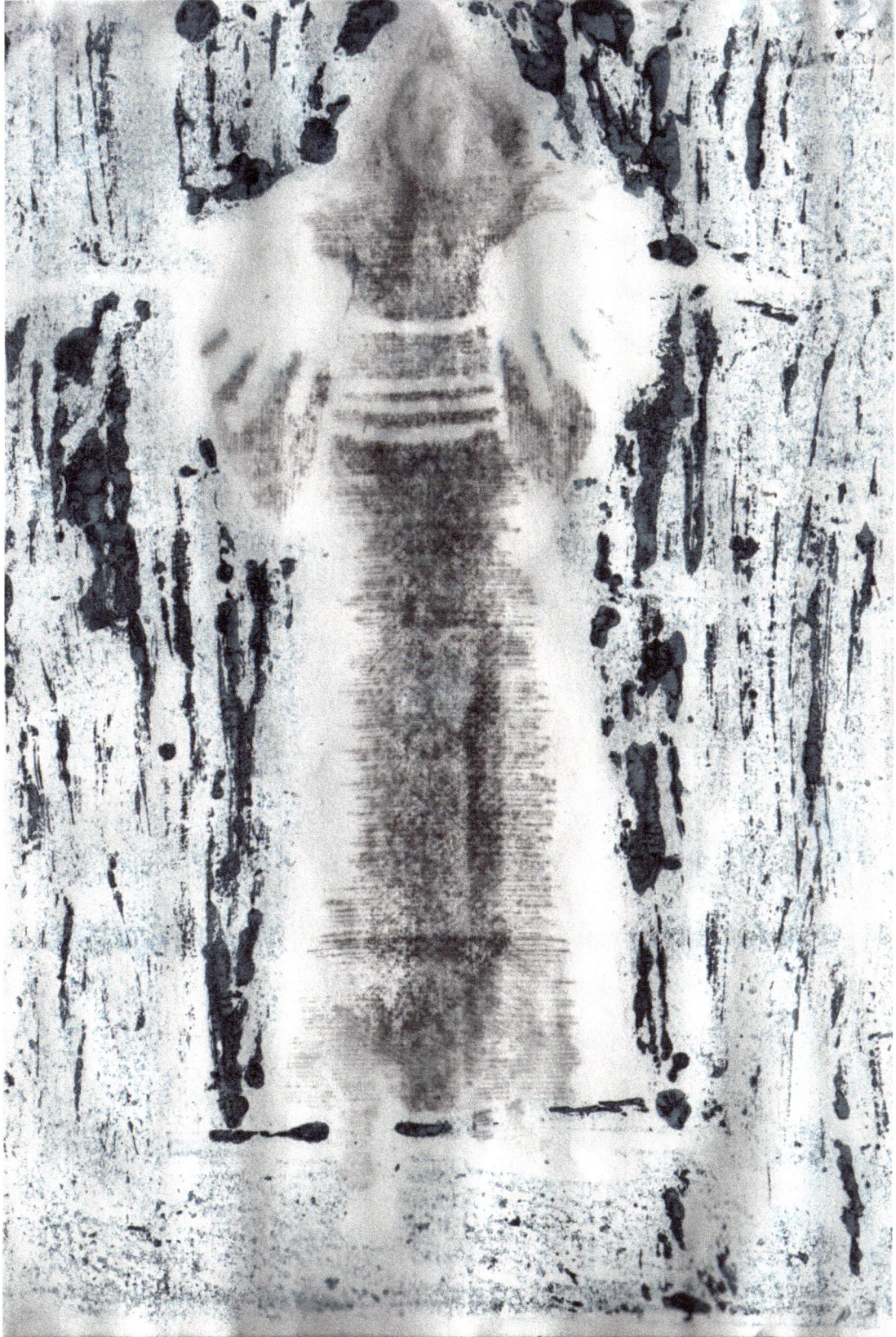

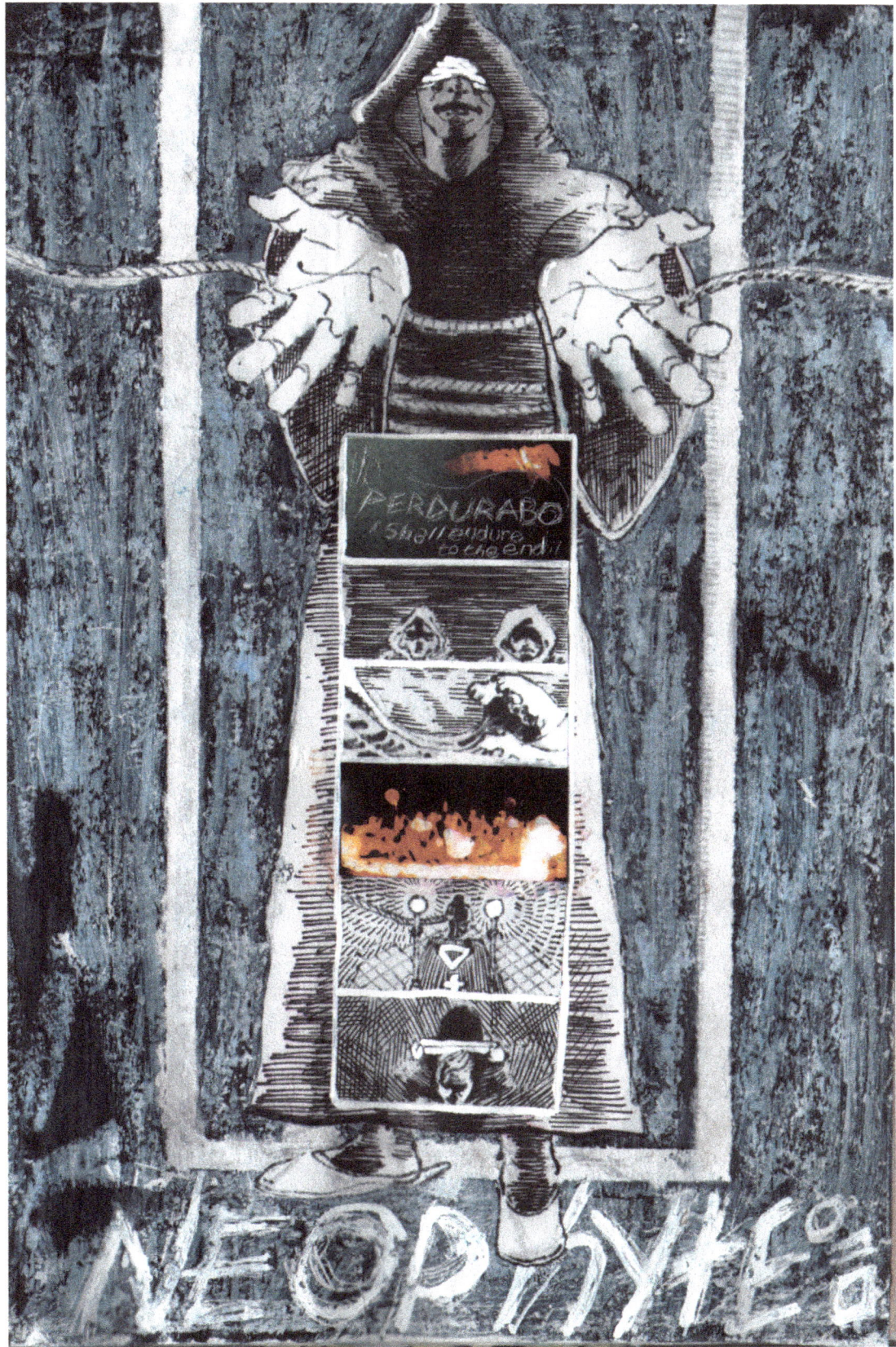

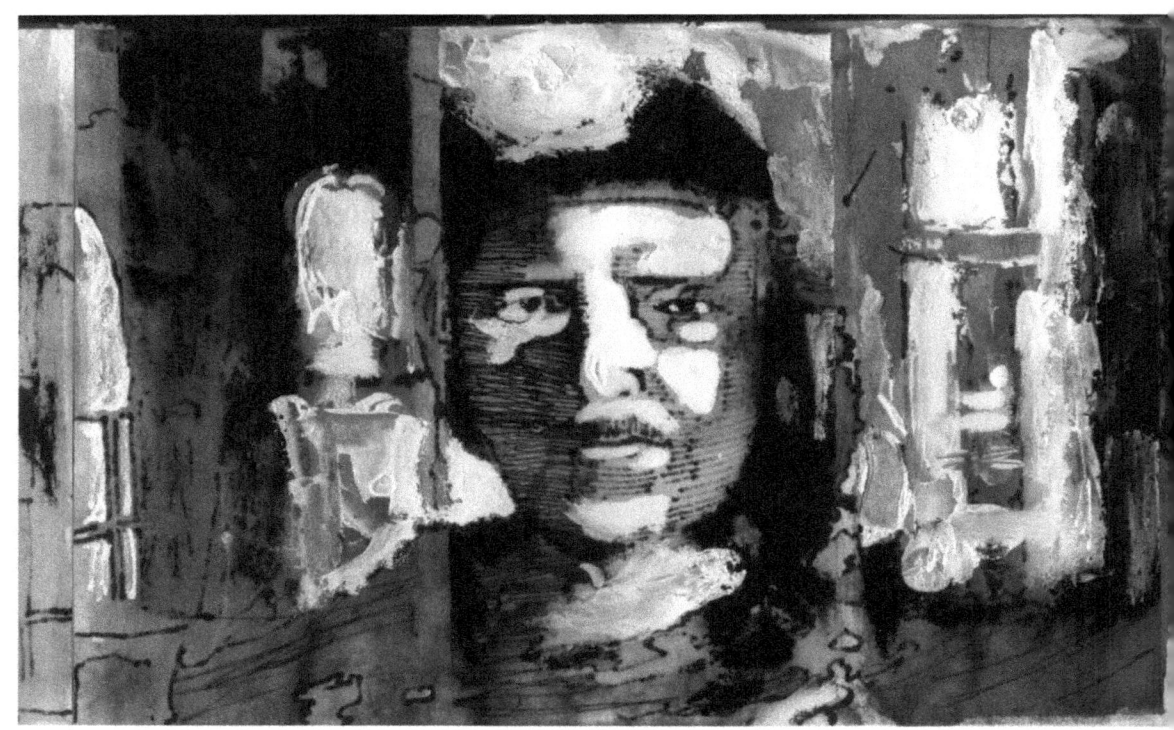

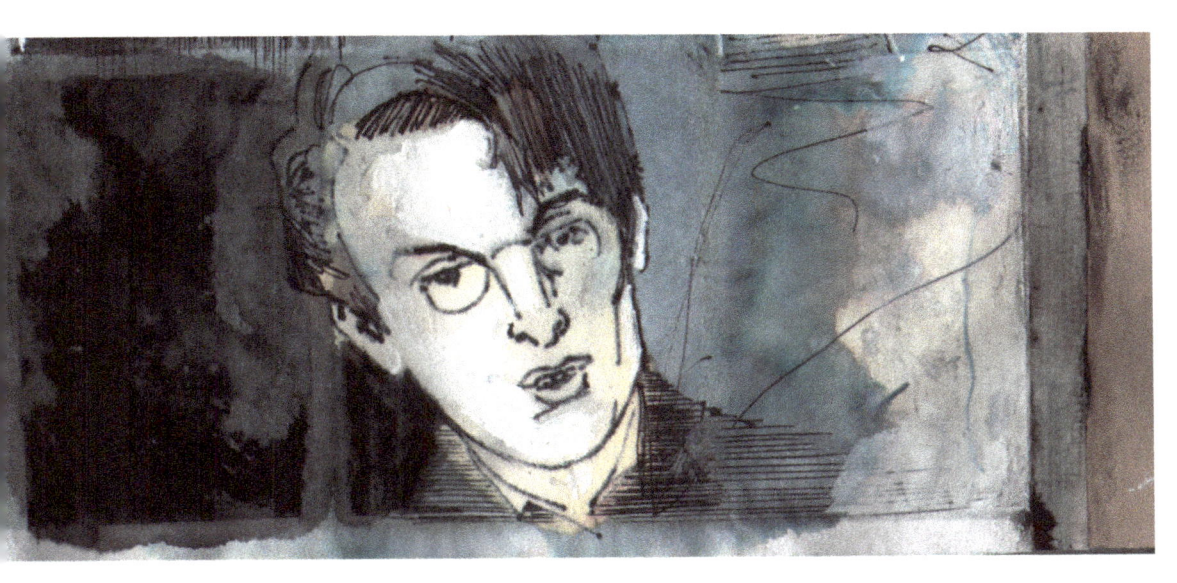

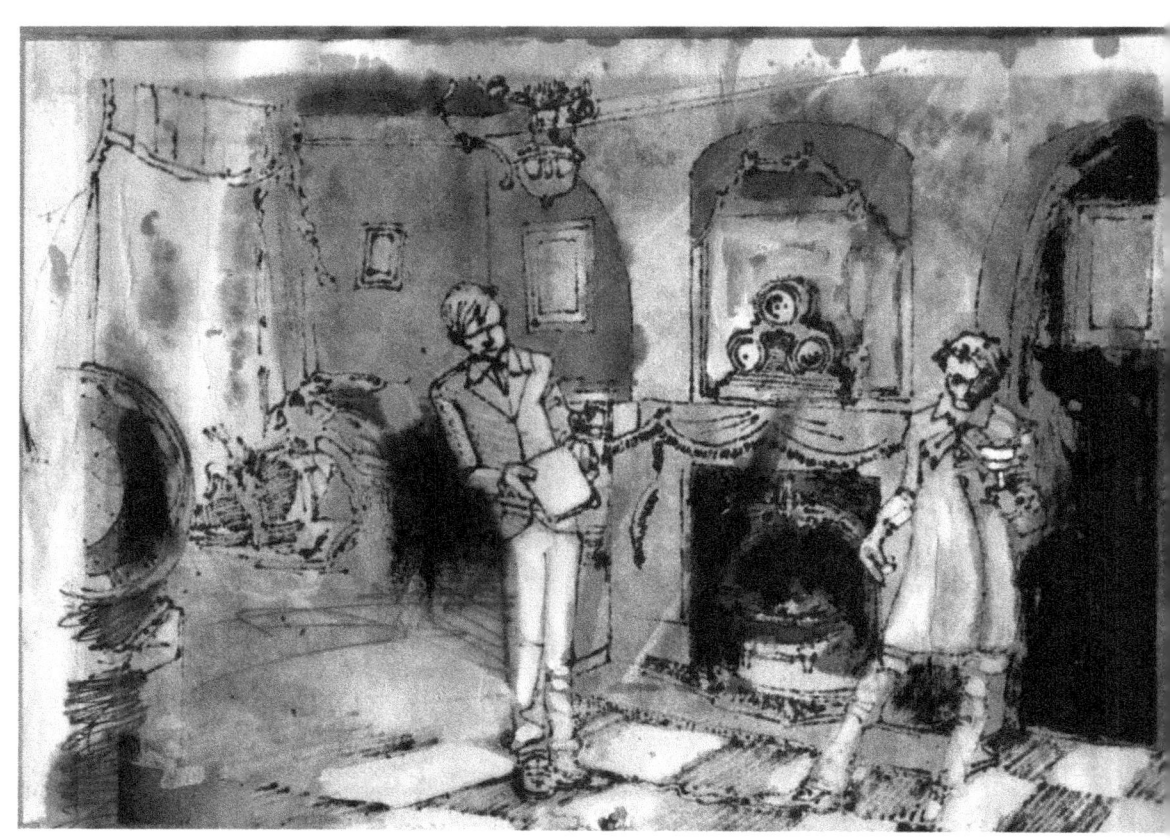

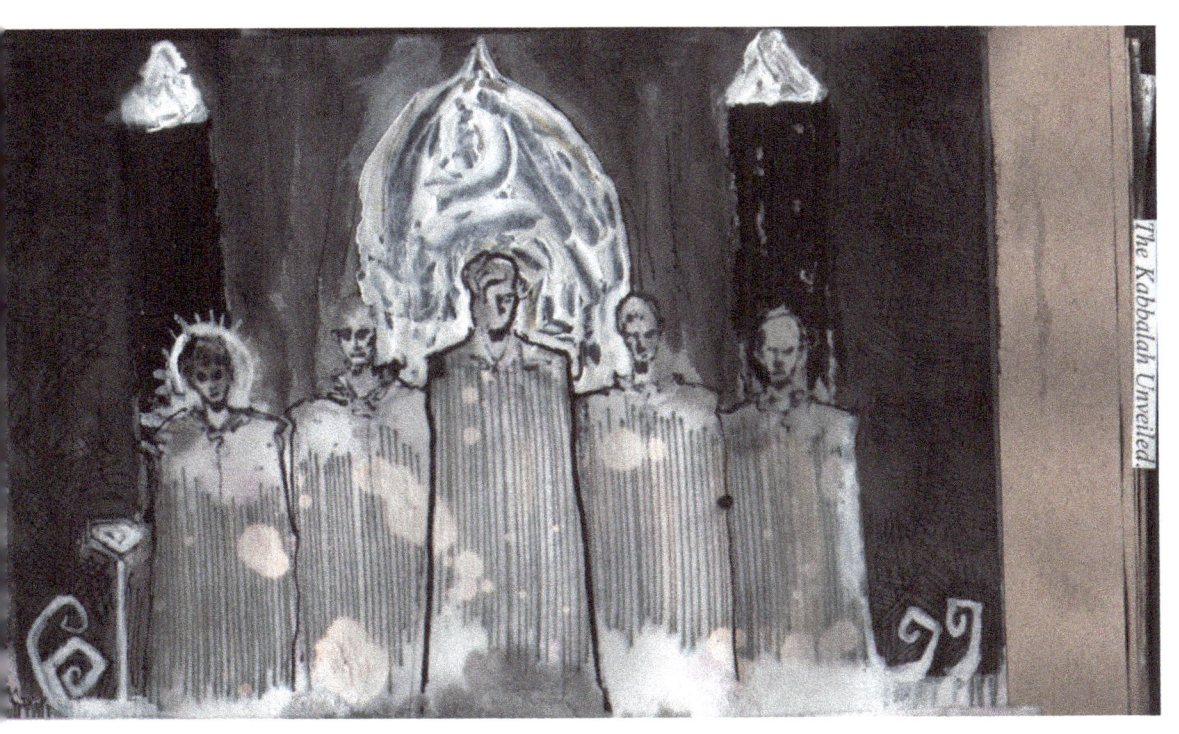

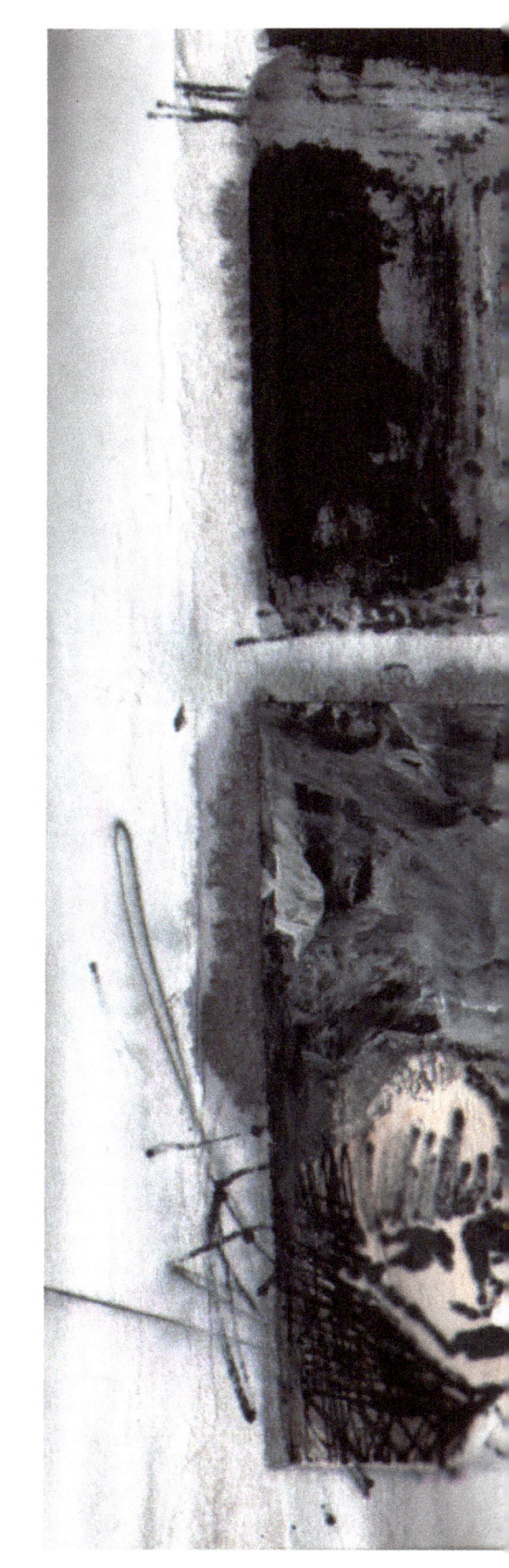

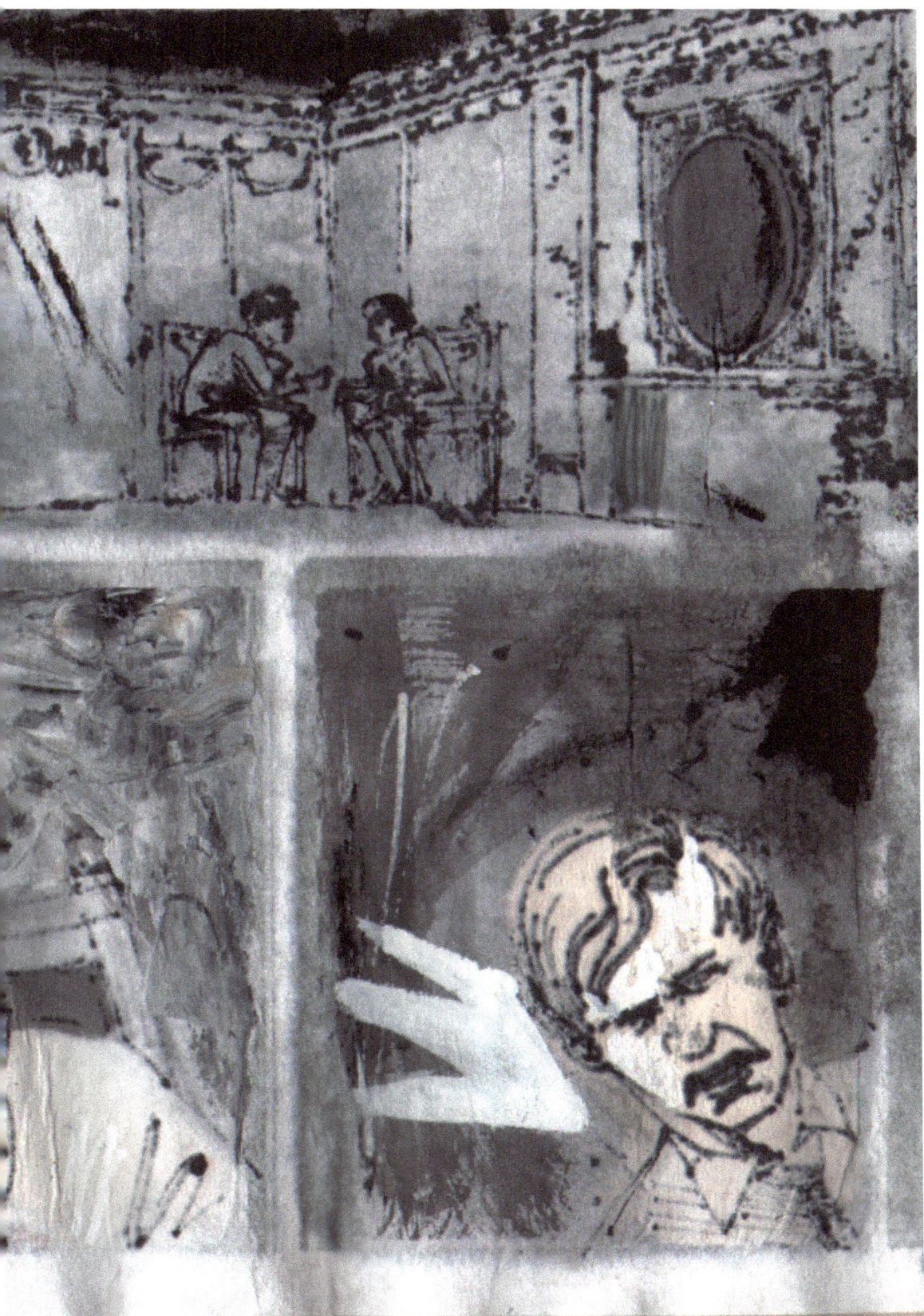

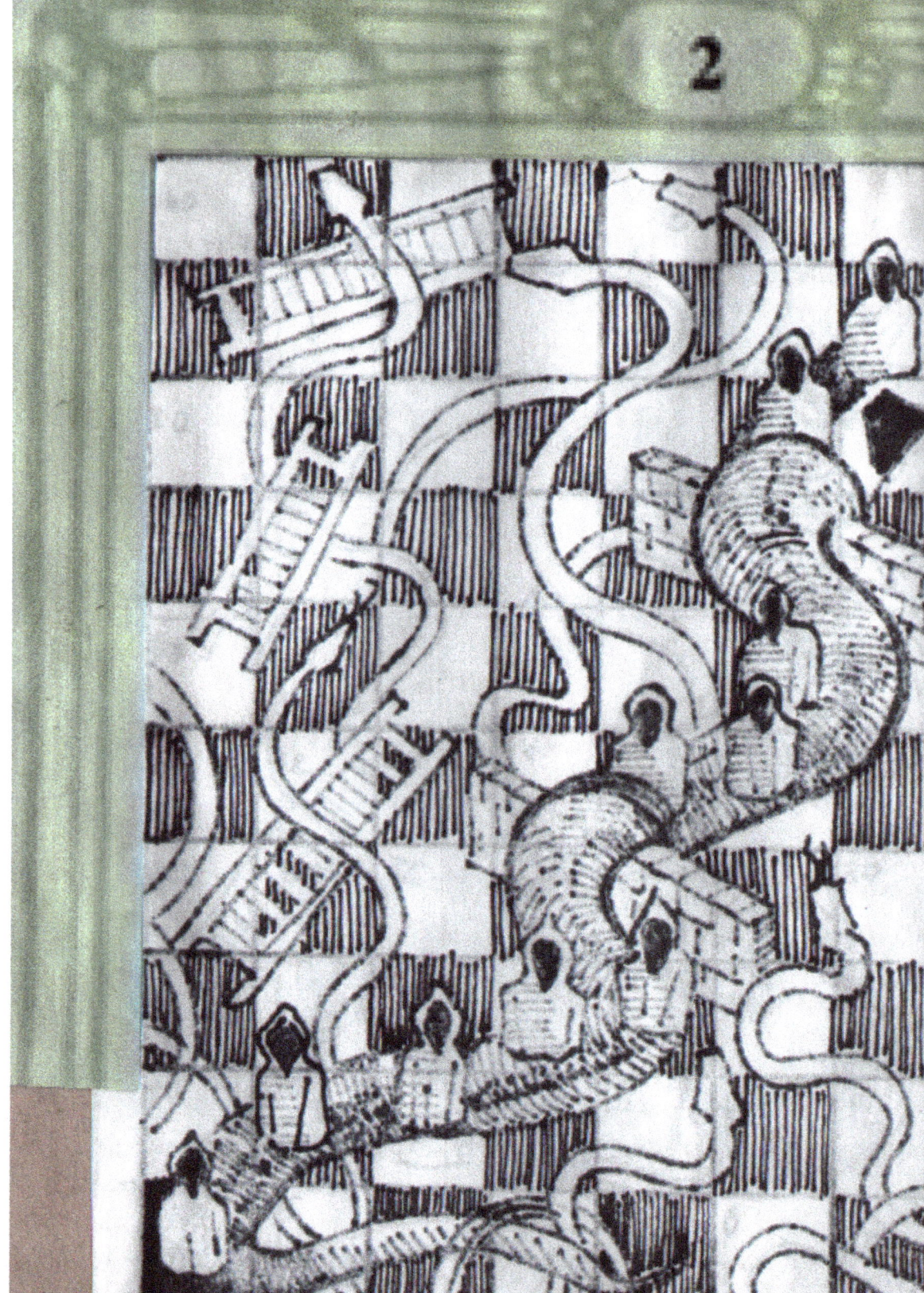

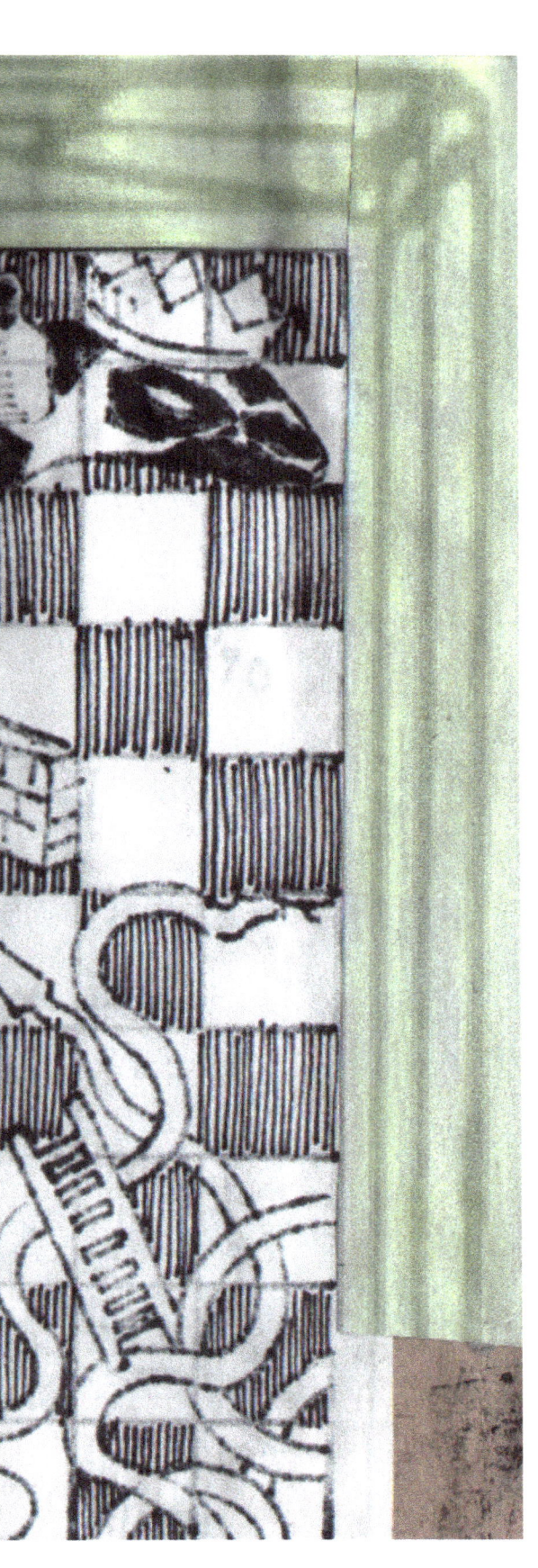

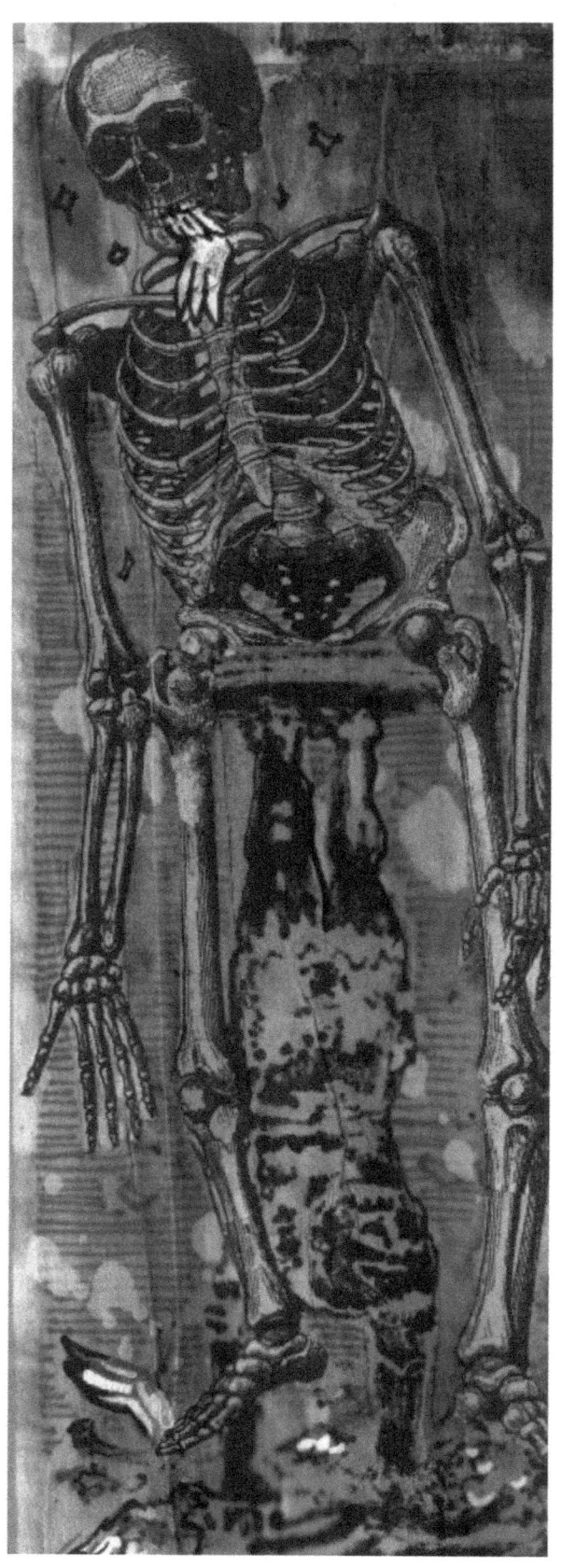

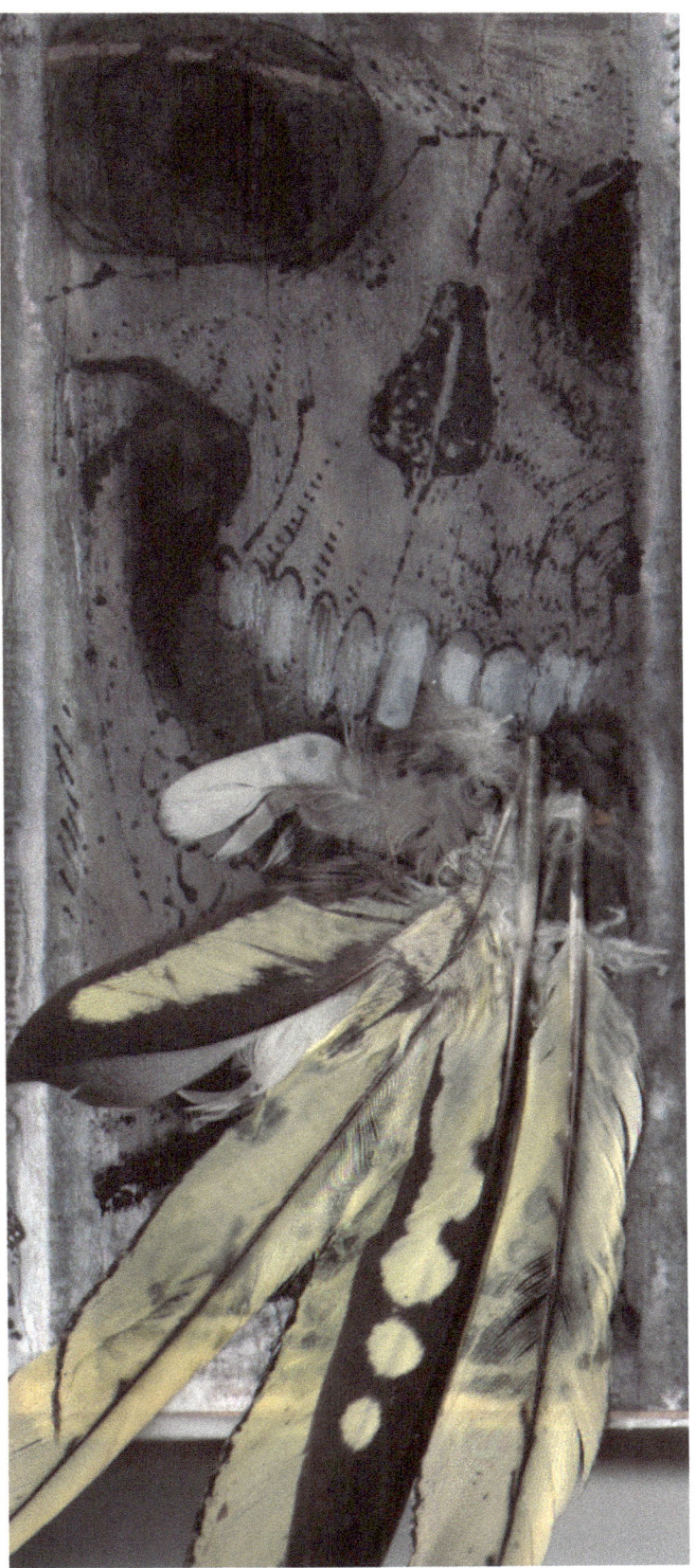

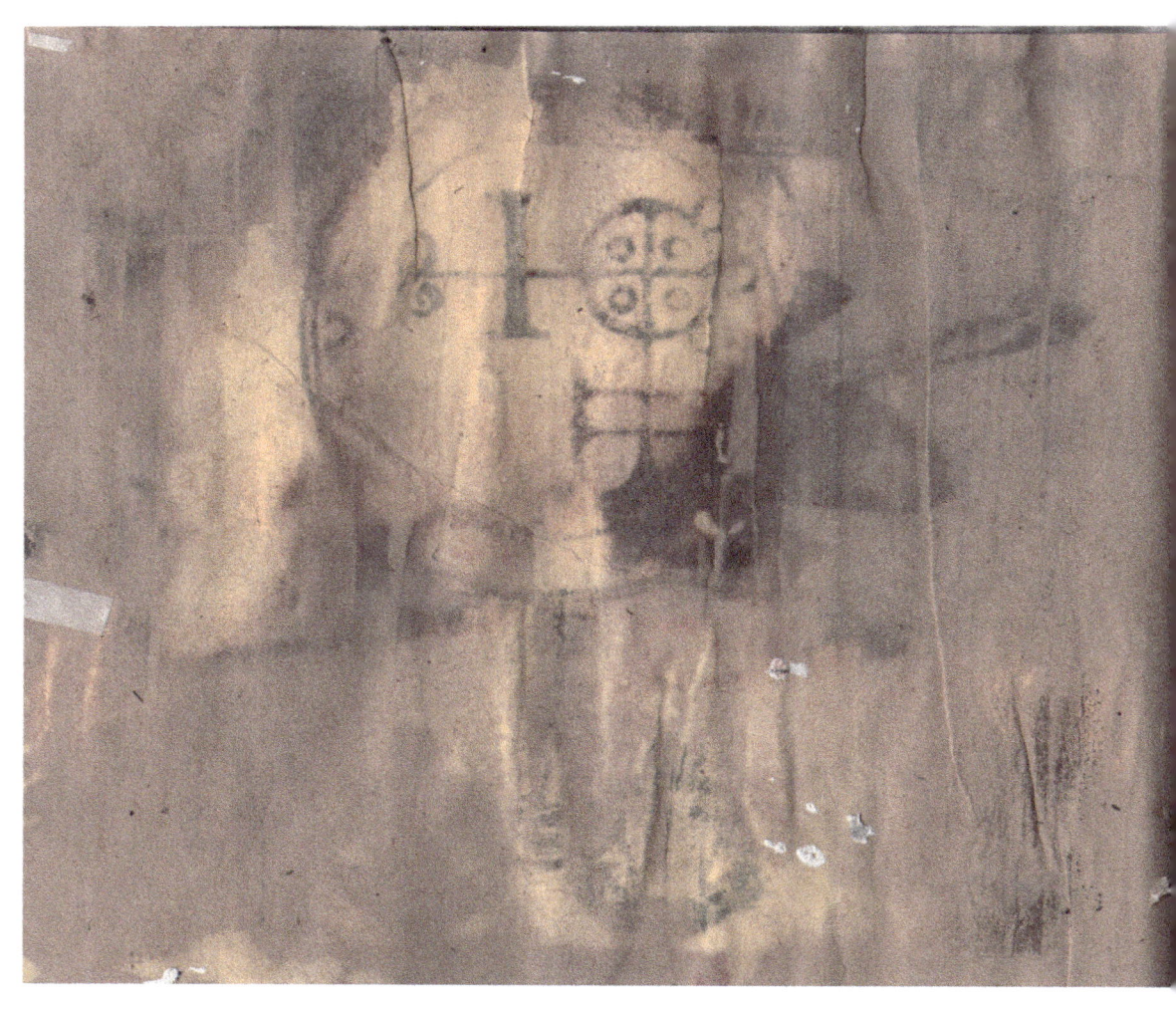

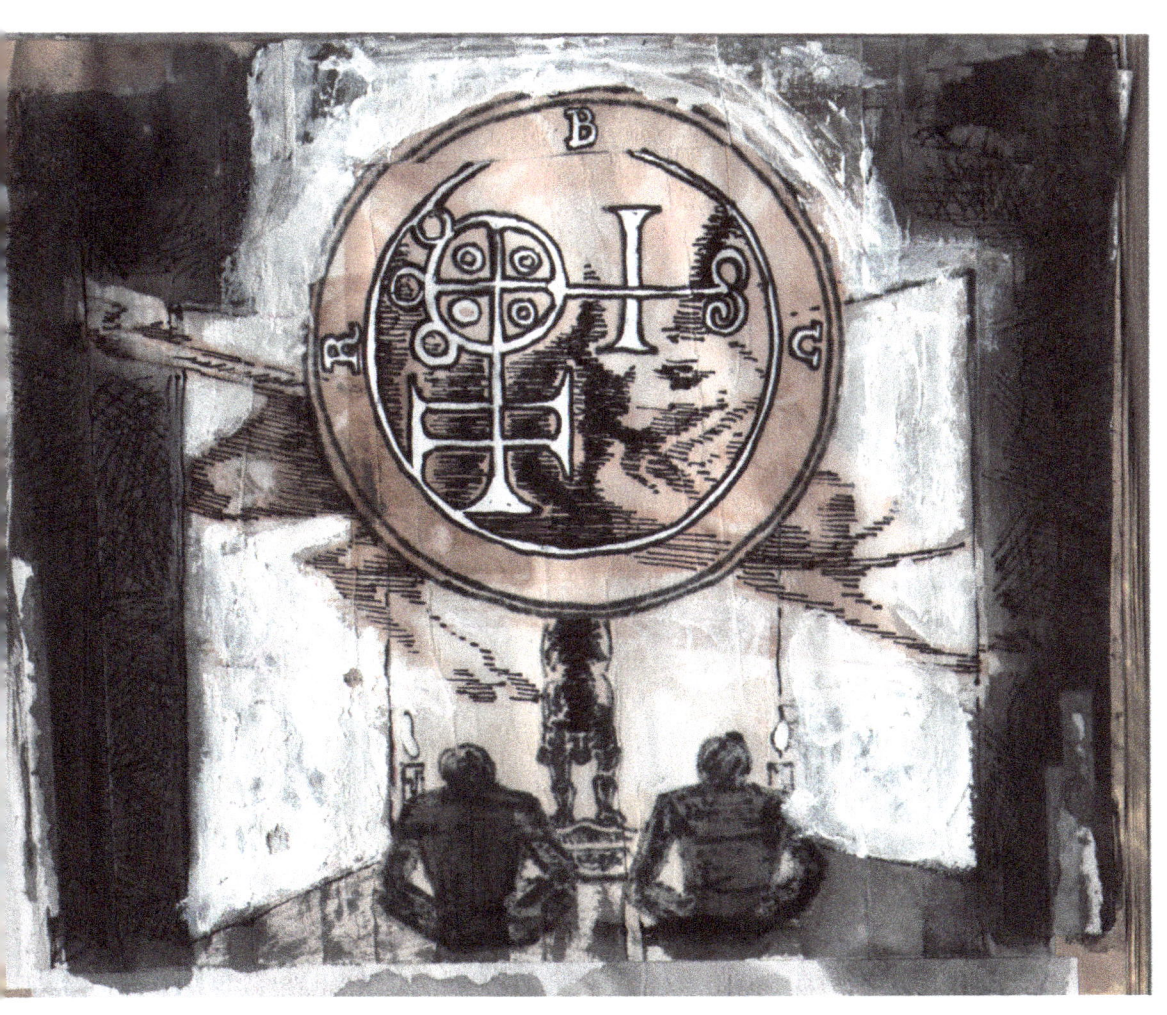

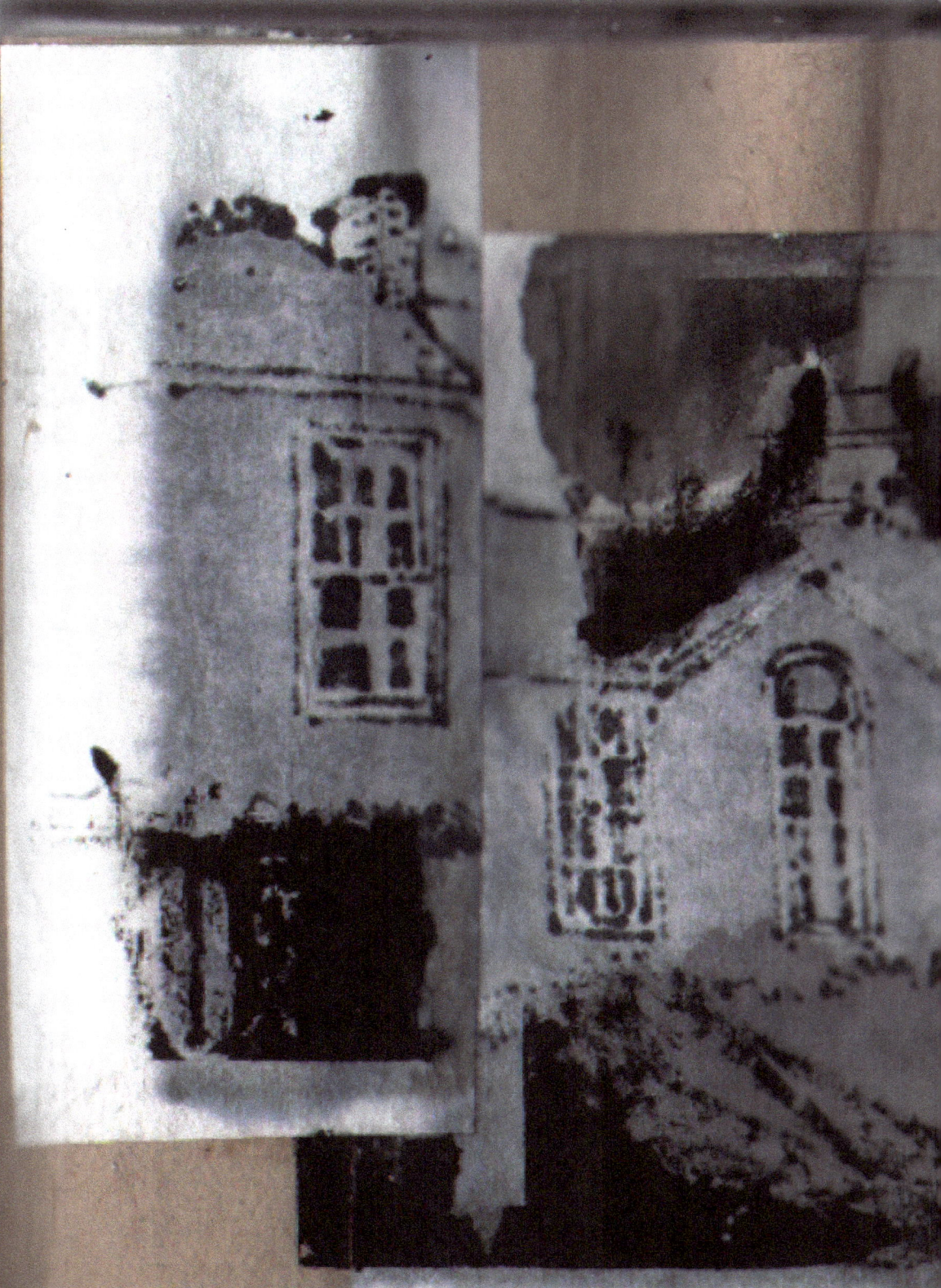

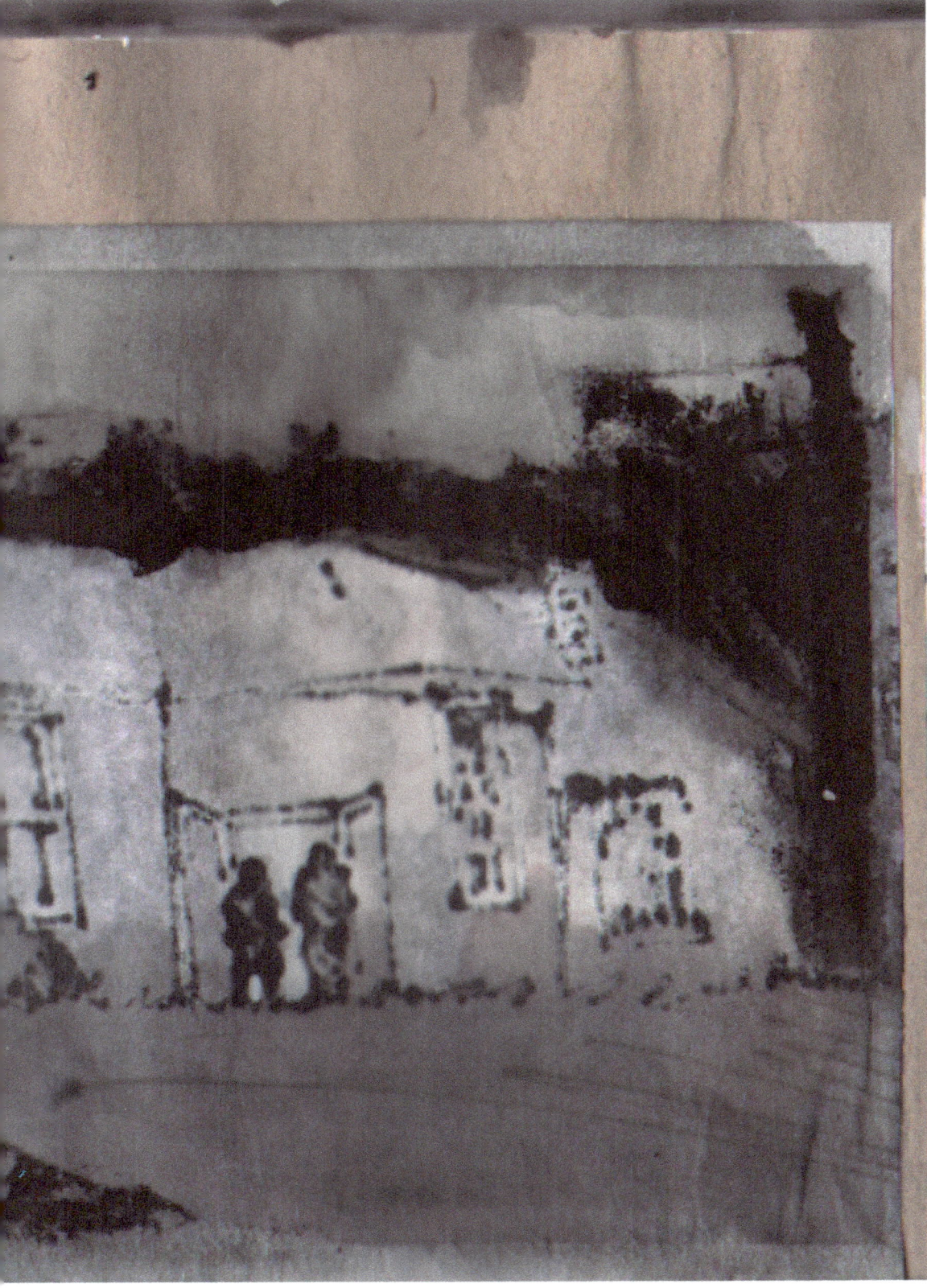

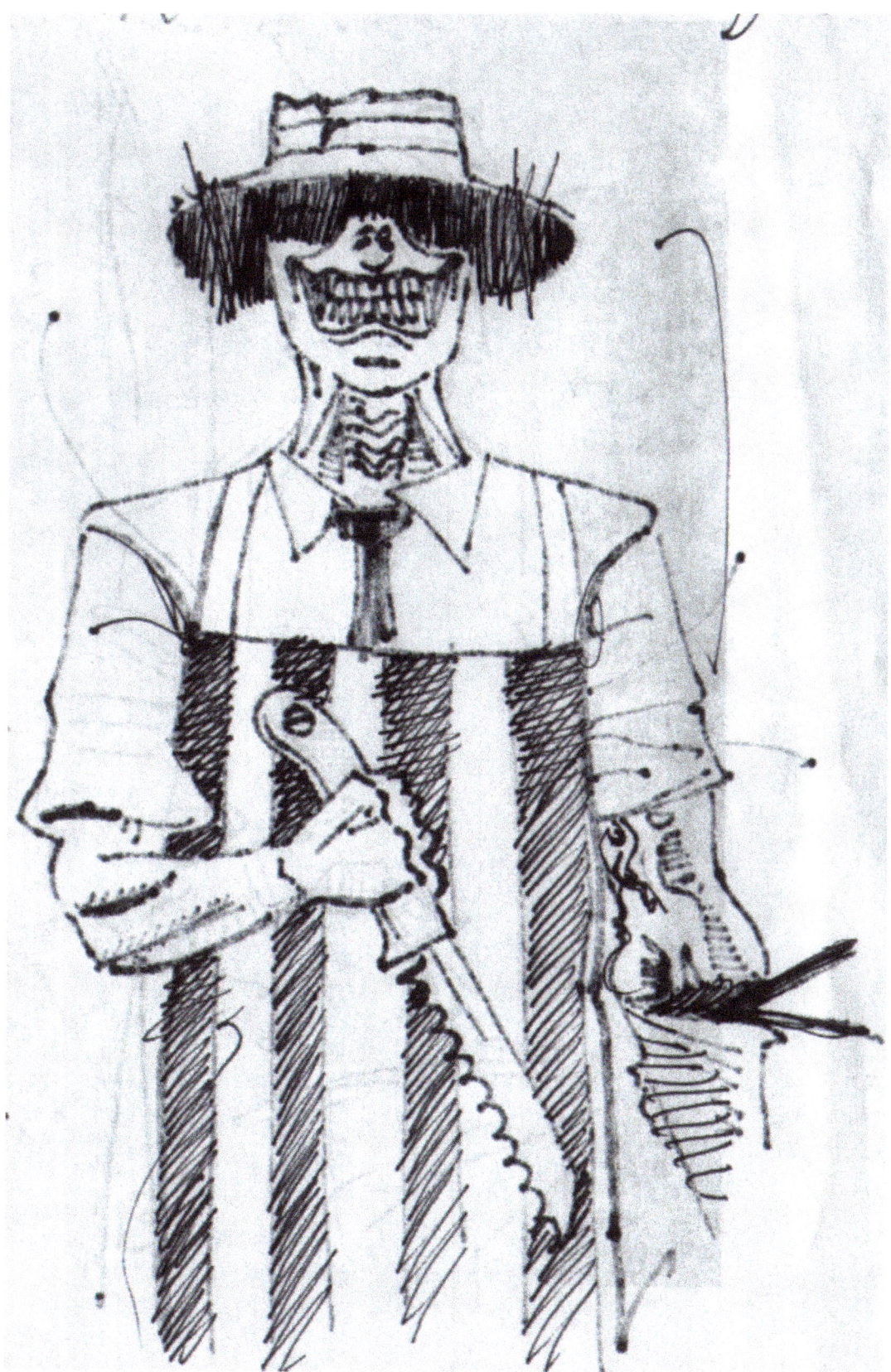

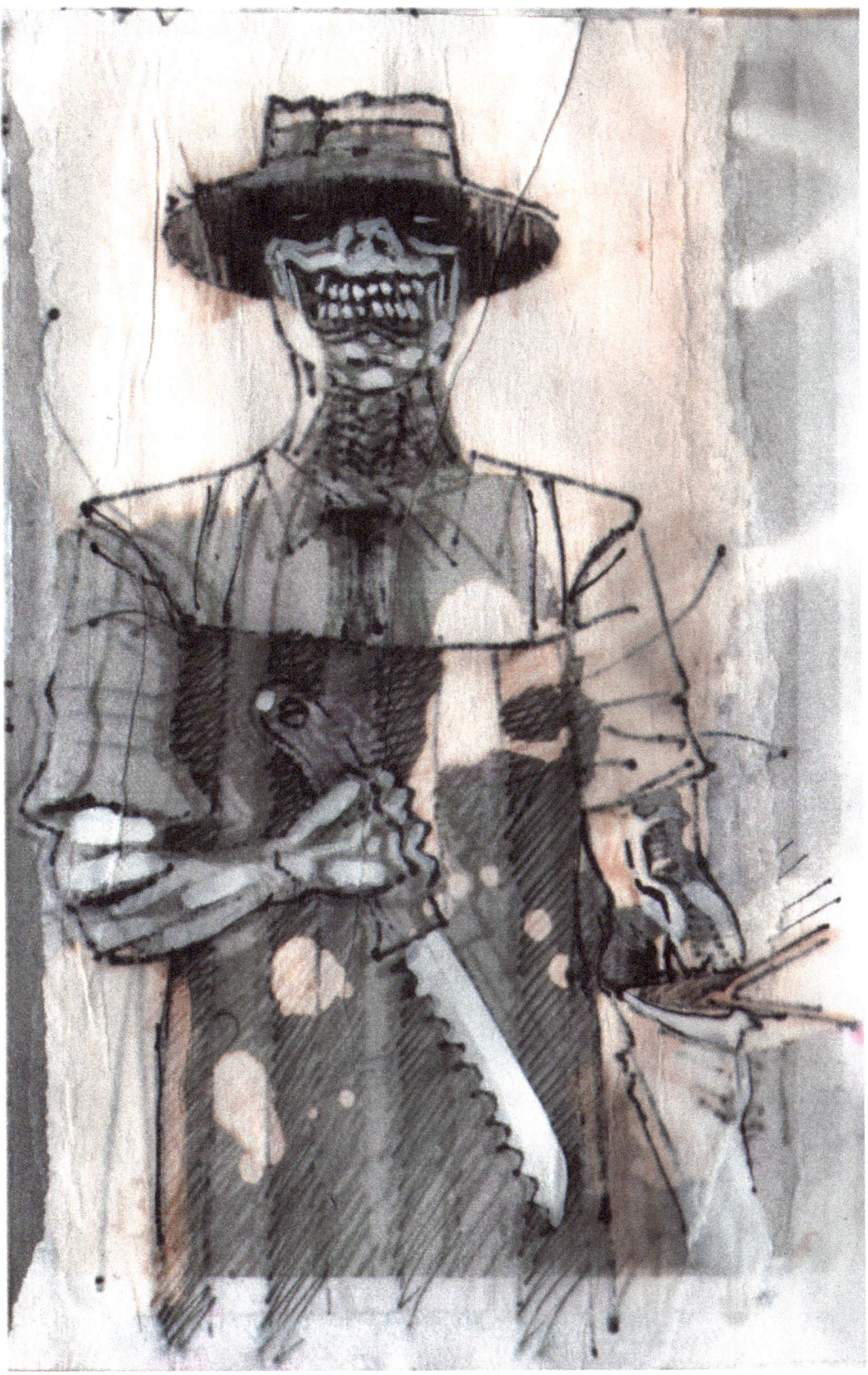

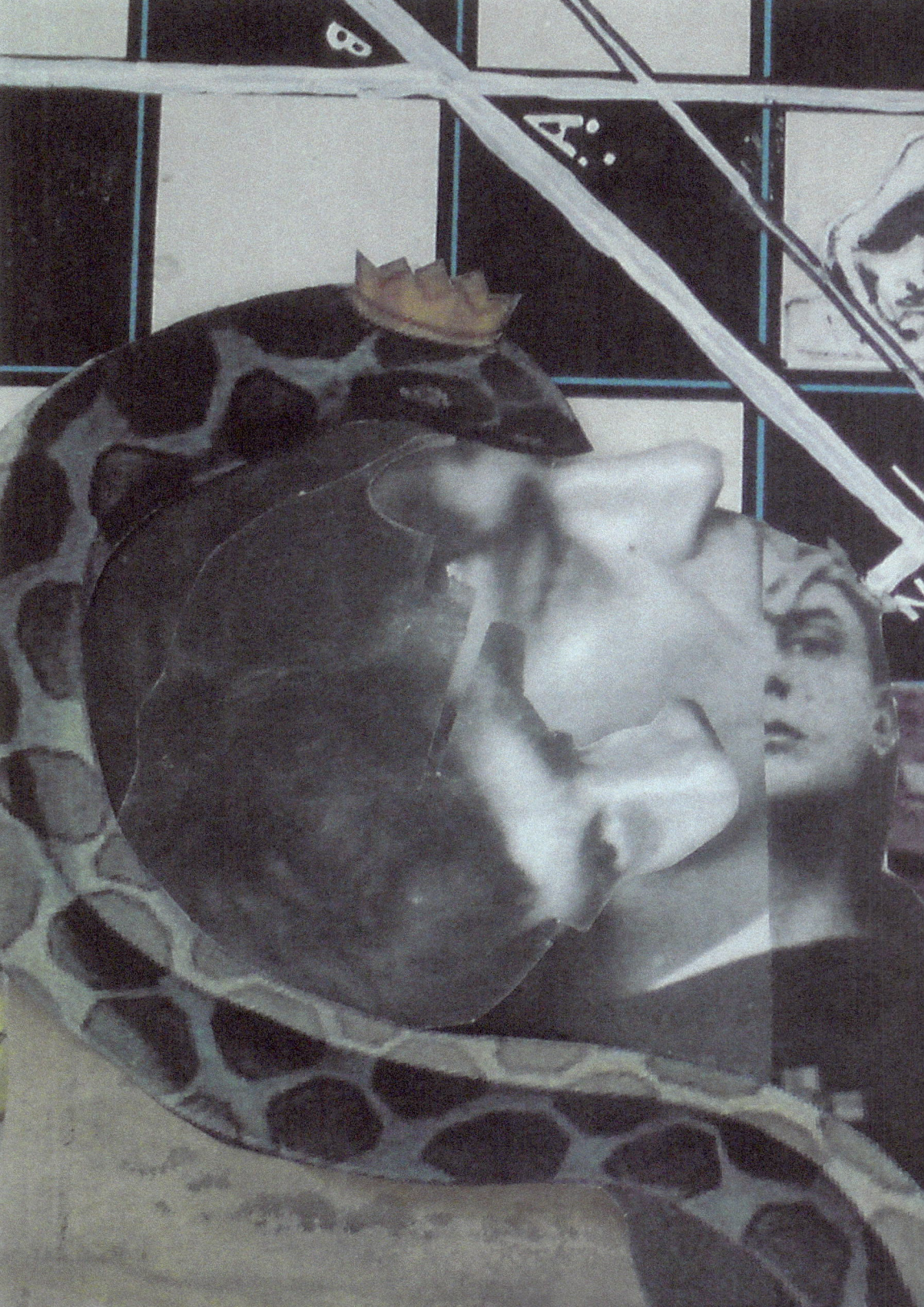

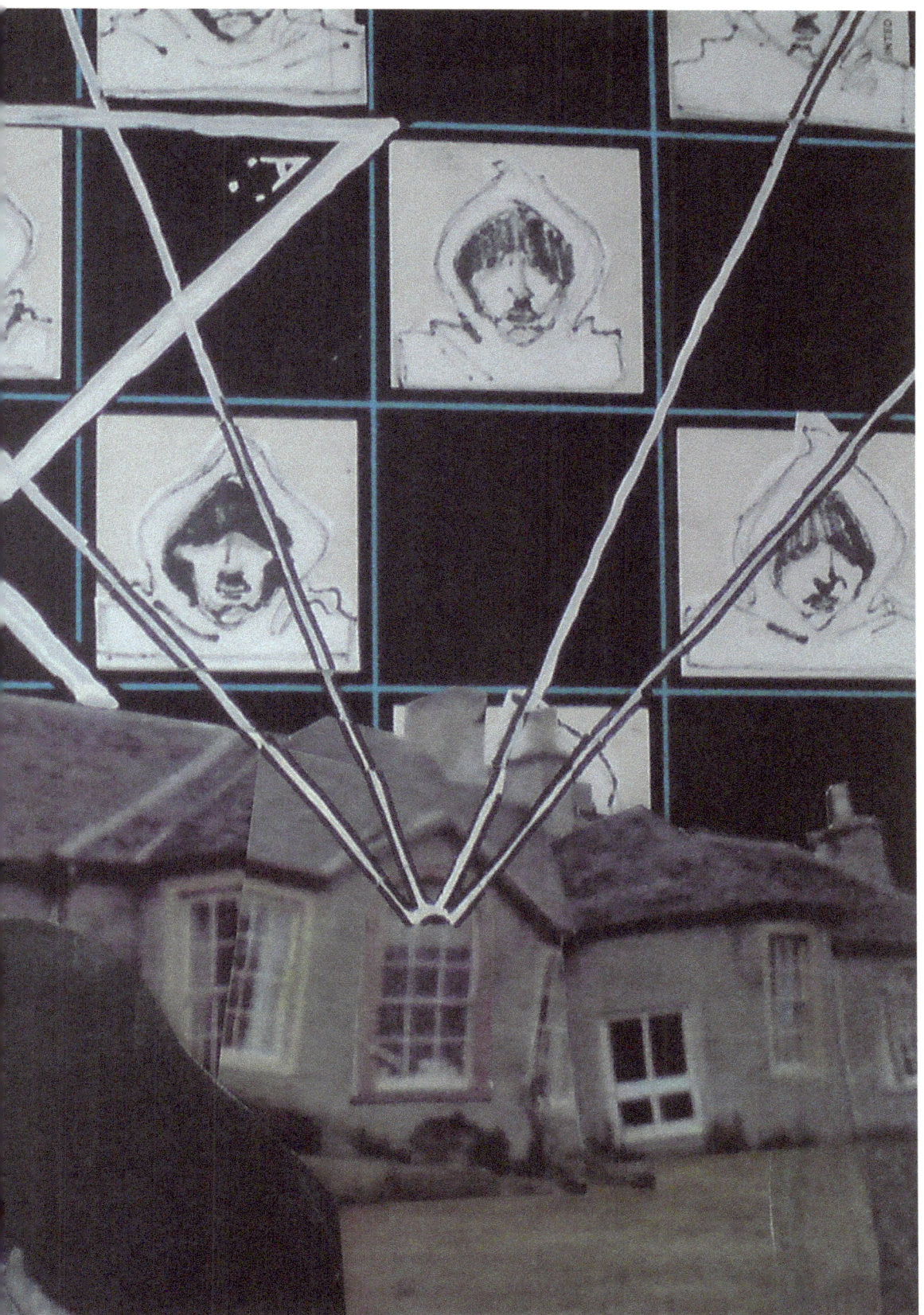

Lord of the Paths in the Portal

ADEPTUS

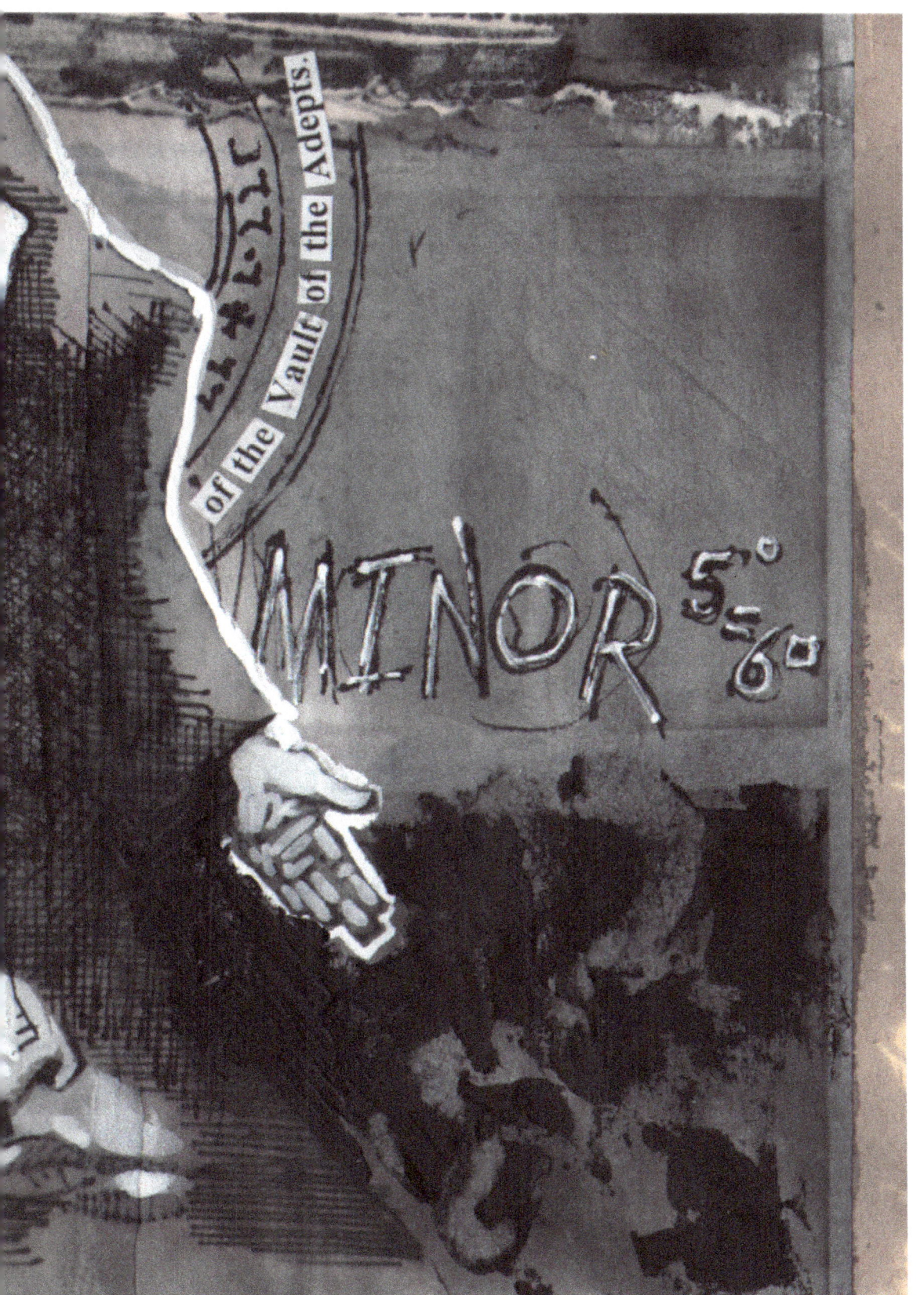

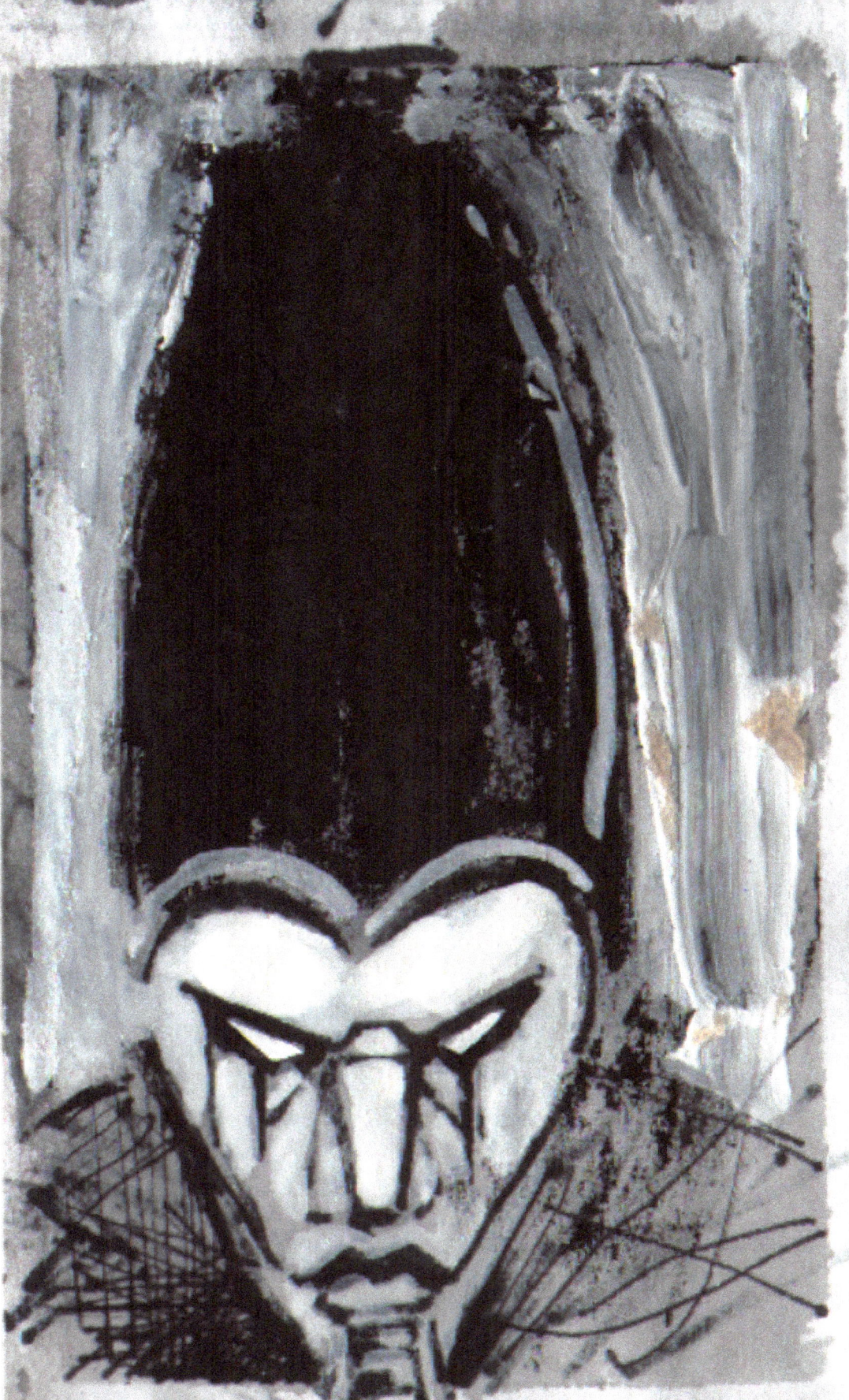

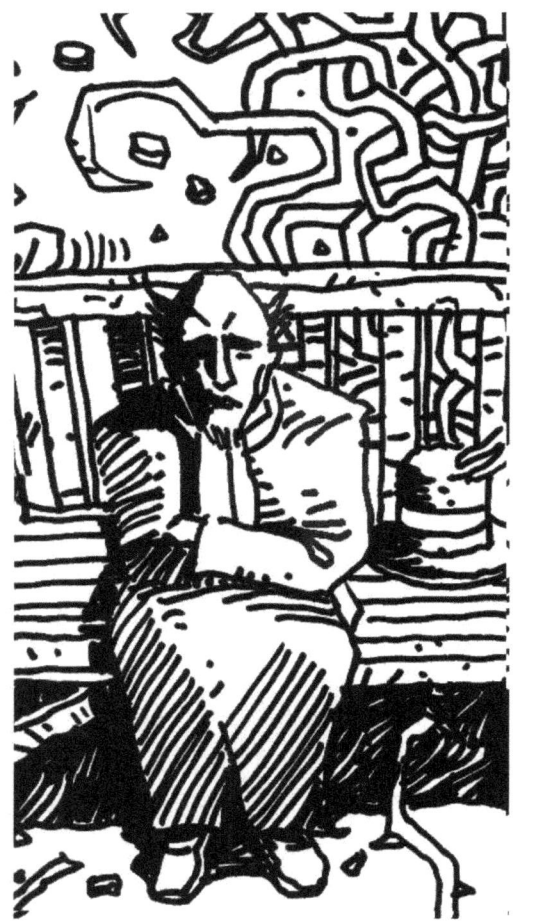 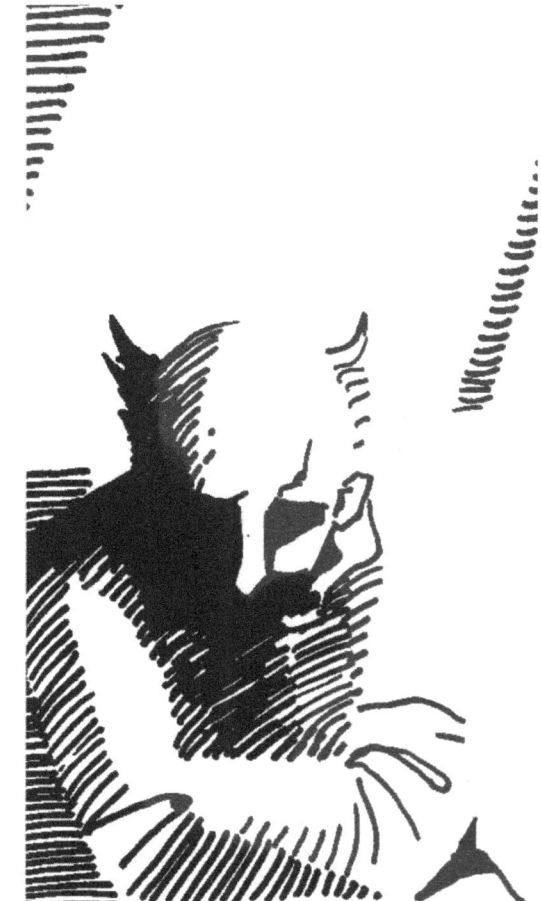

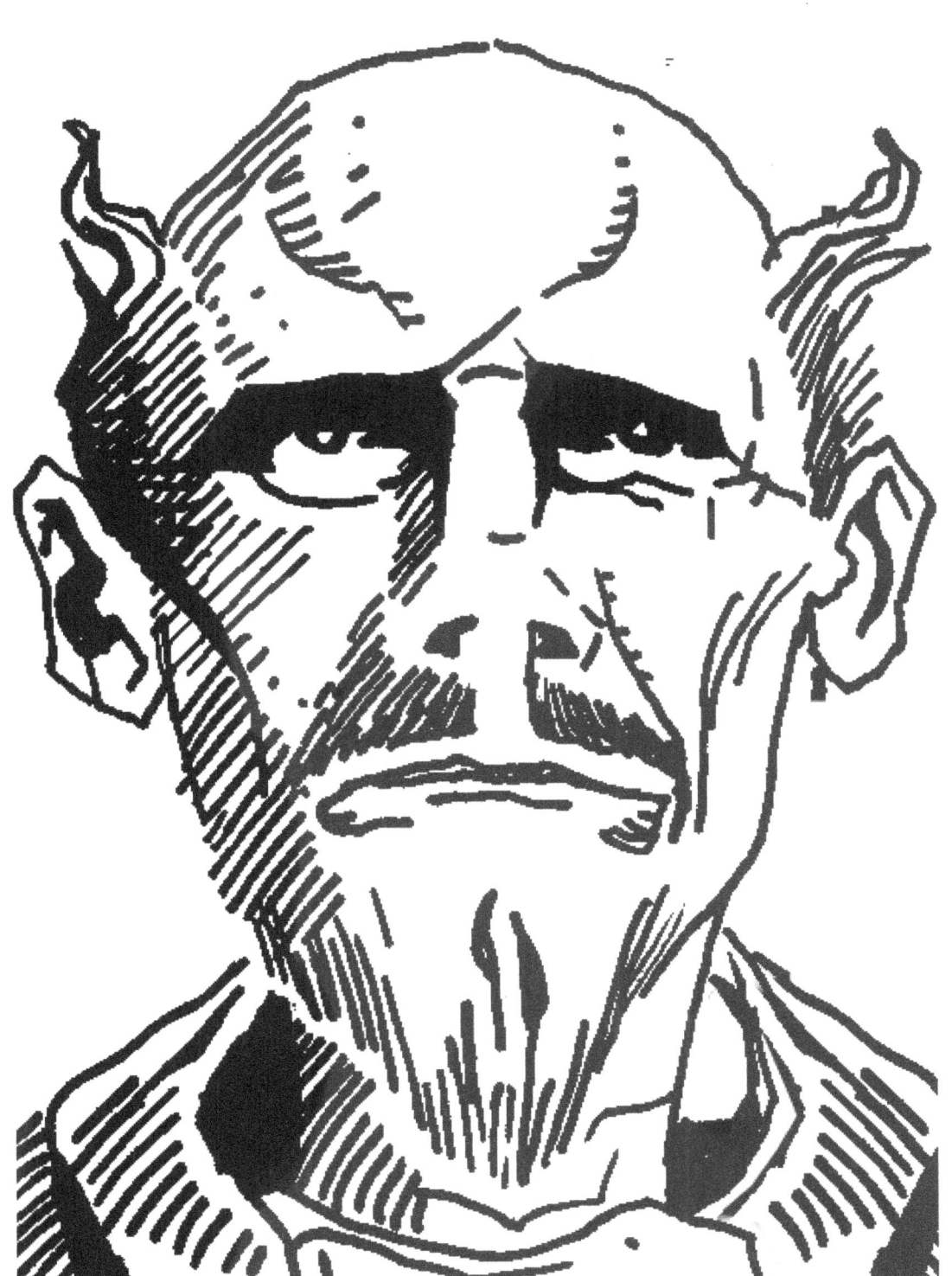

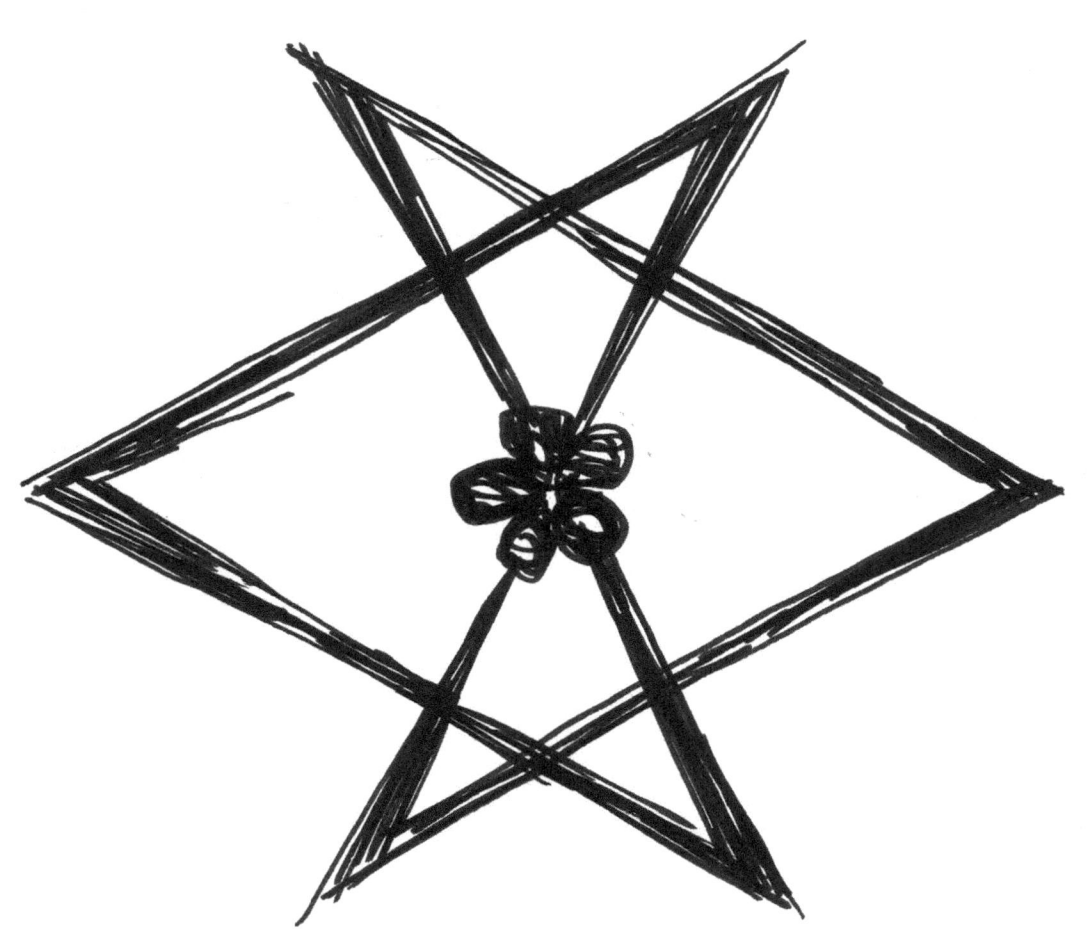

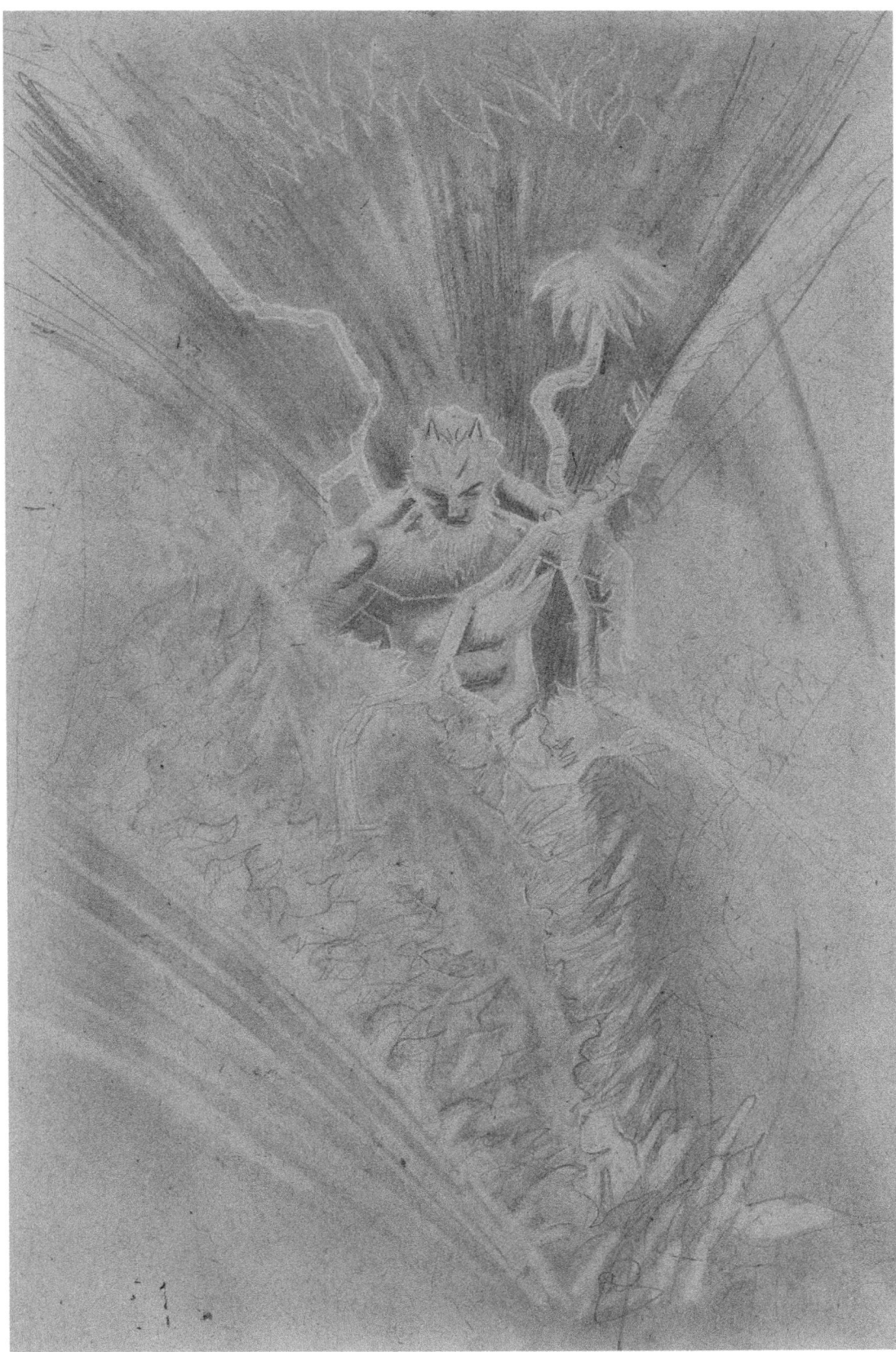

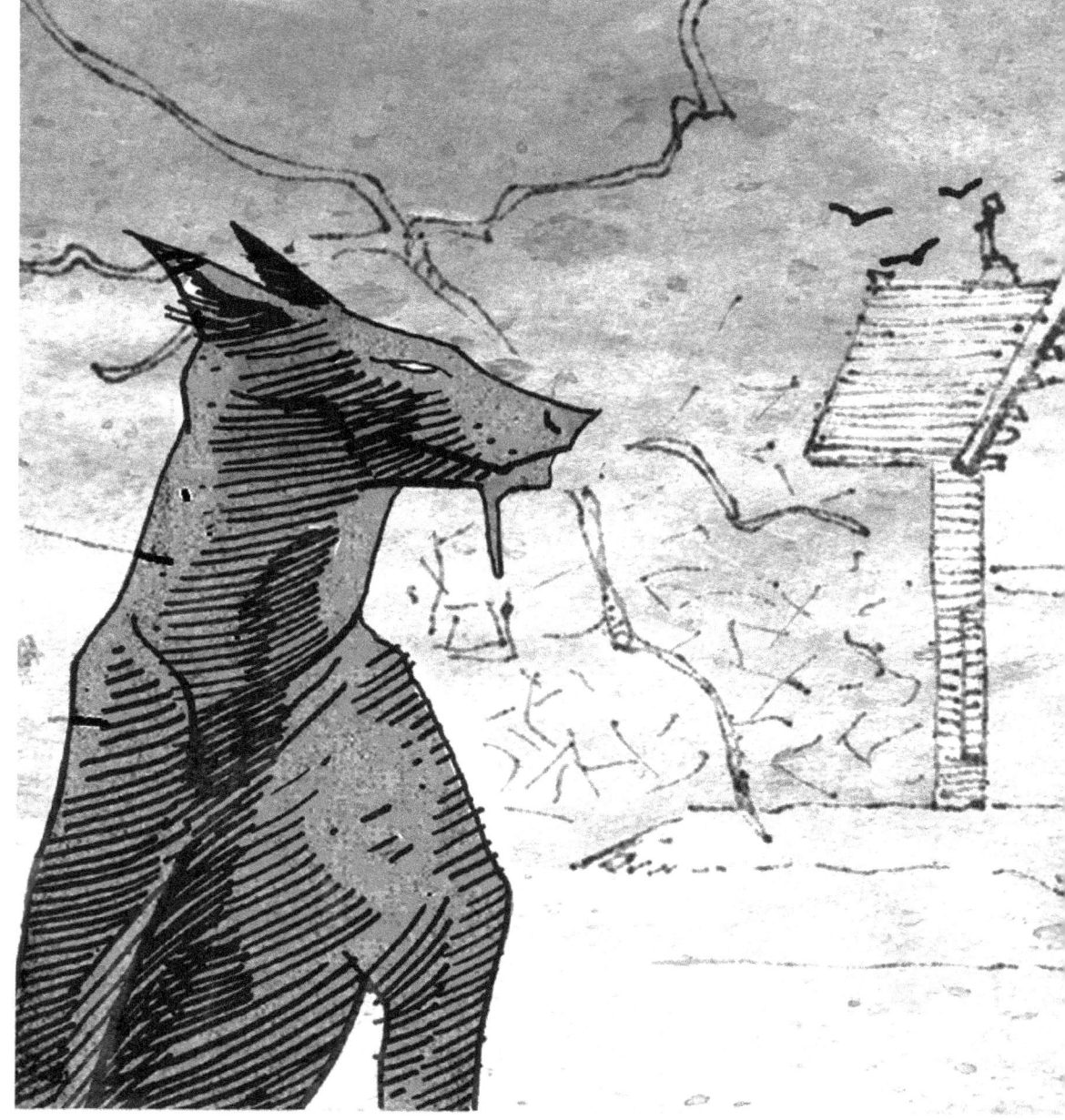

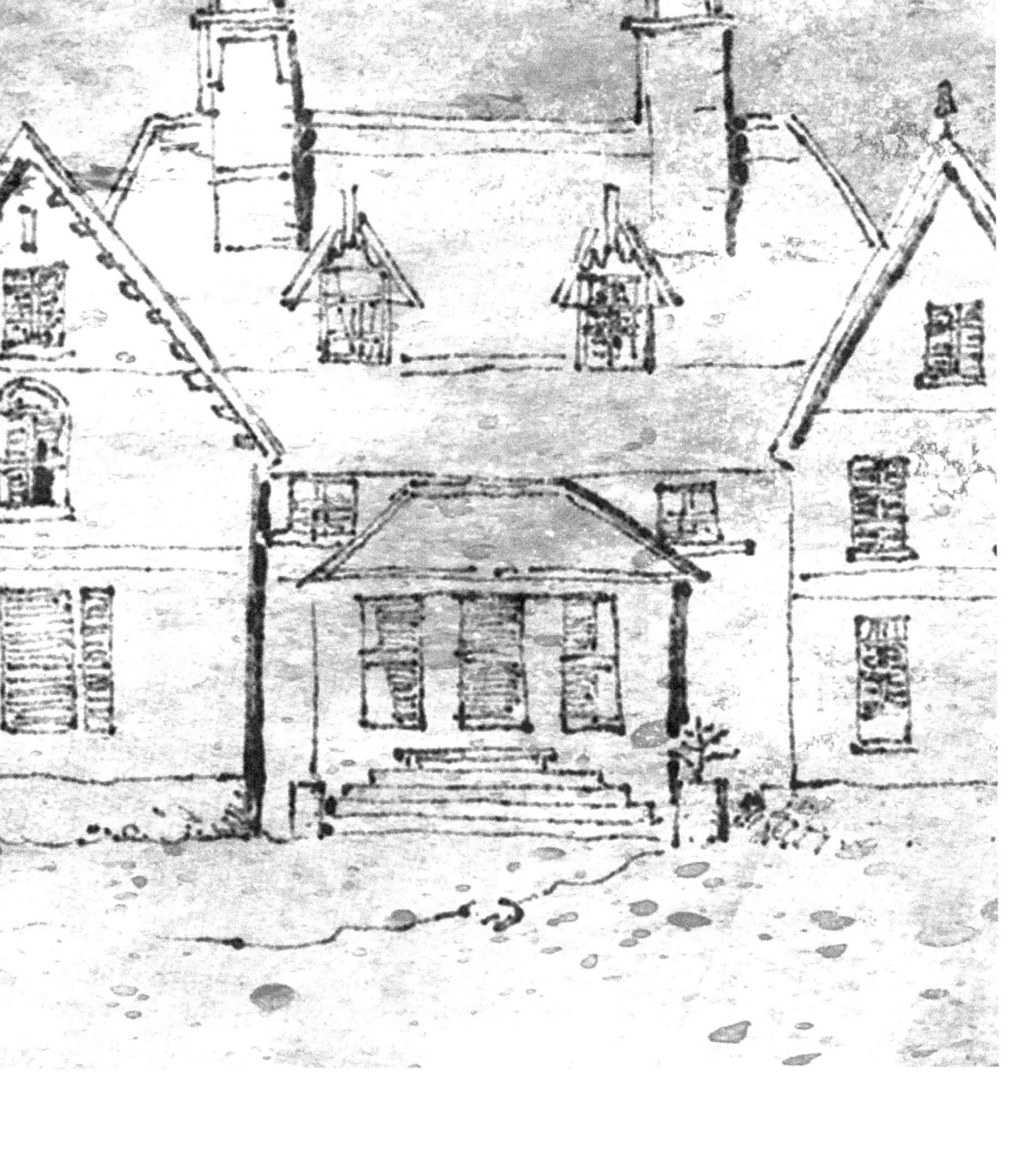

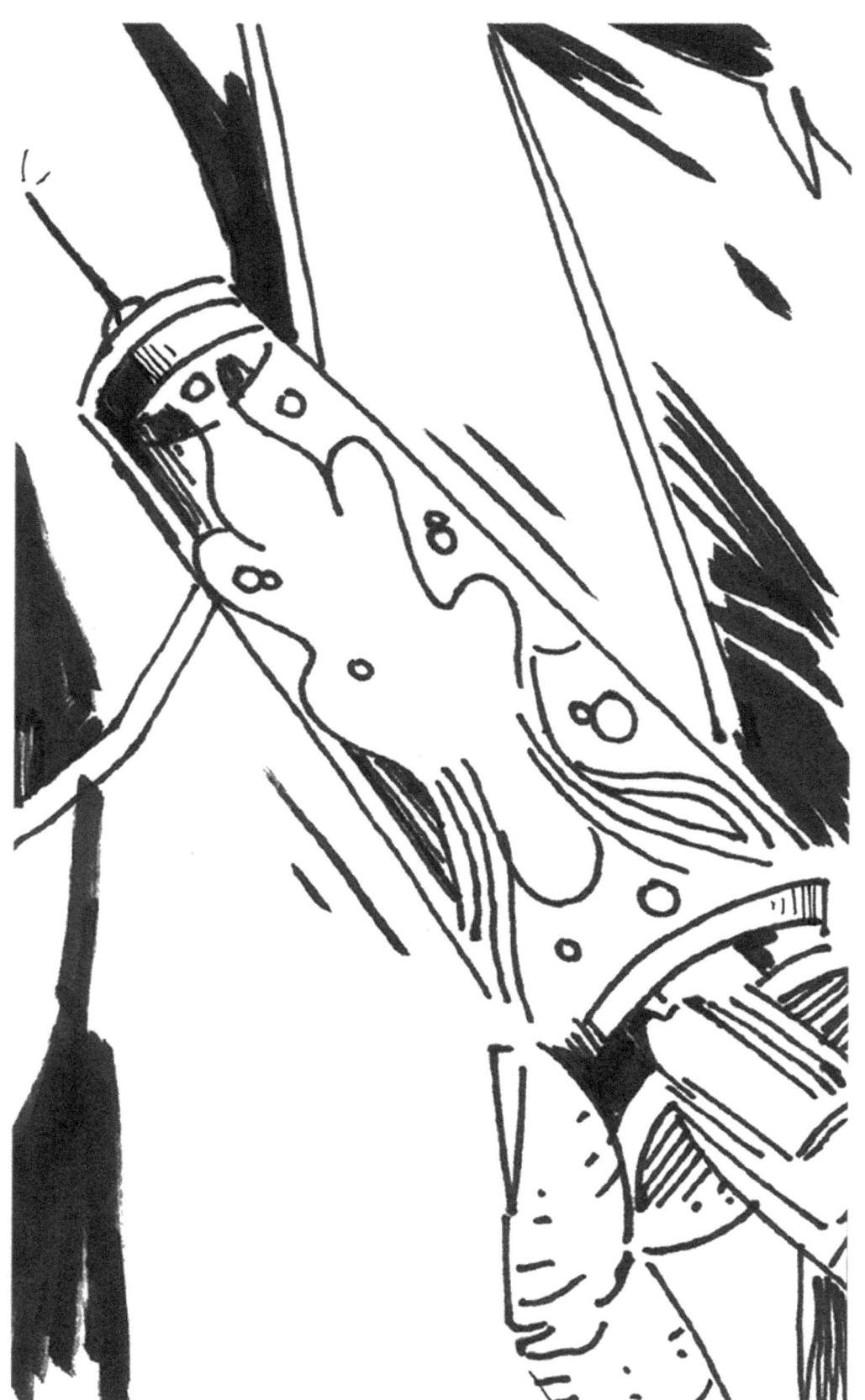

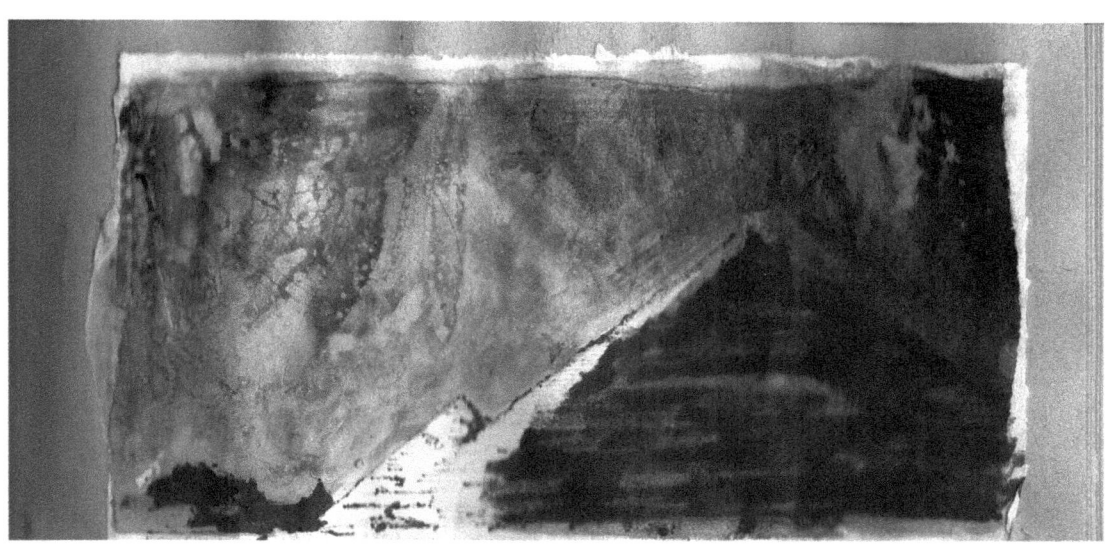

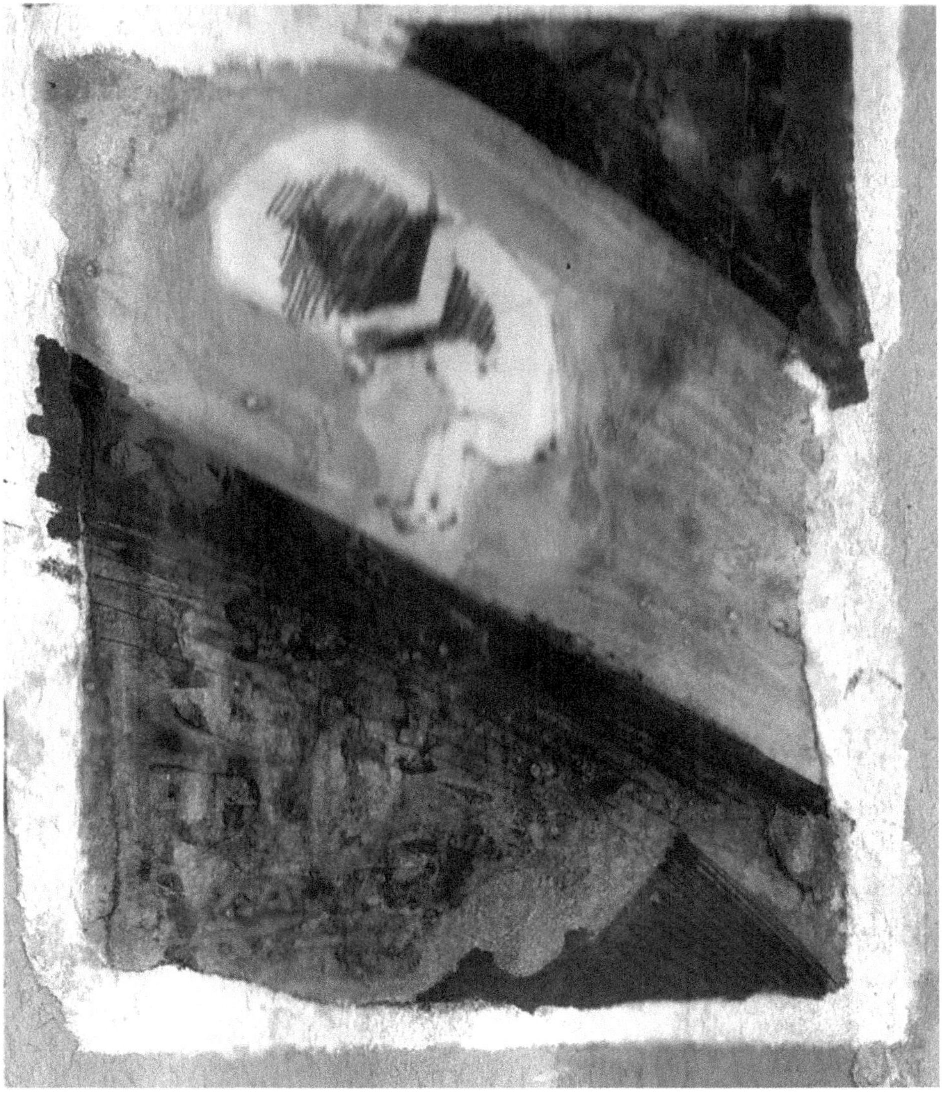

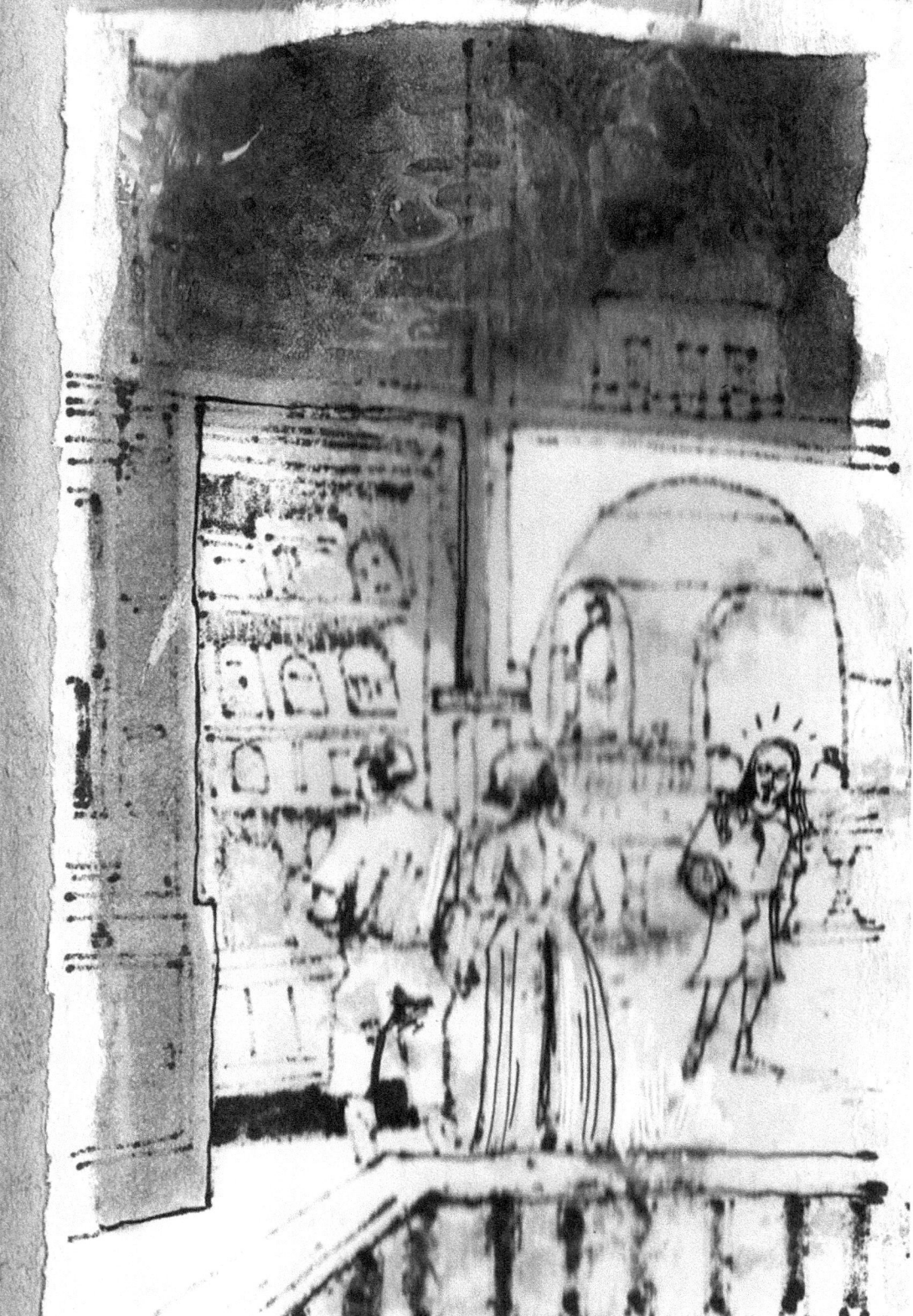

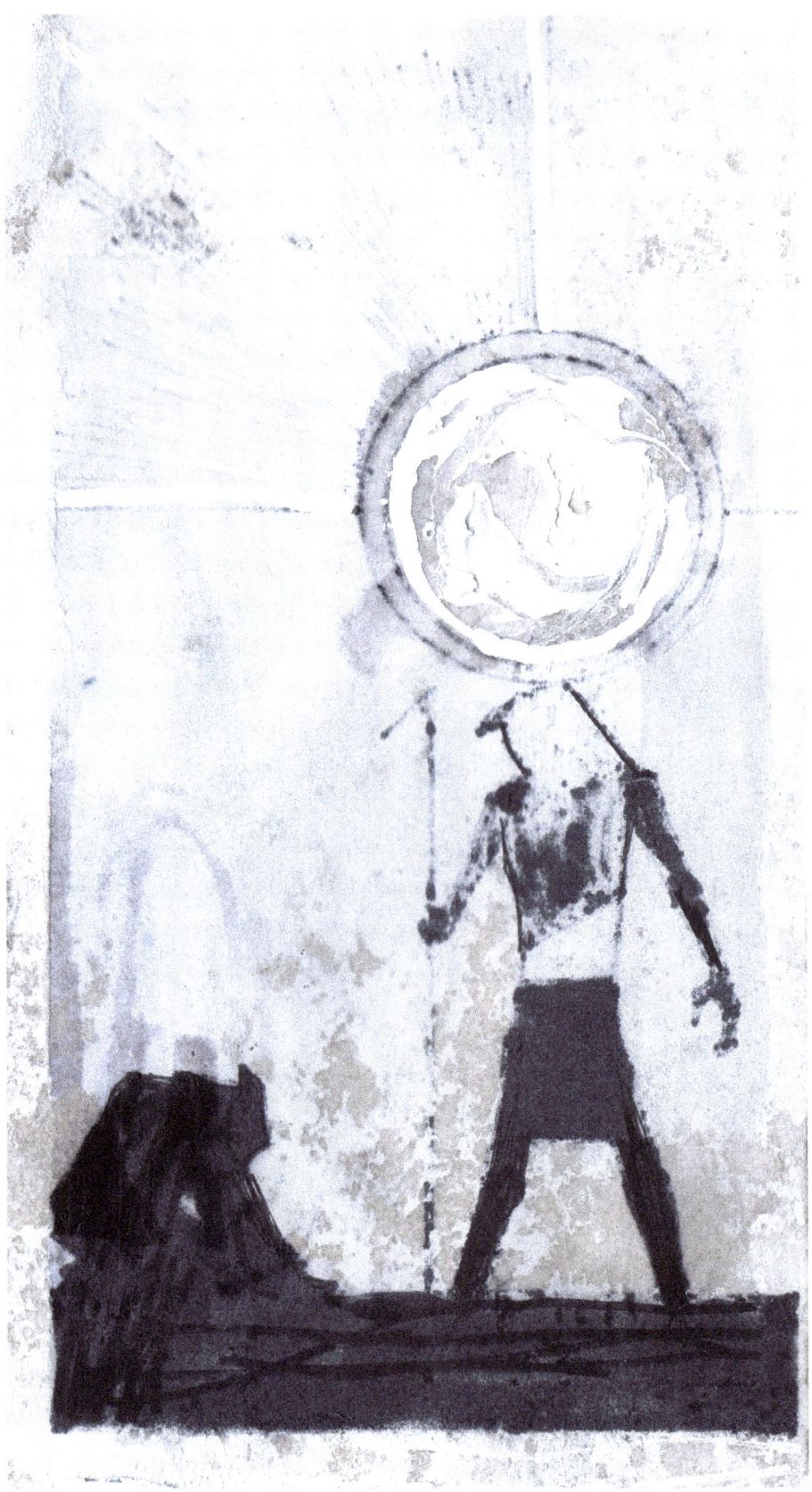

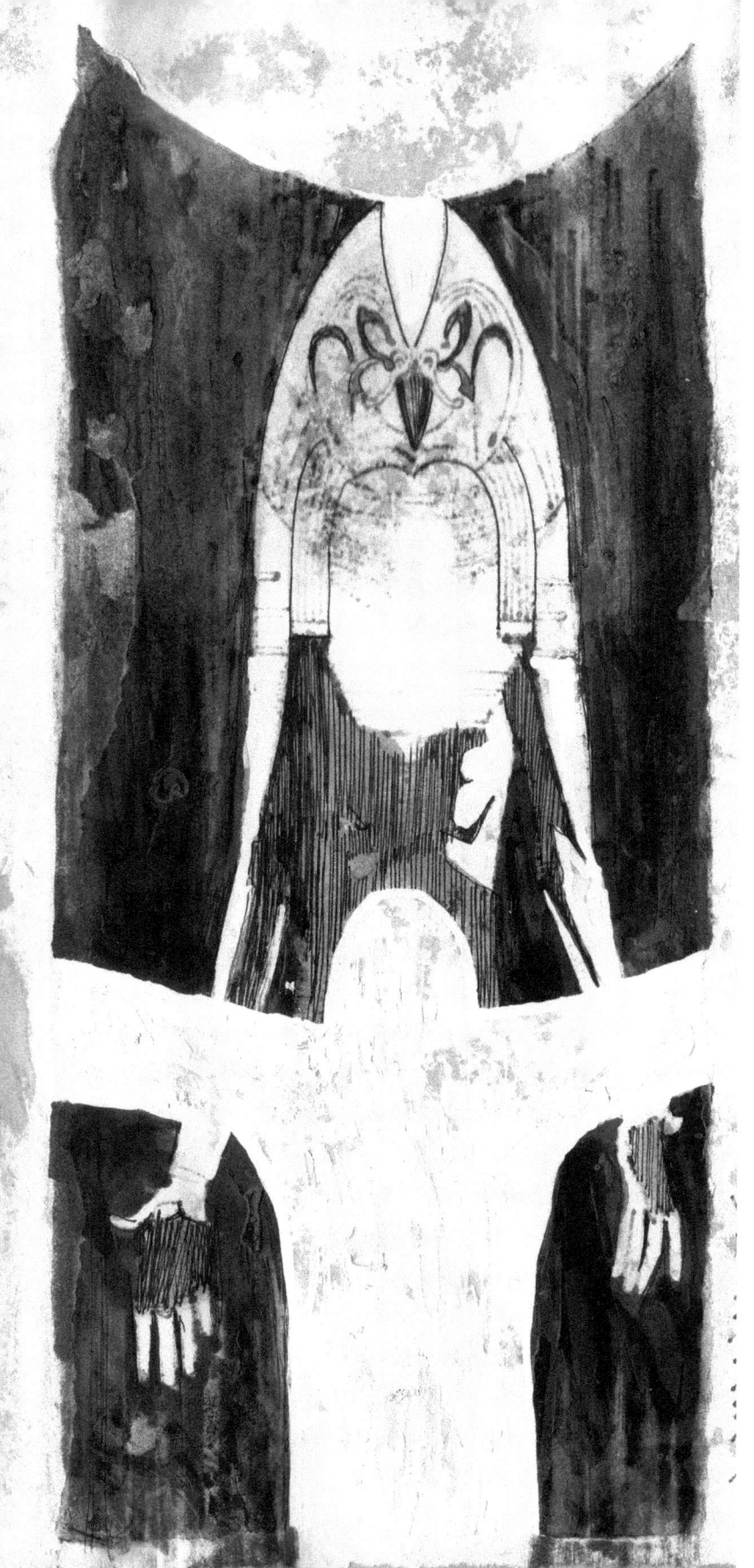

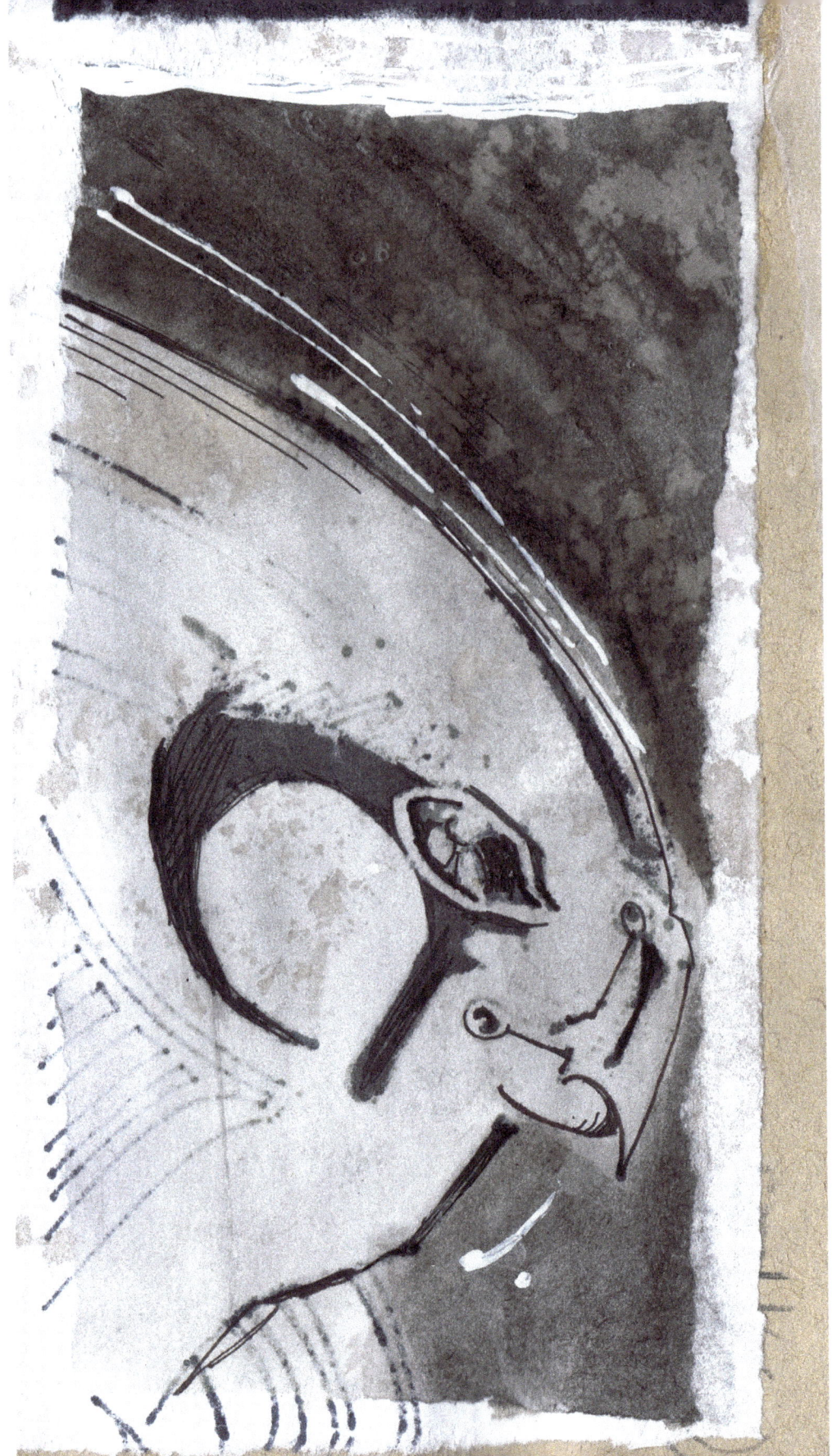

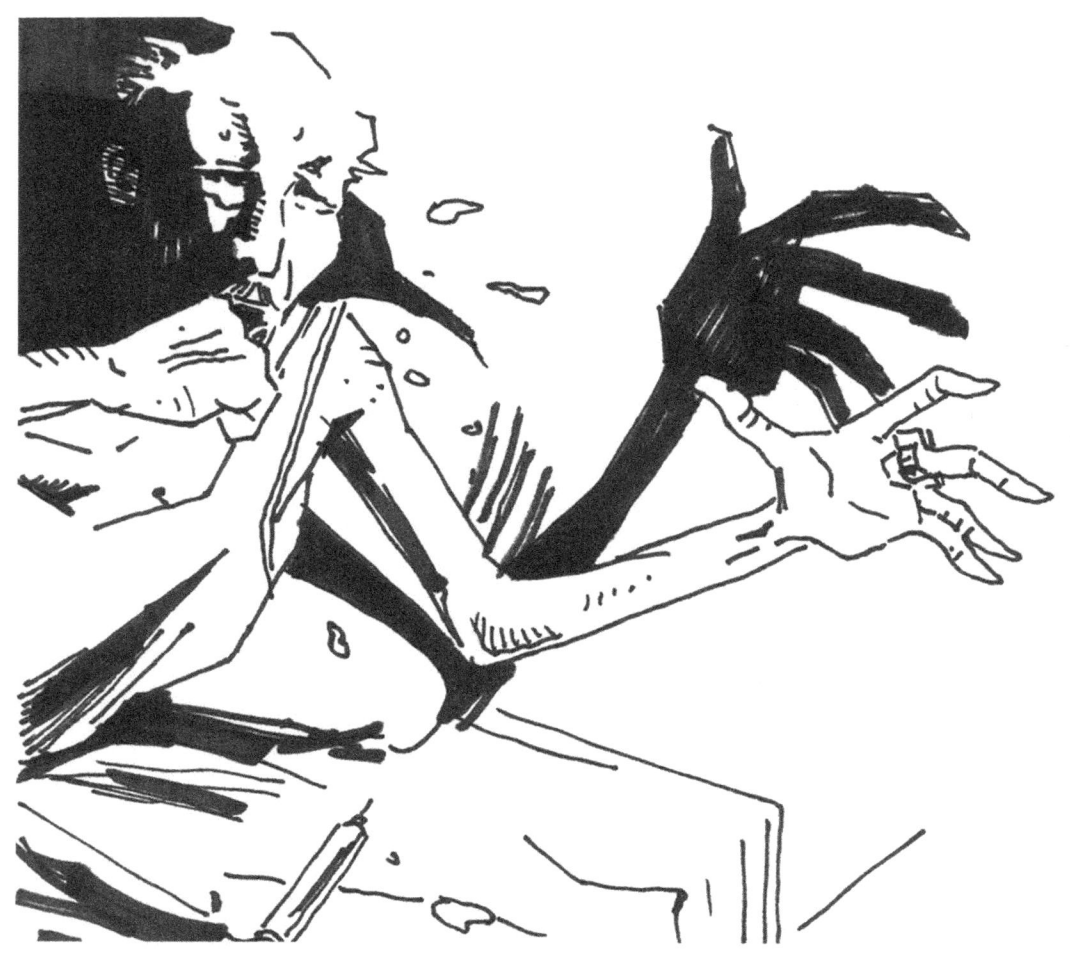

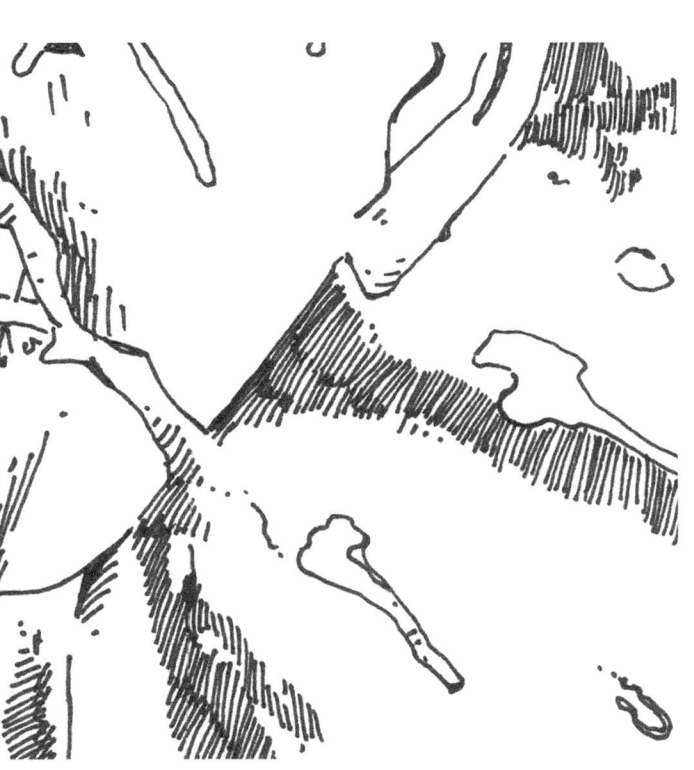

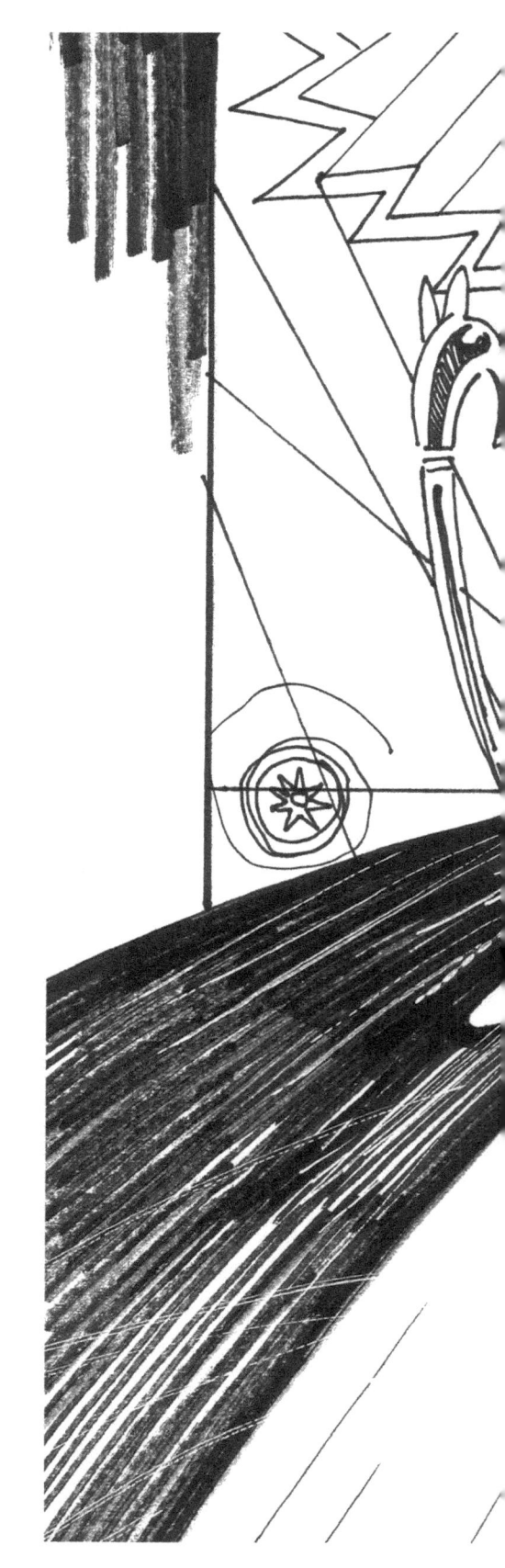

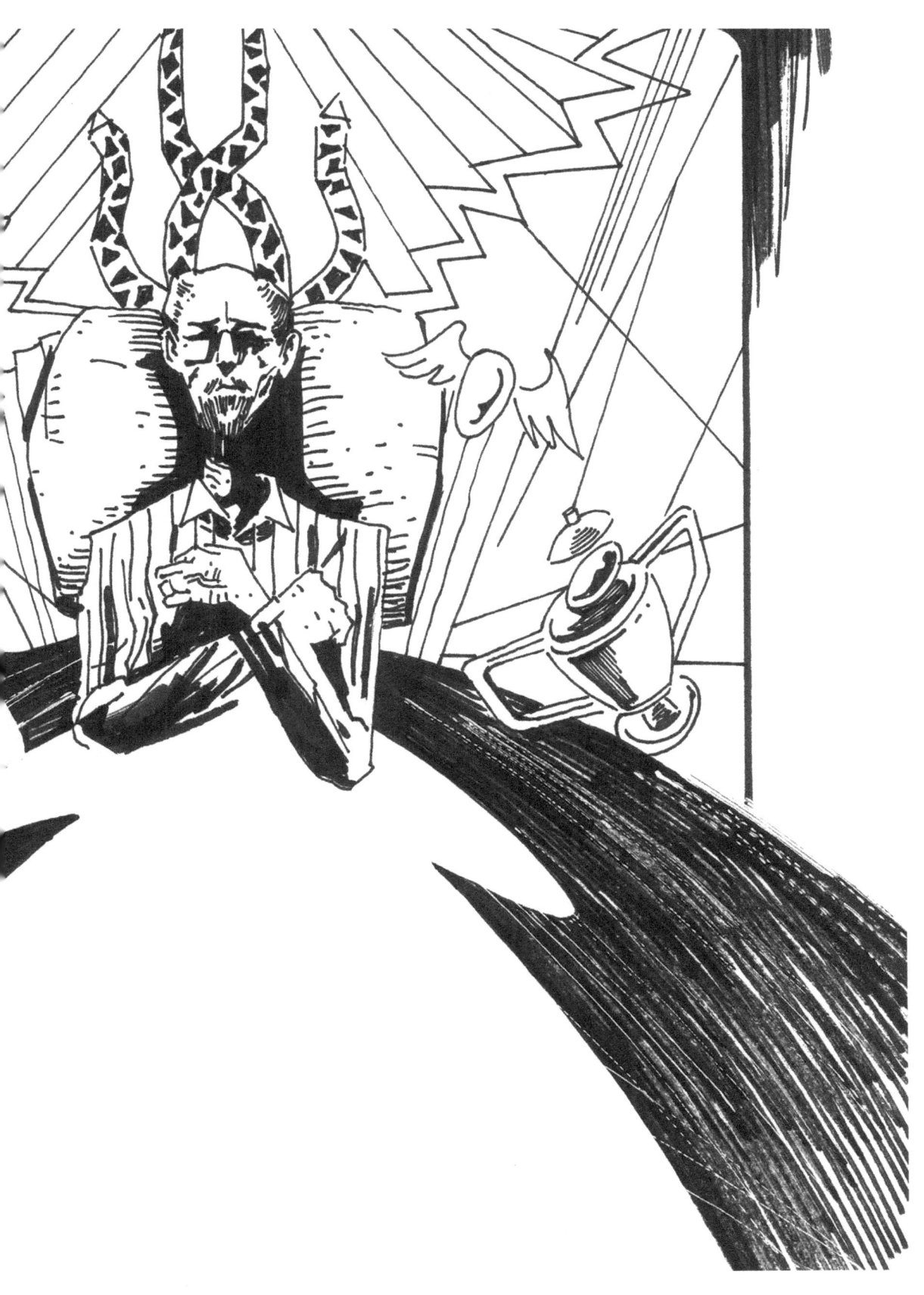

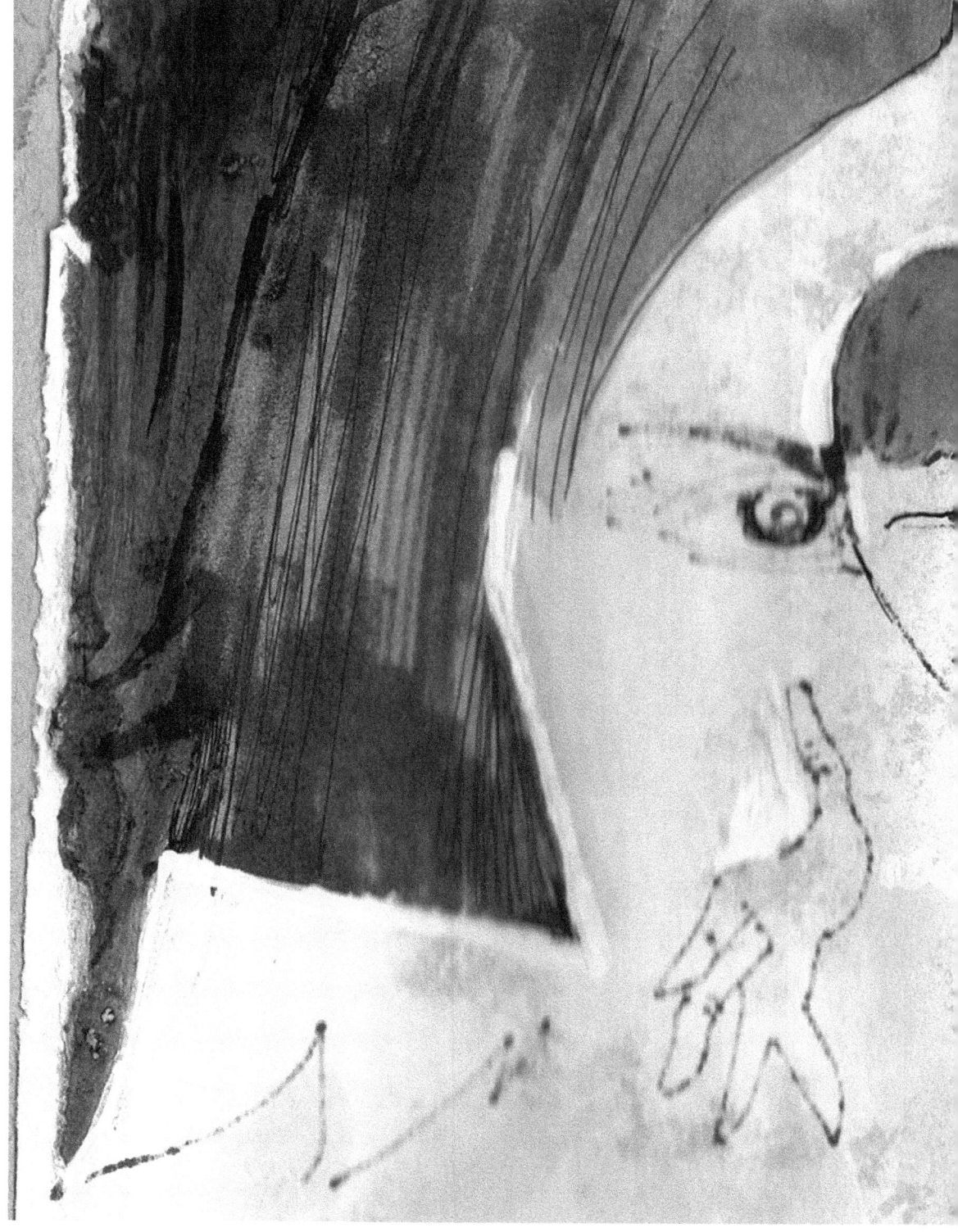

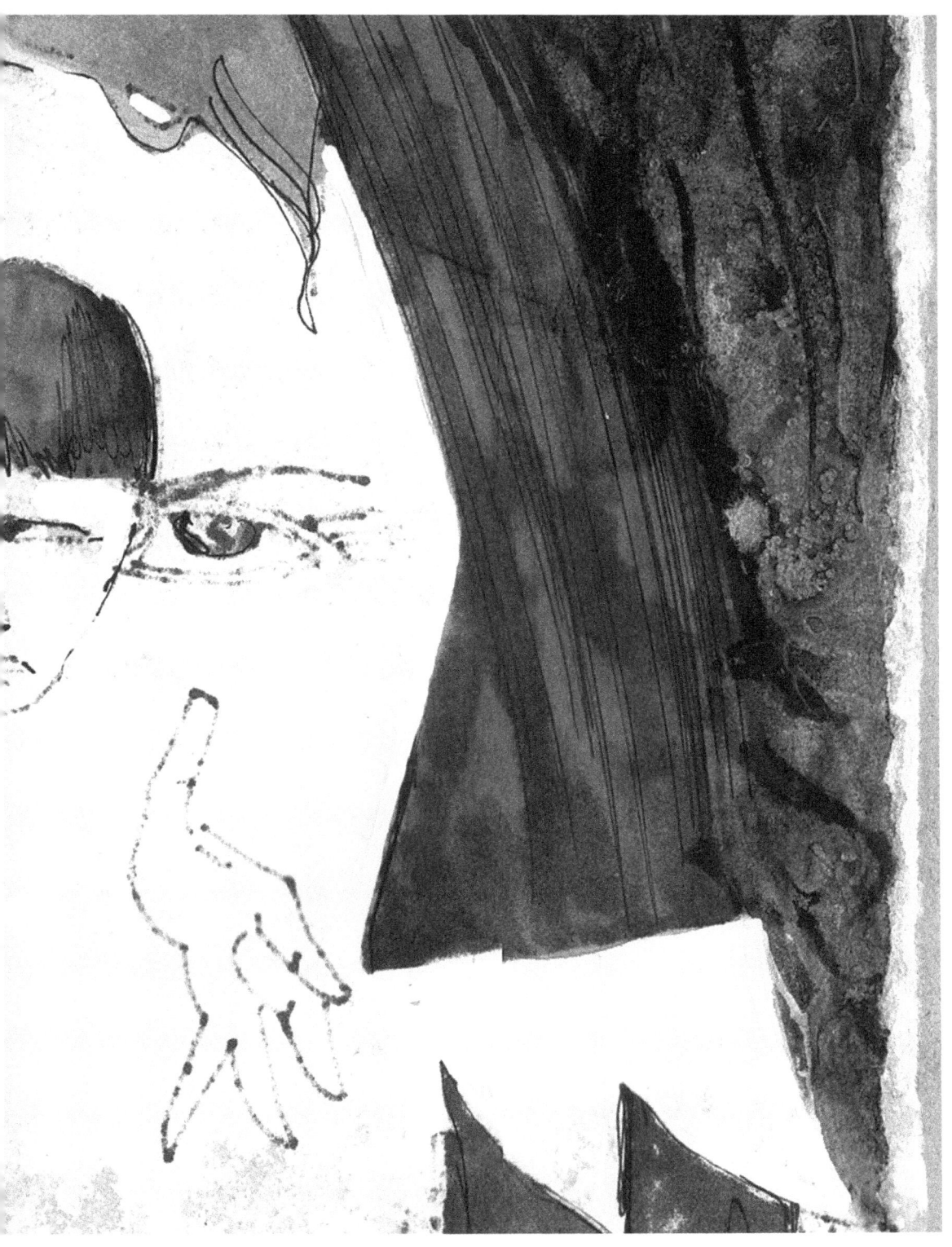

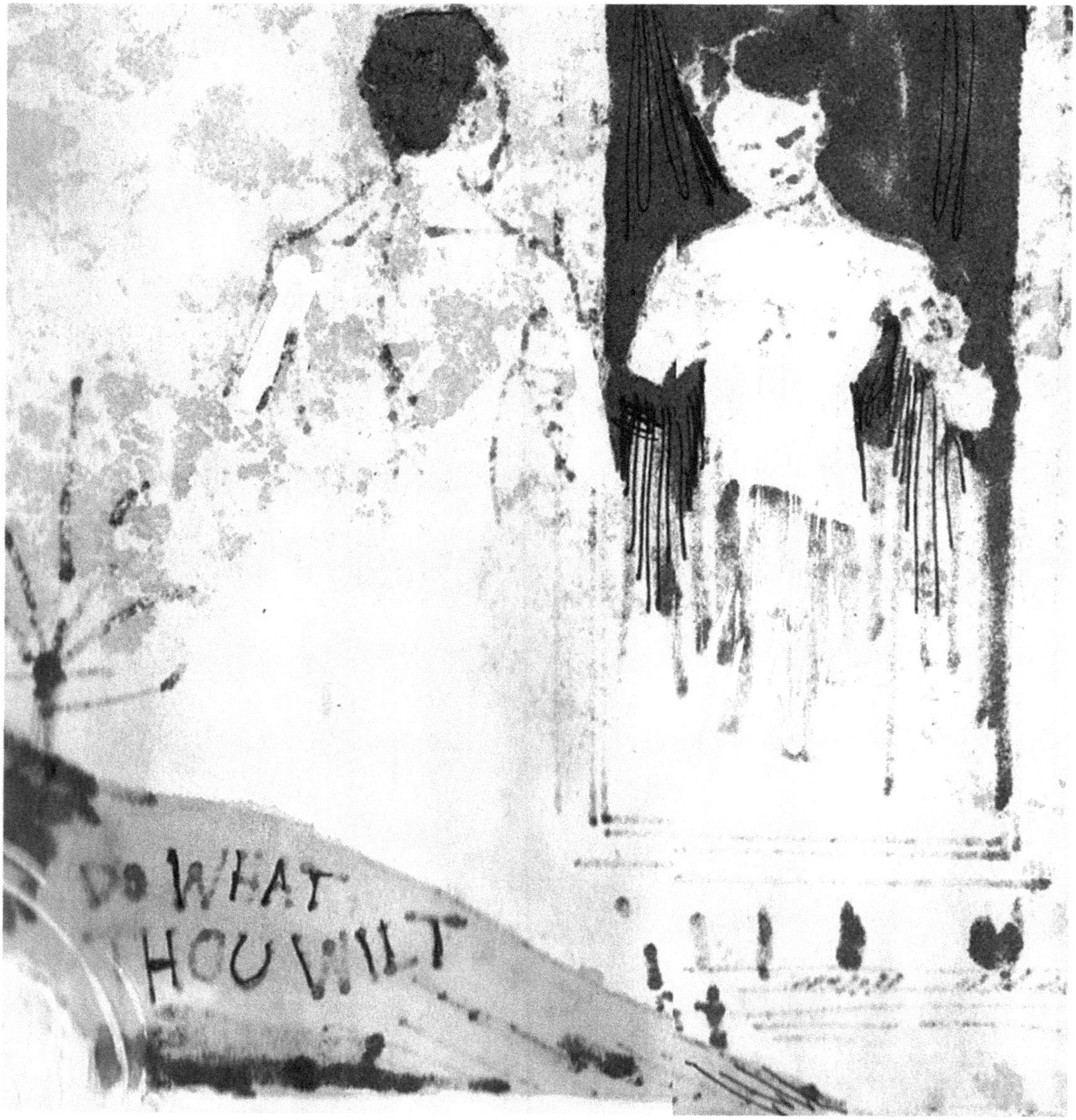

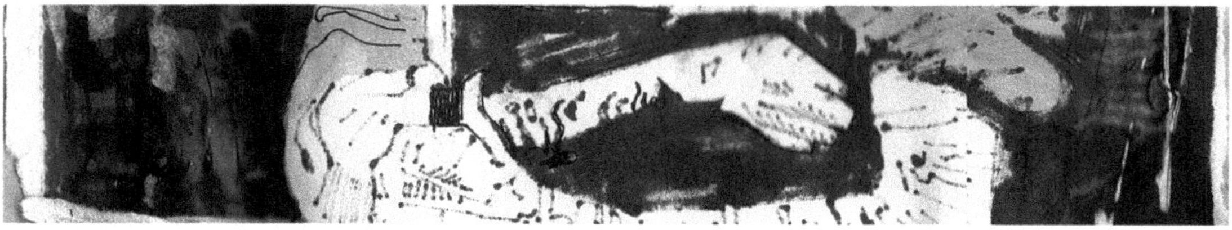

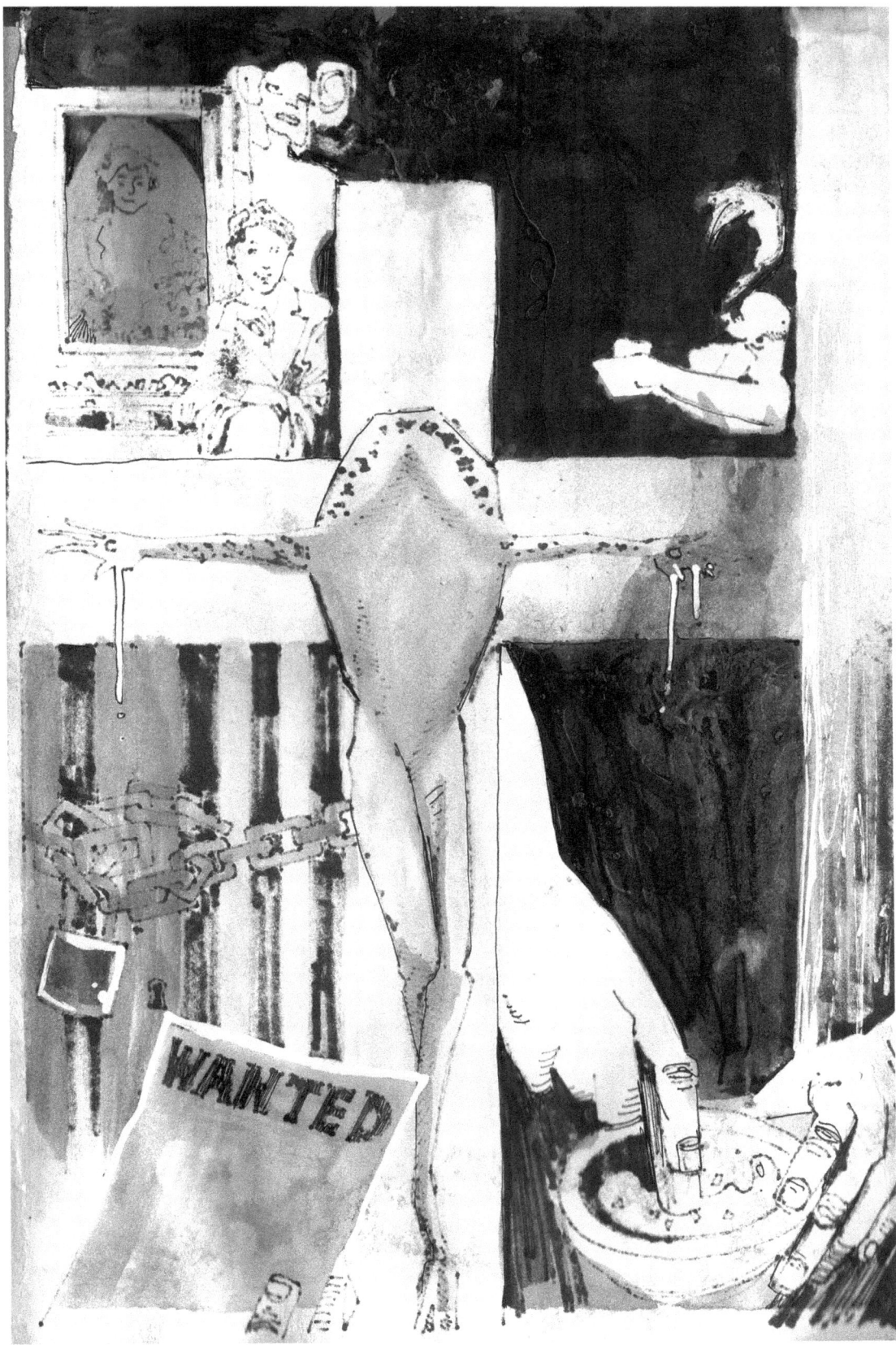

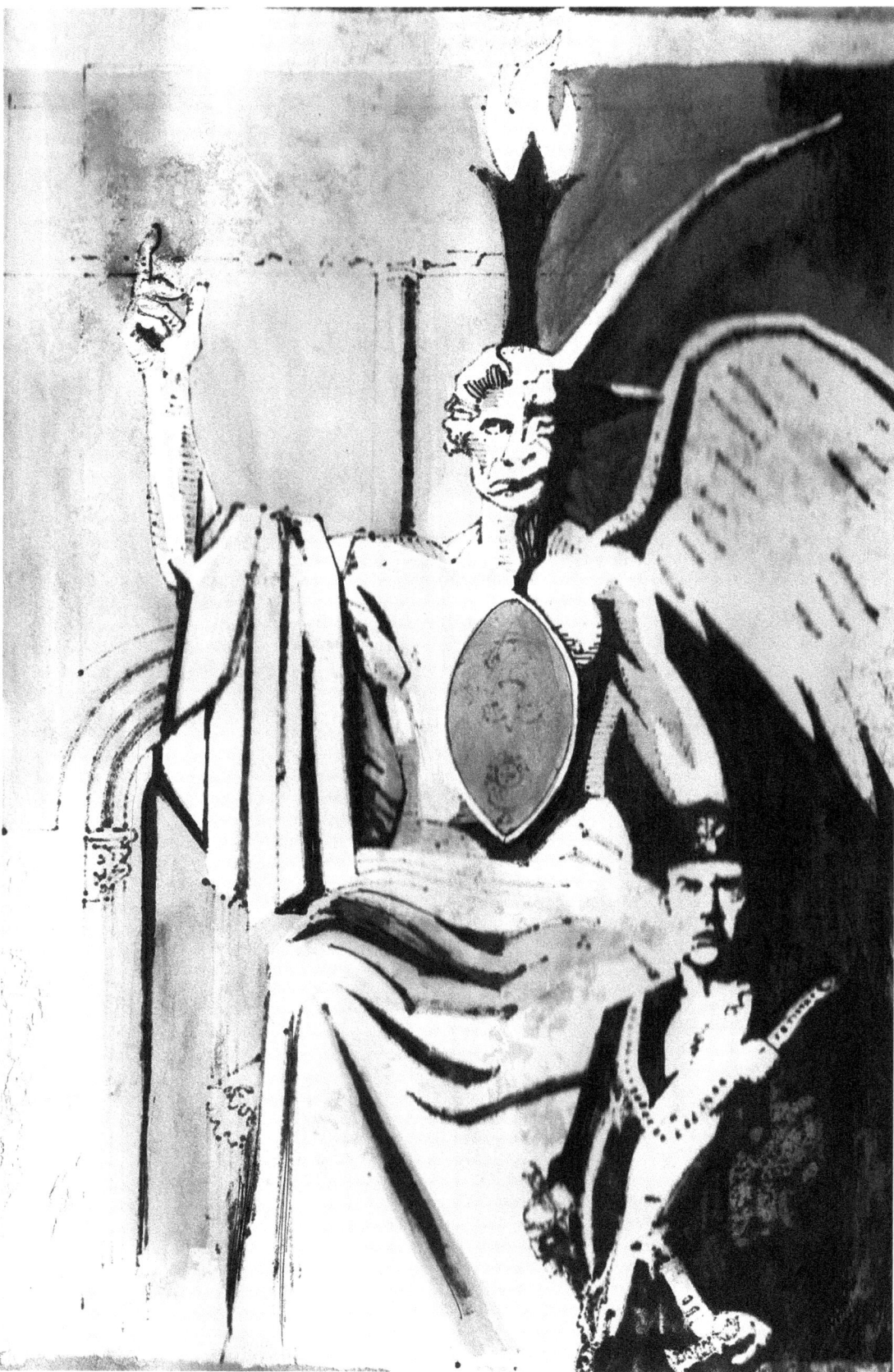

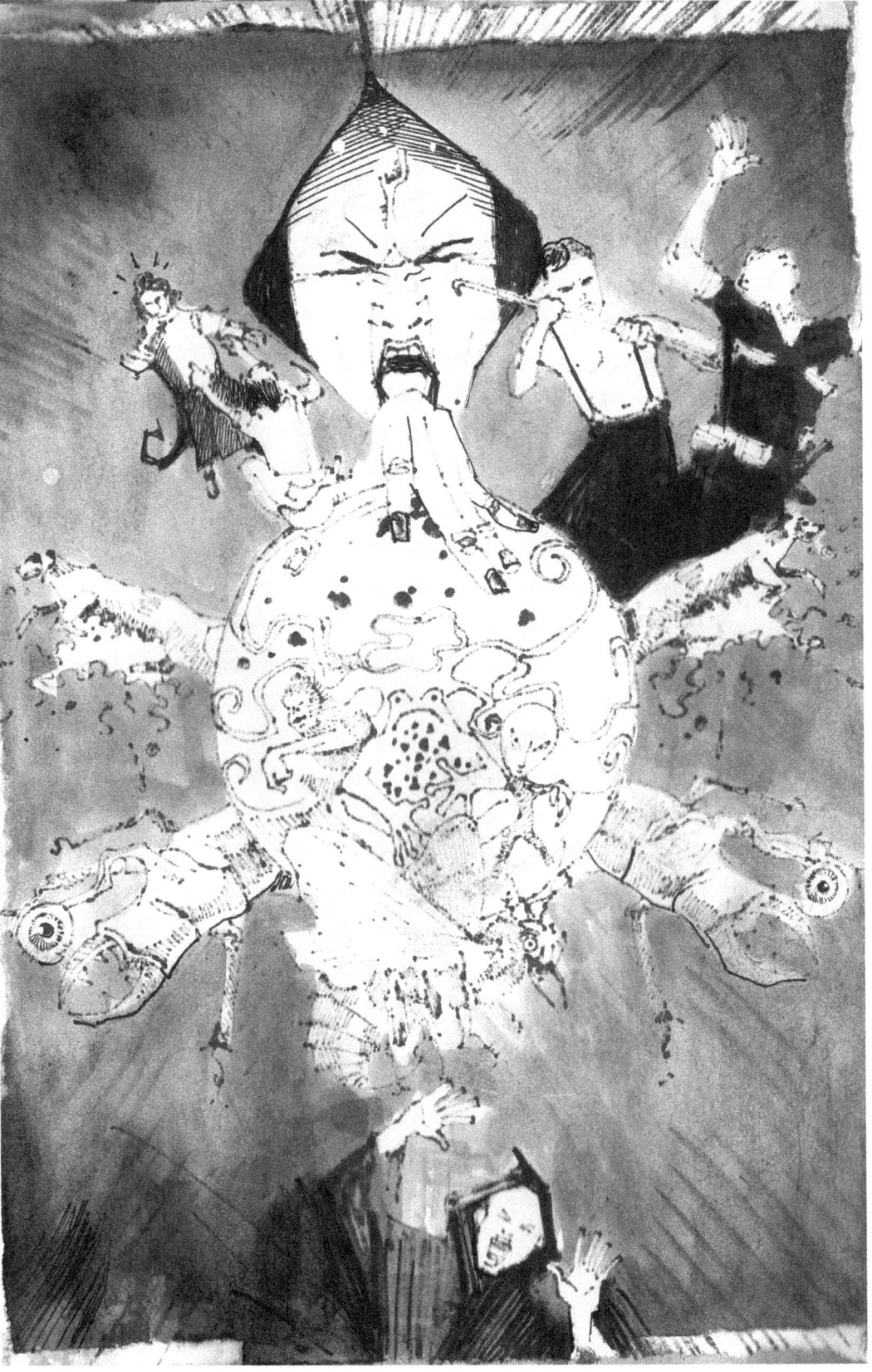

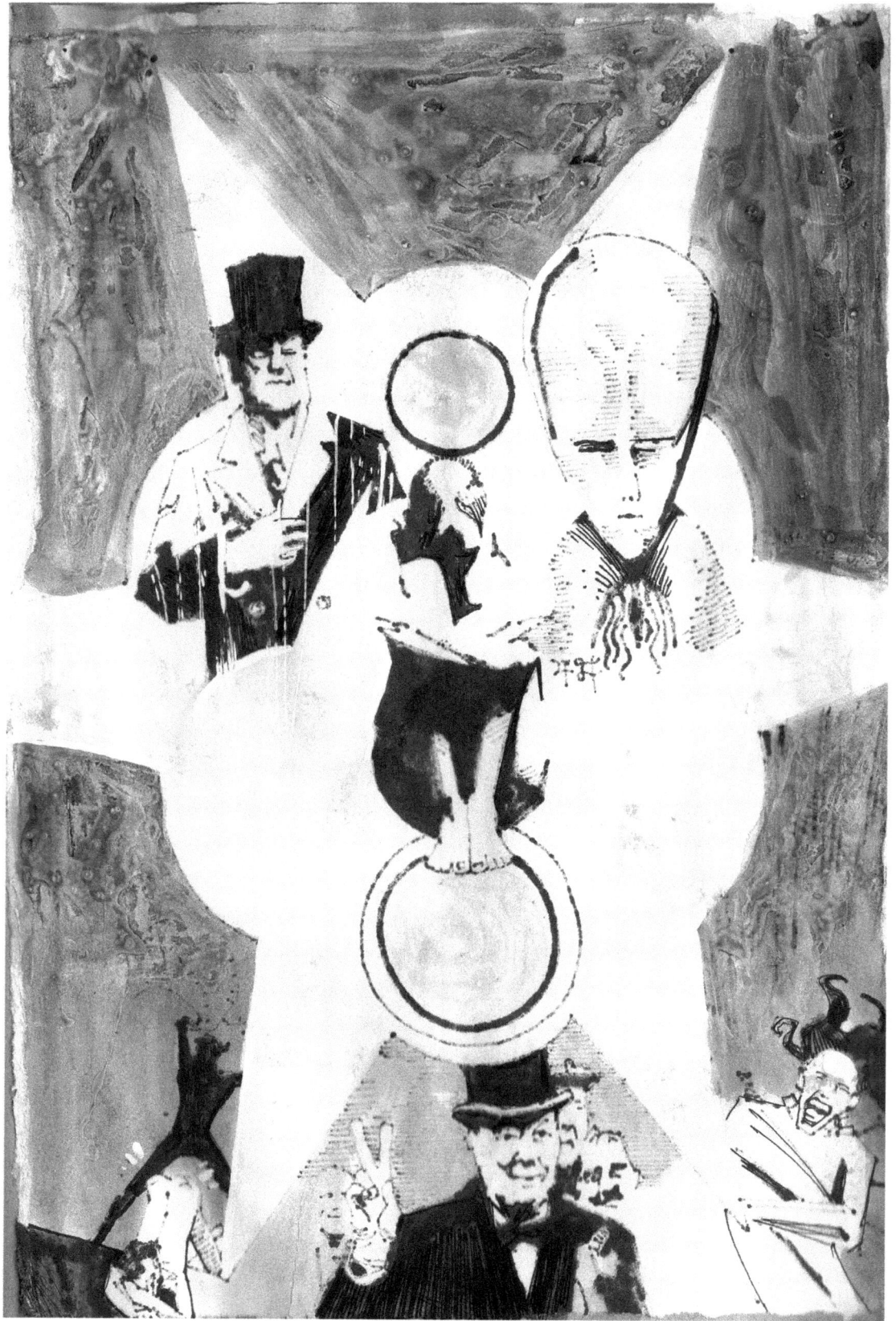

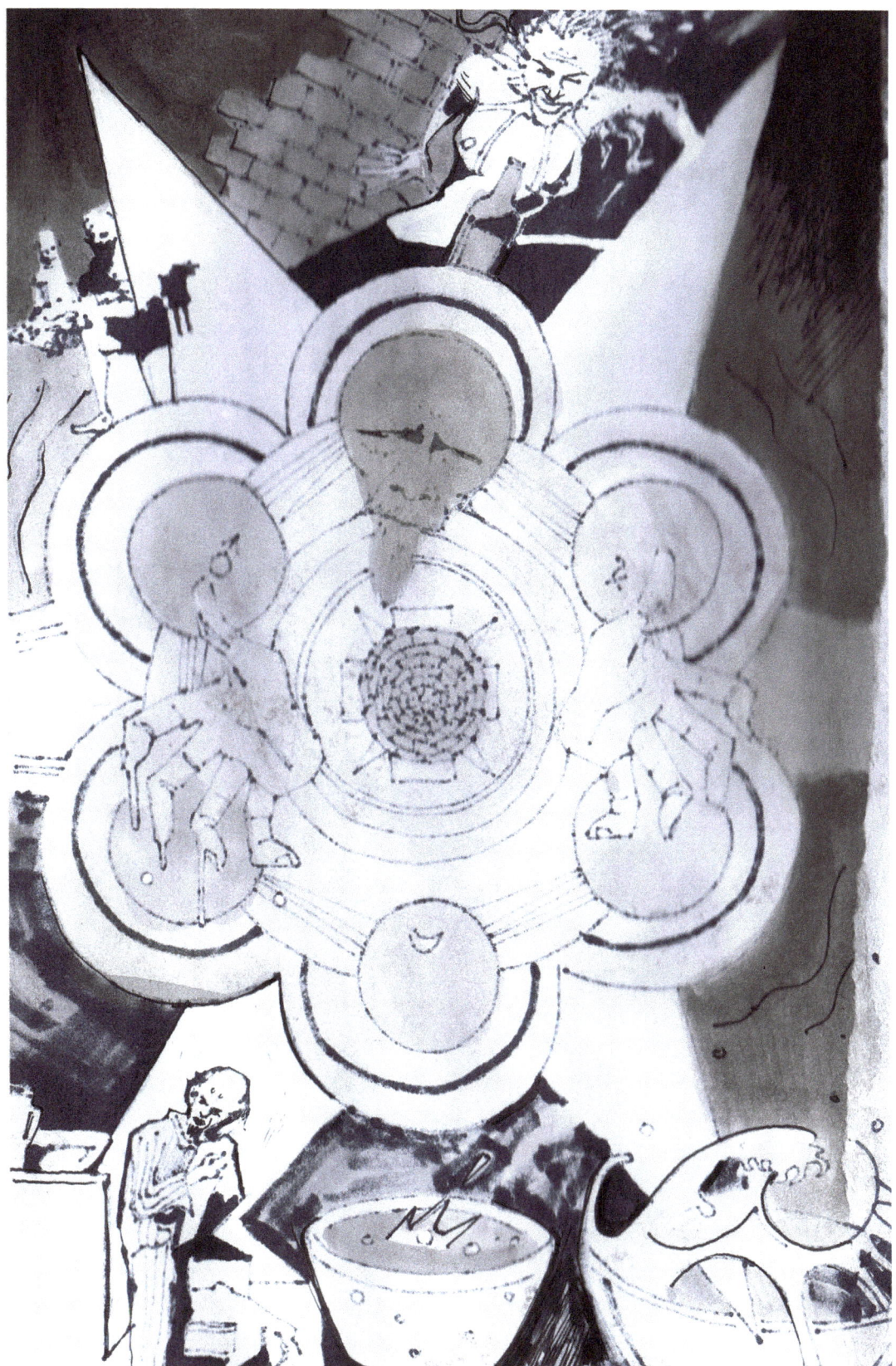

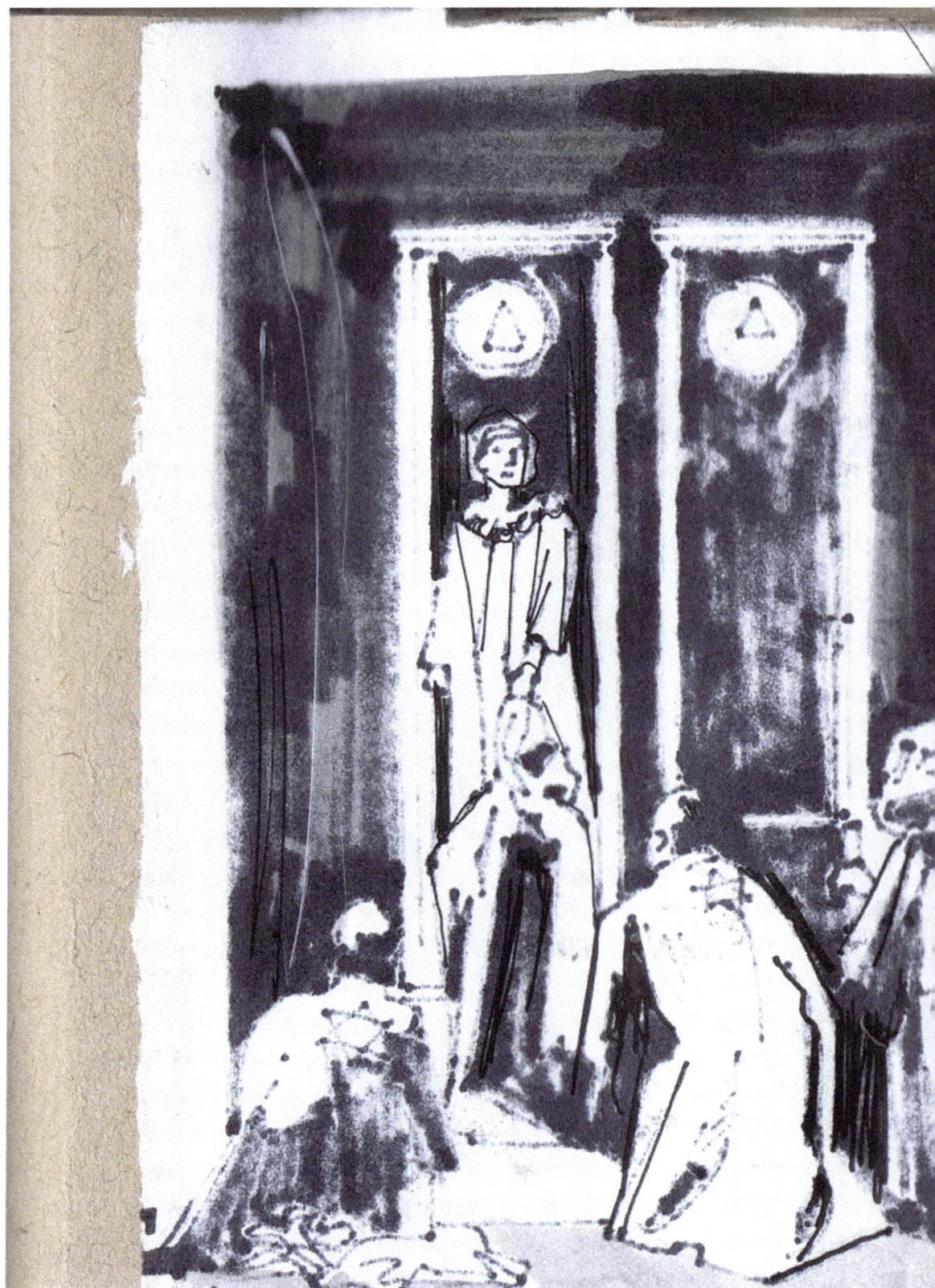

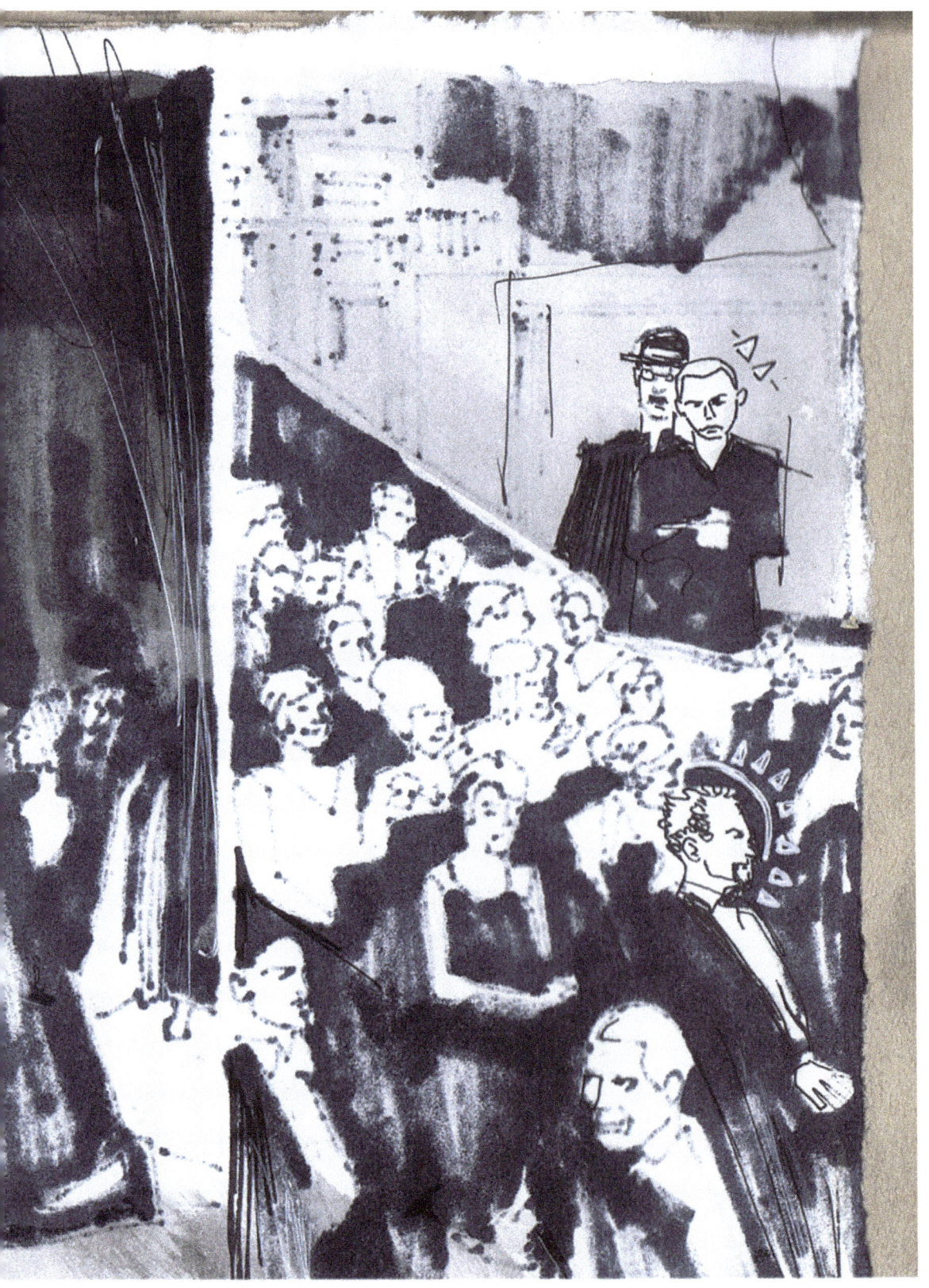

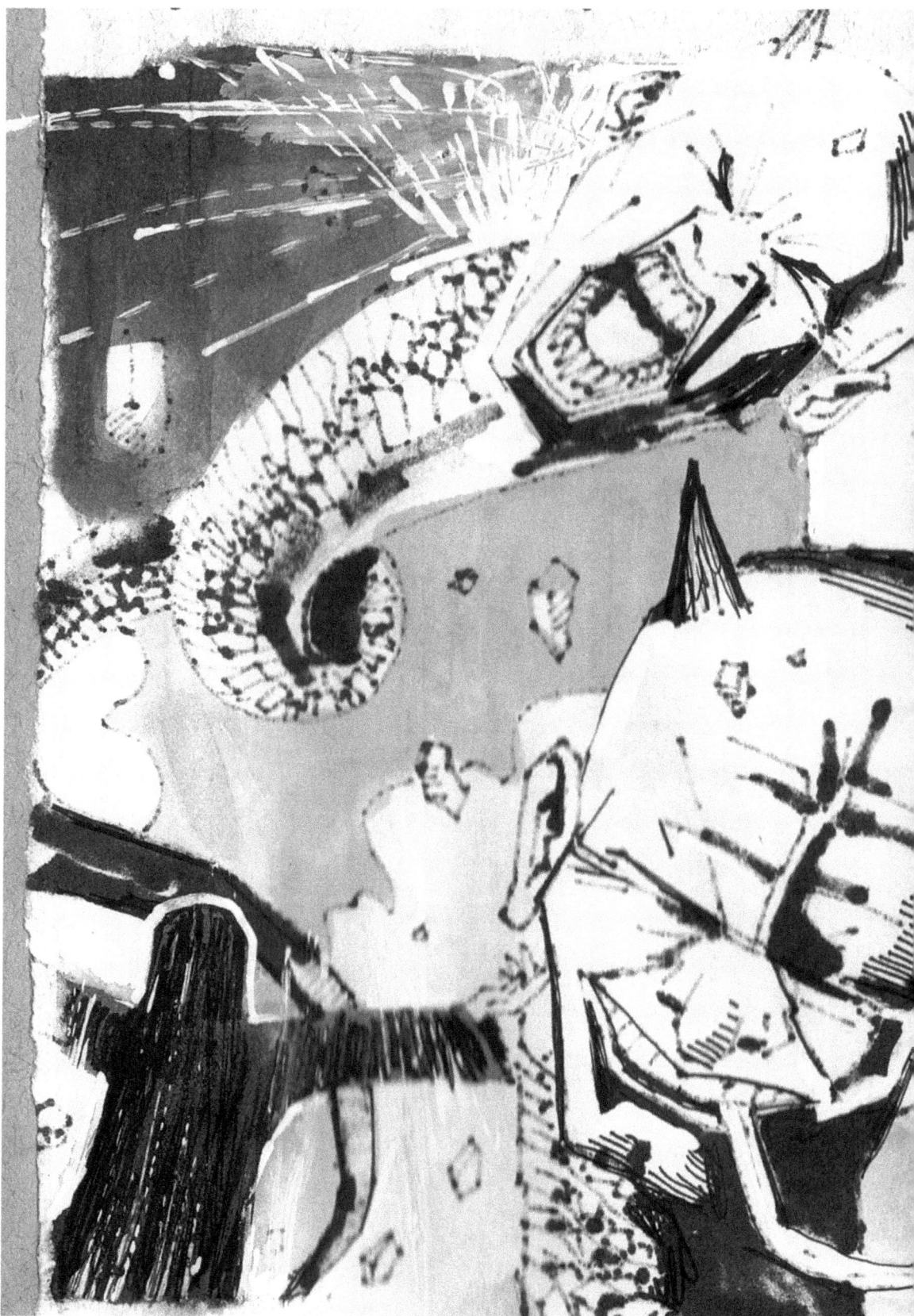

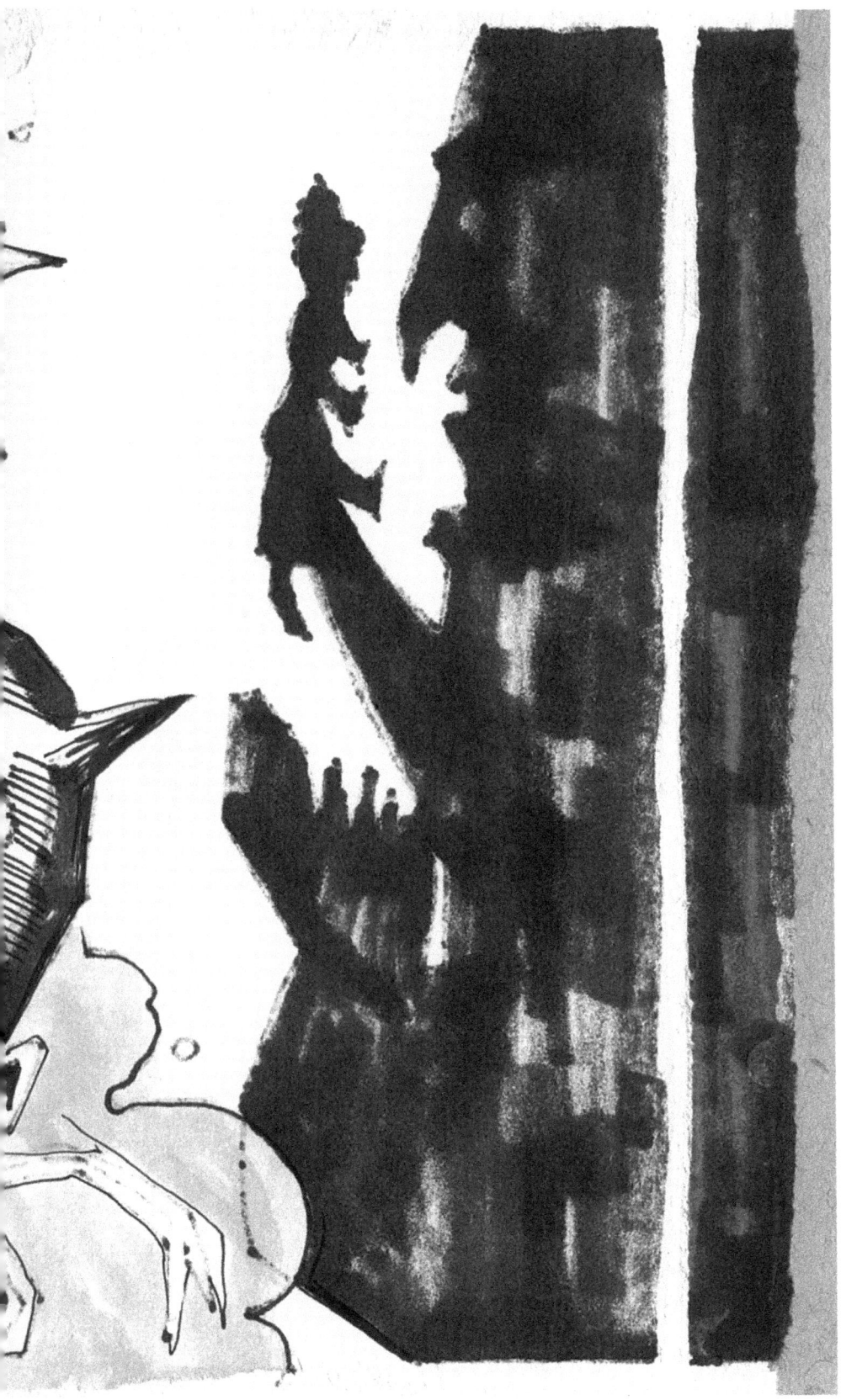

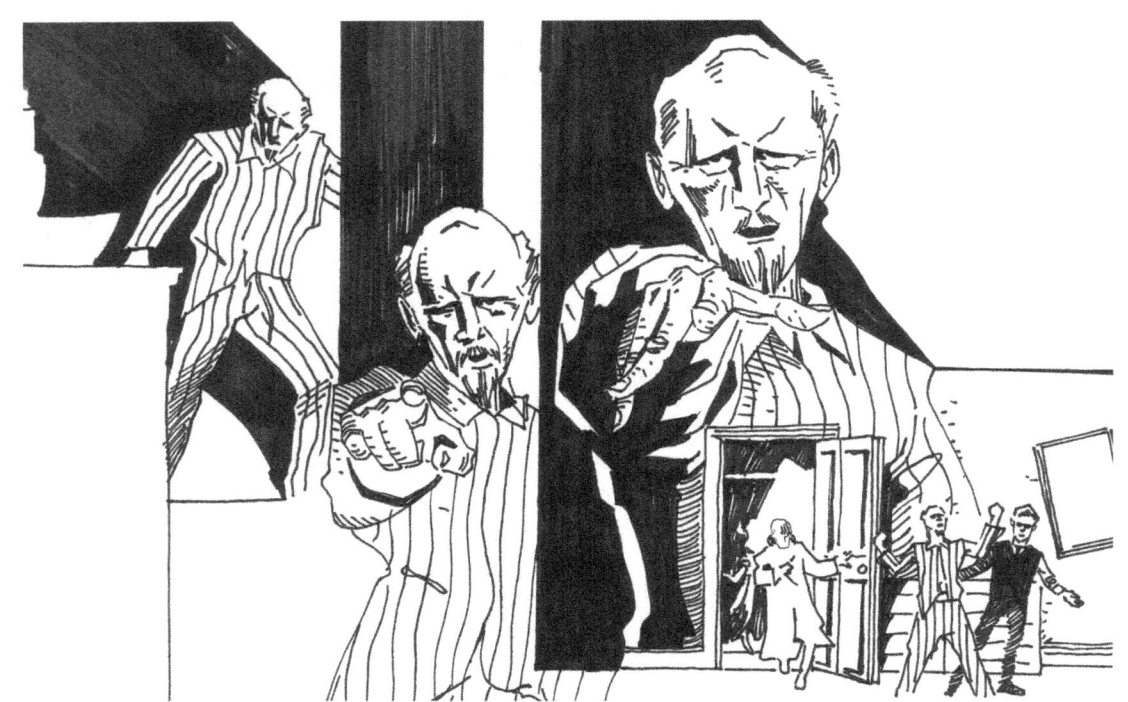

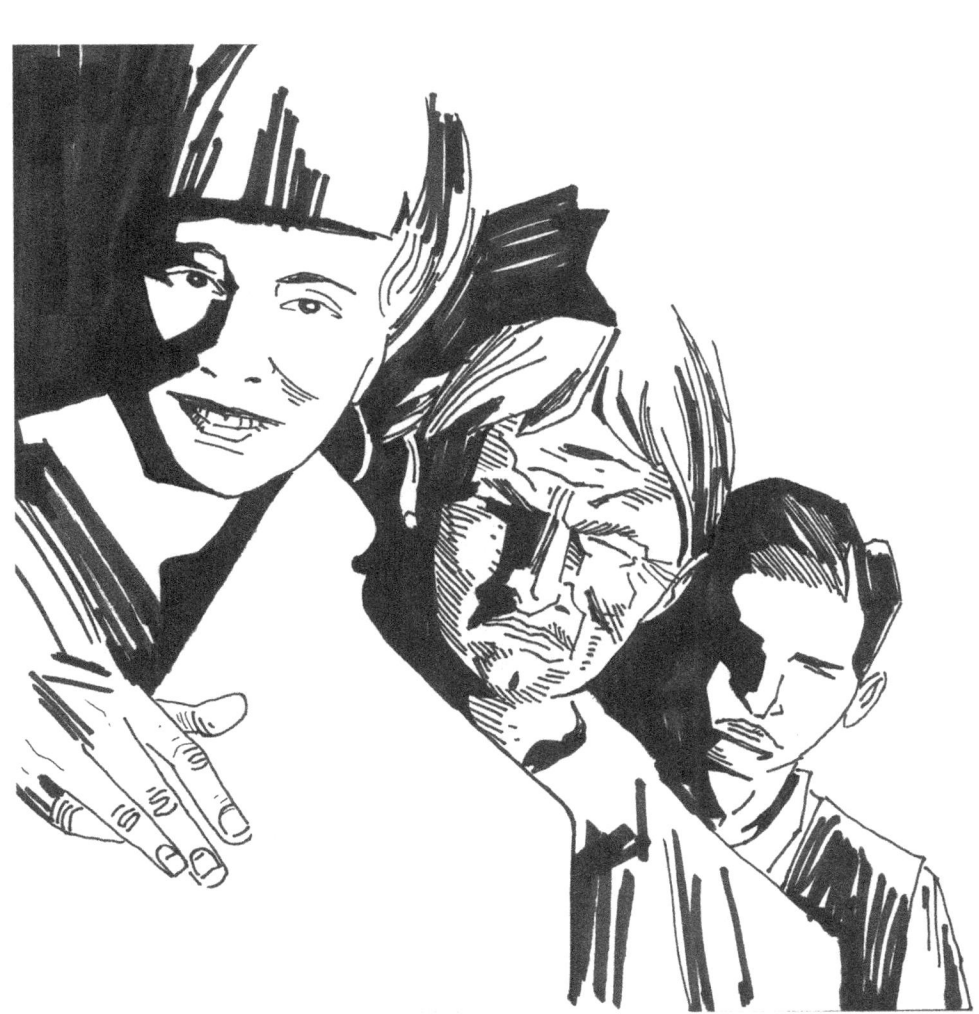

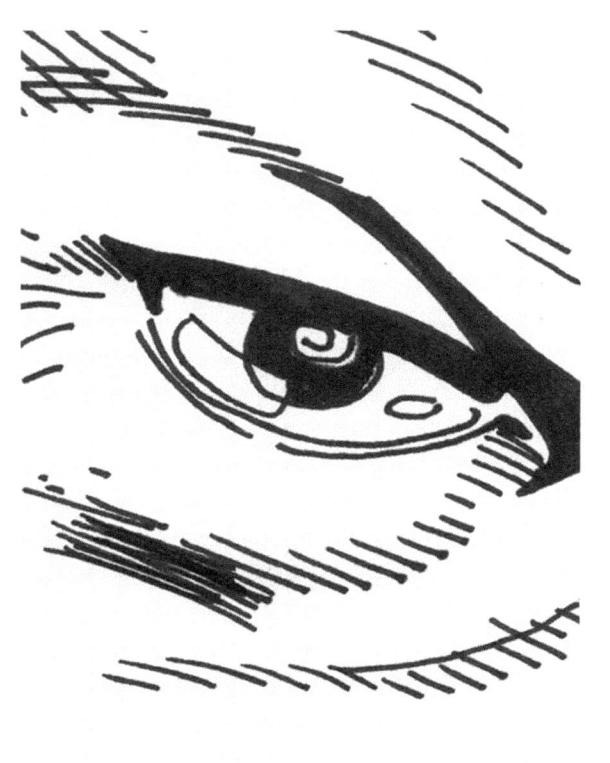
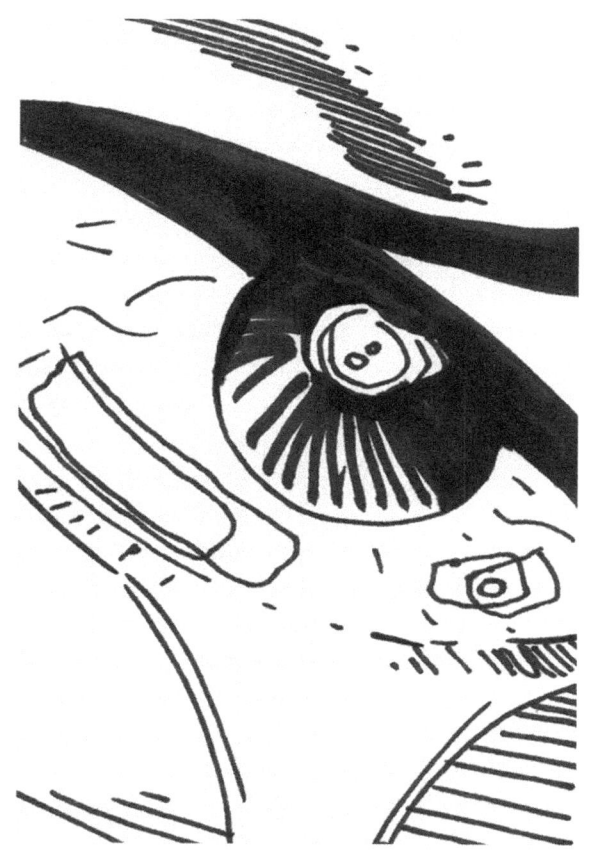

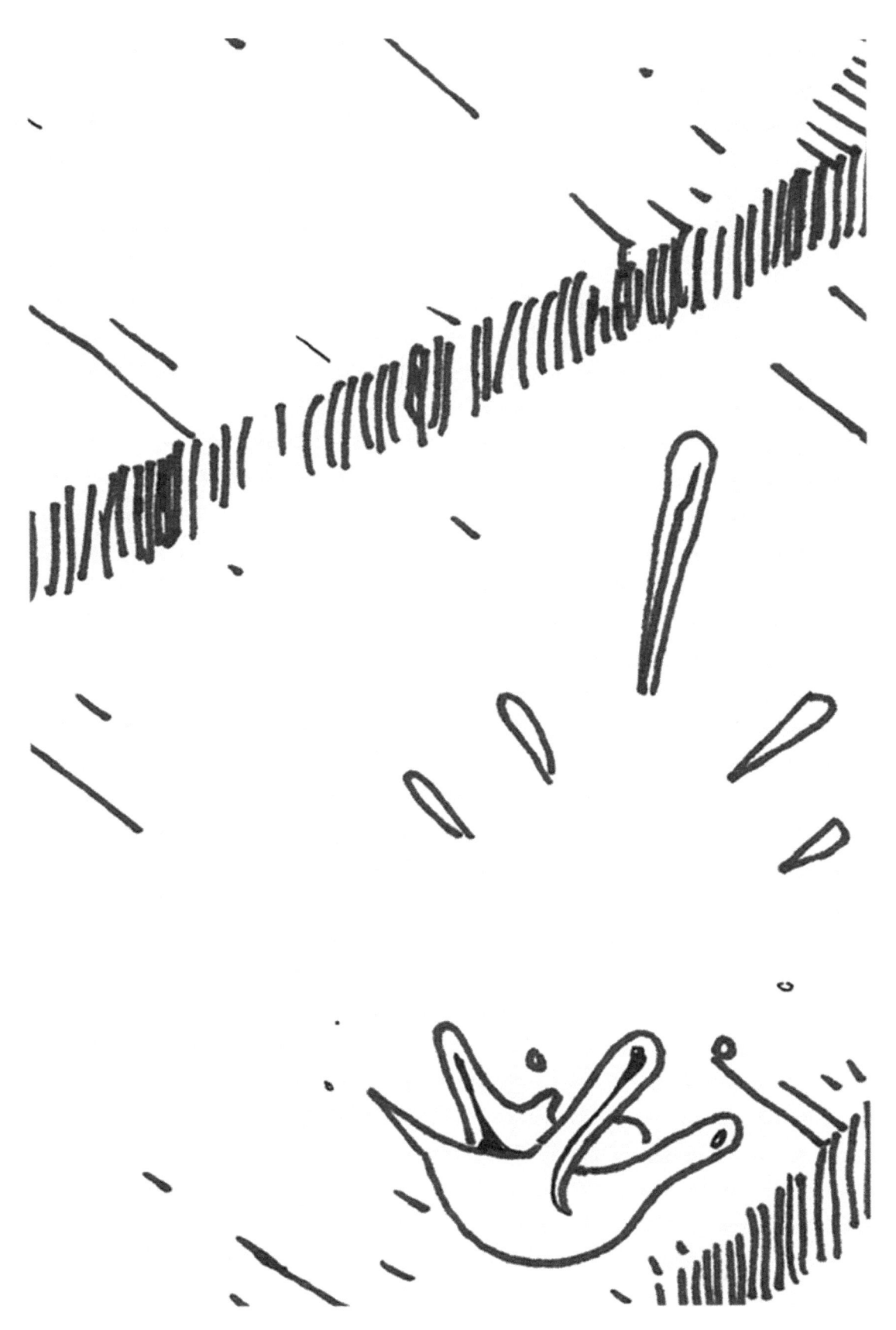

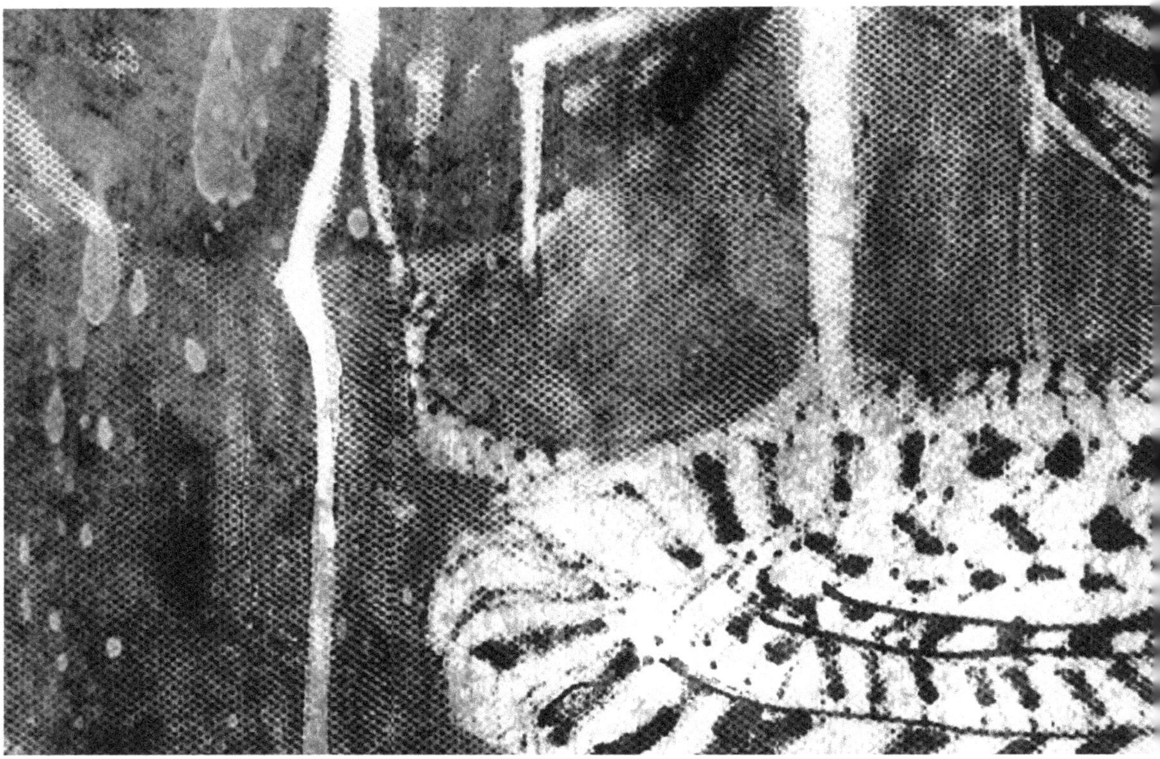

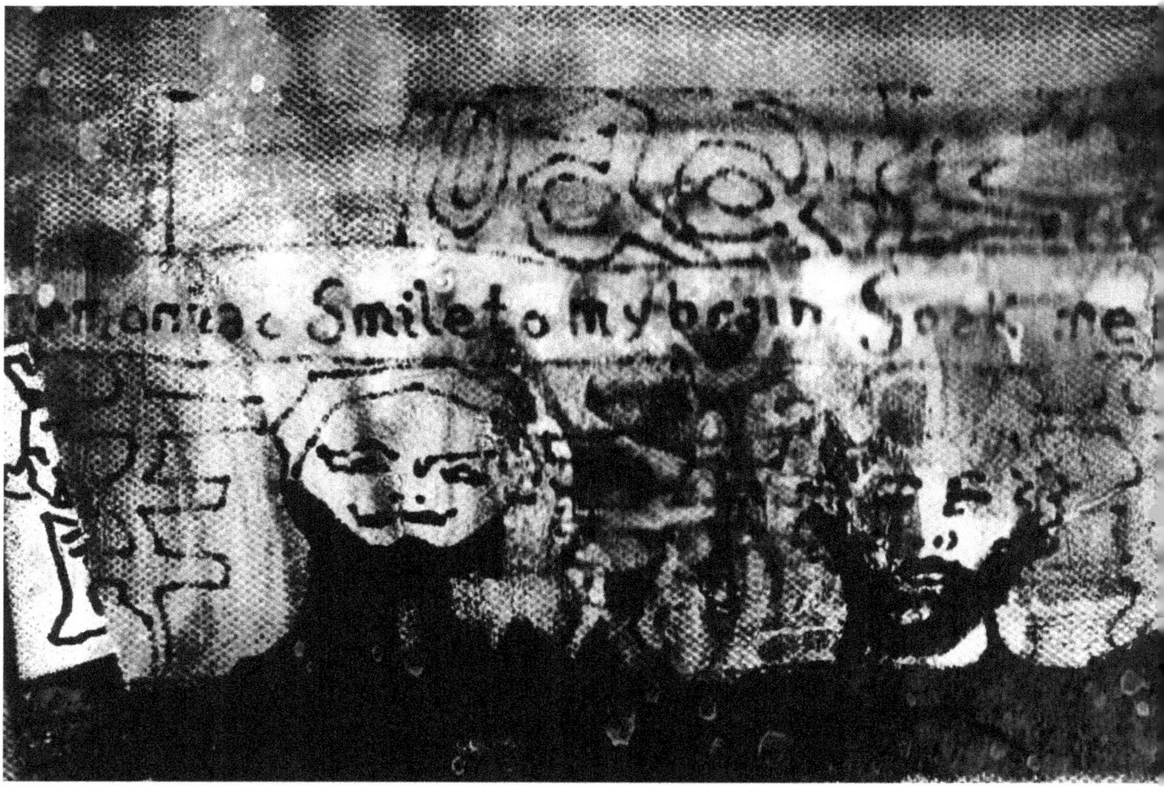

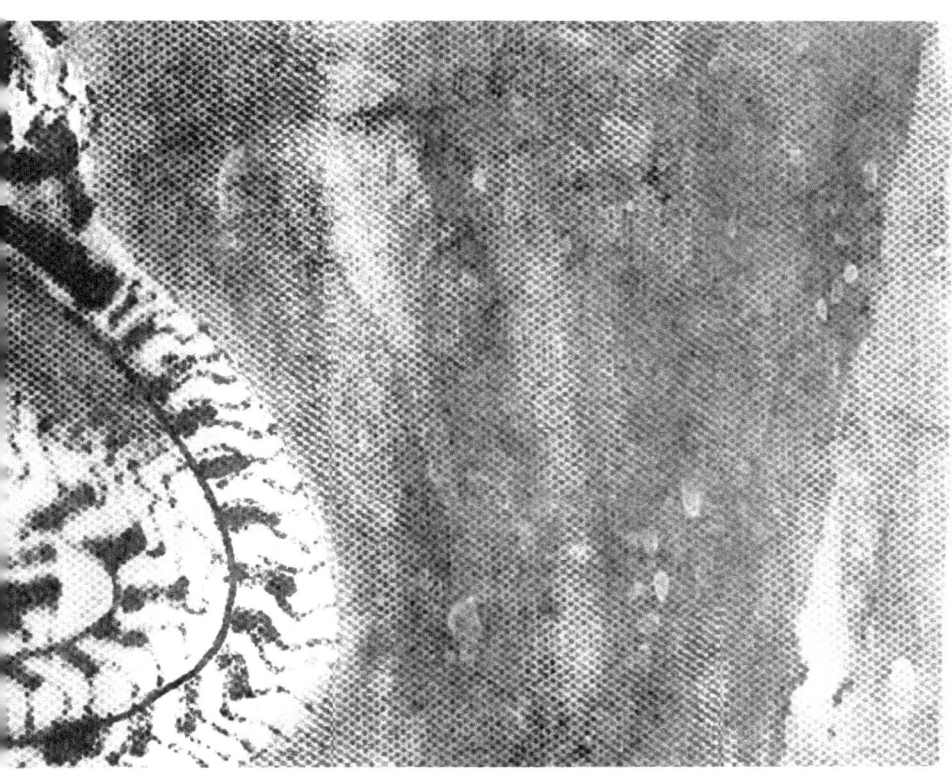

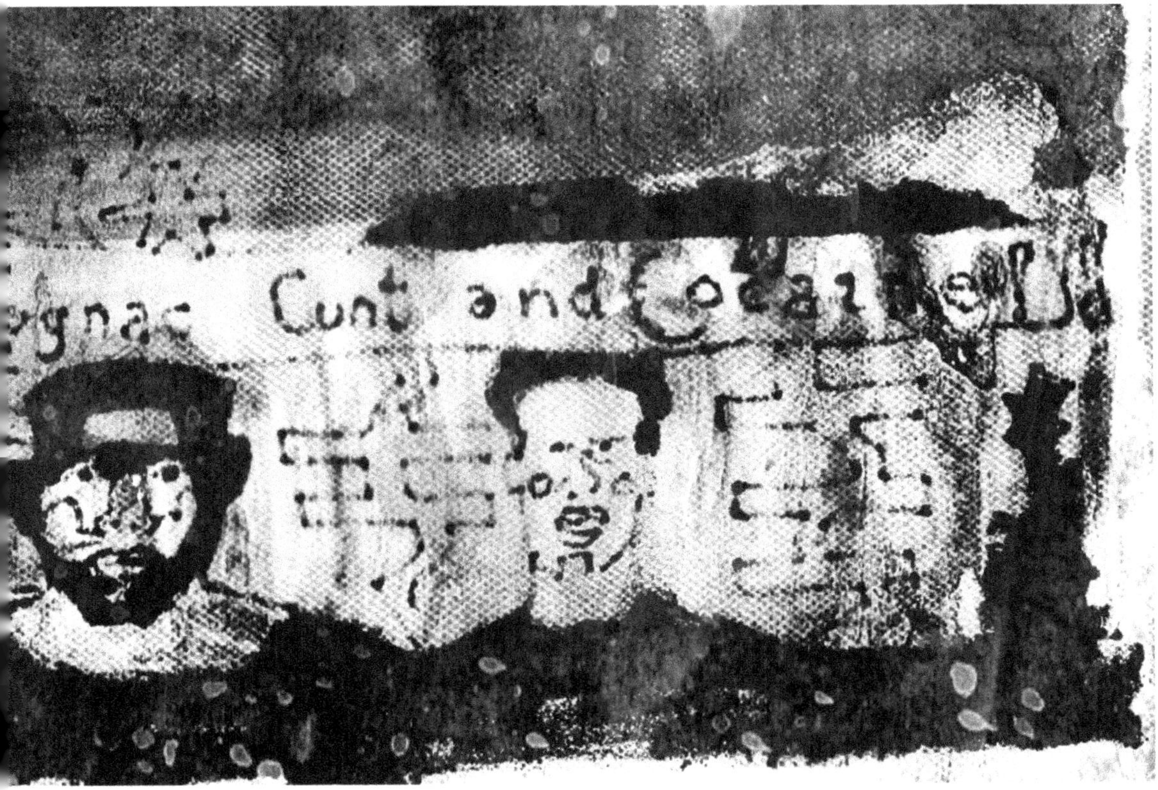

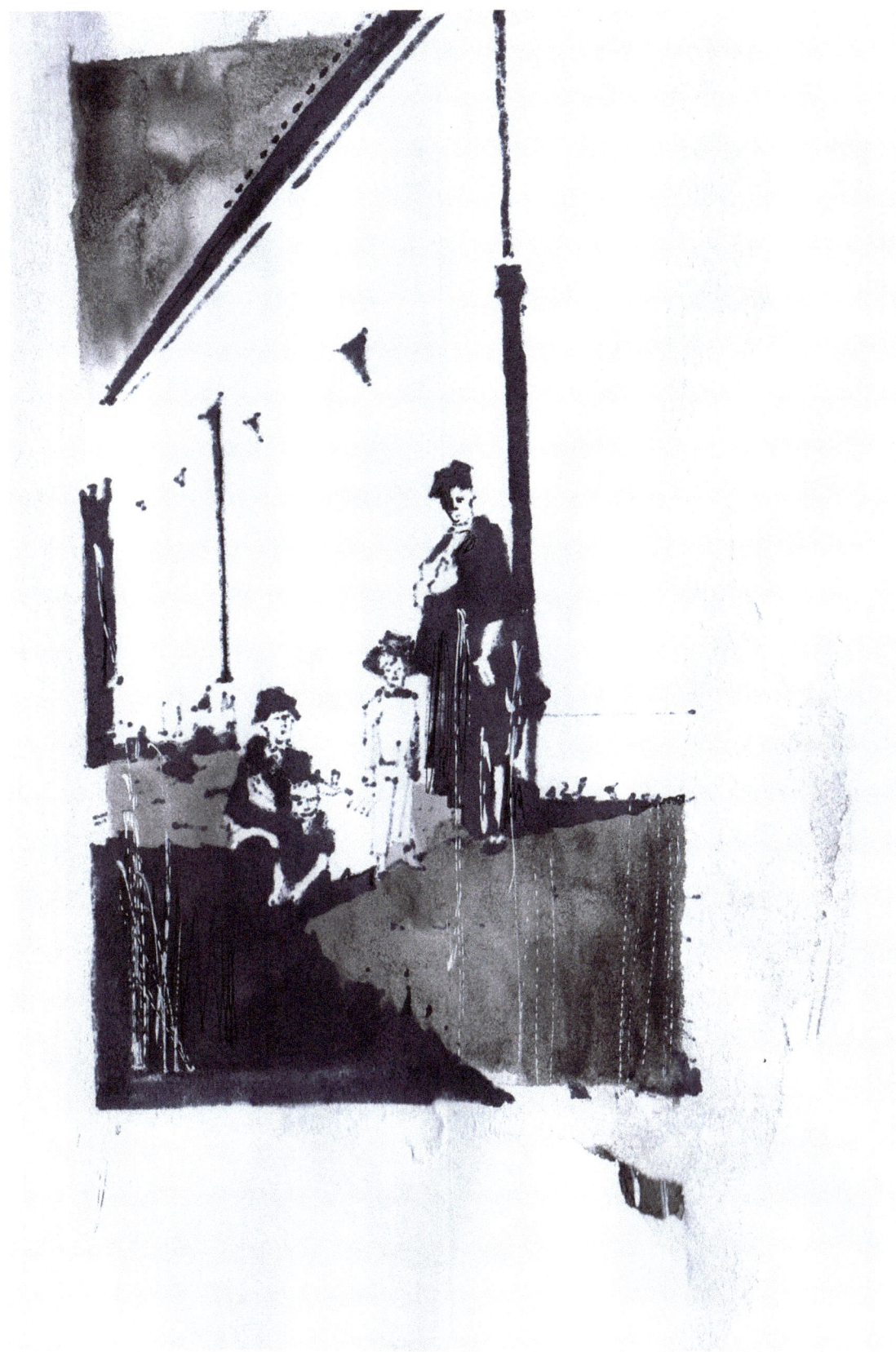

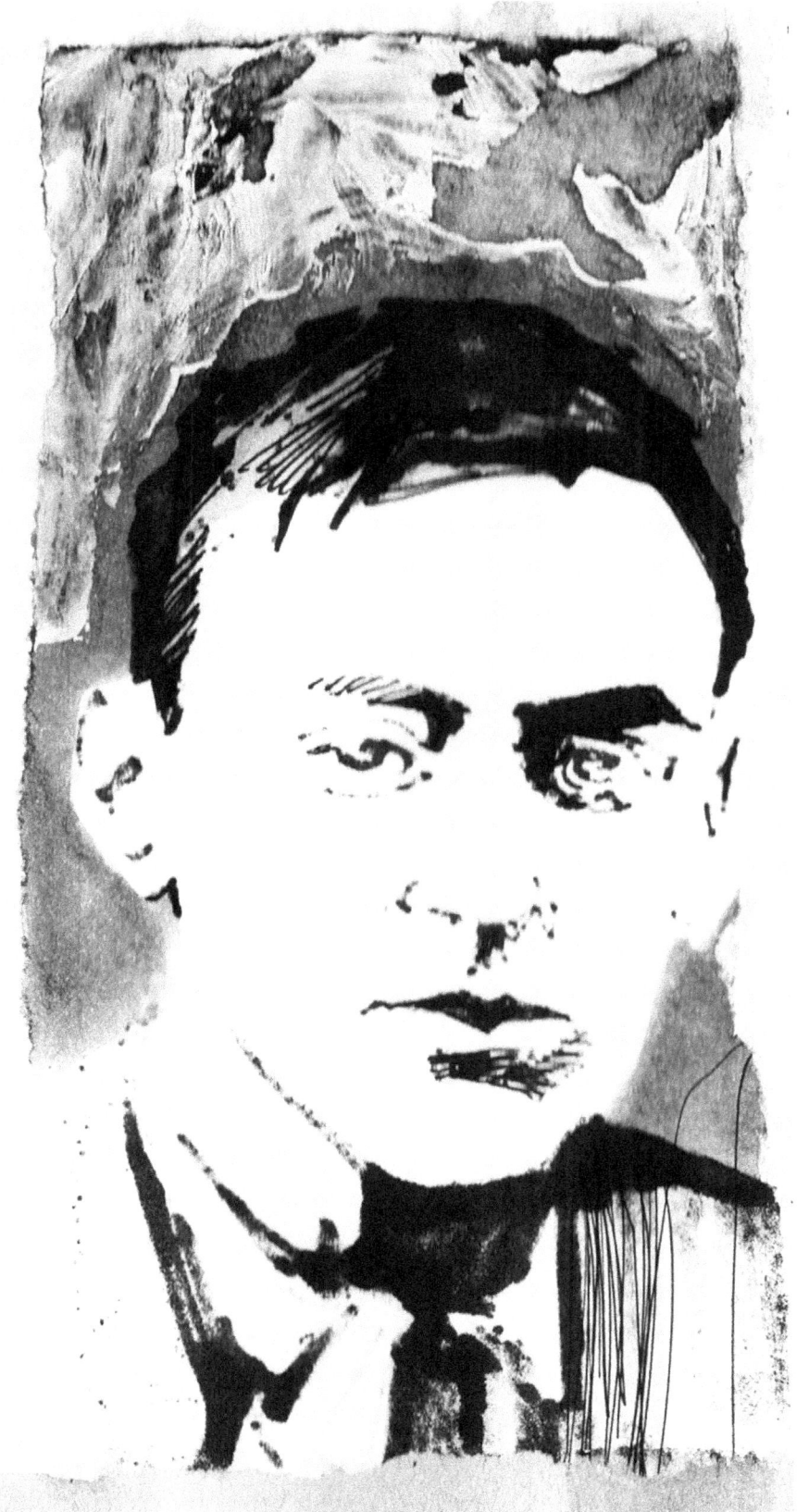

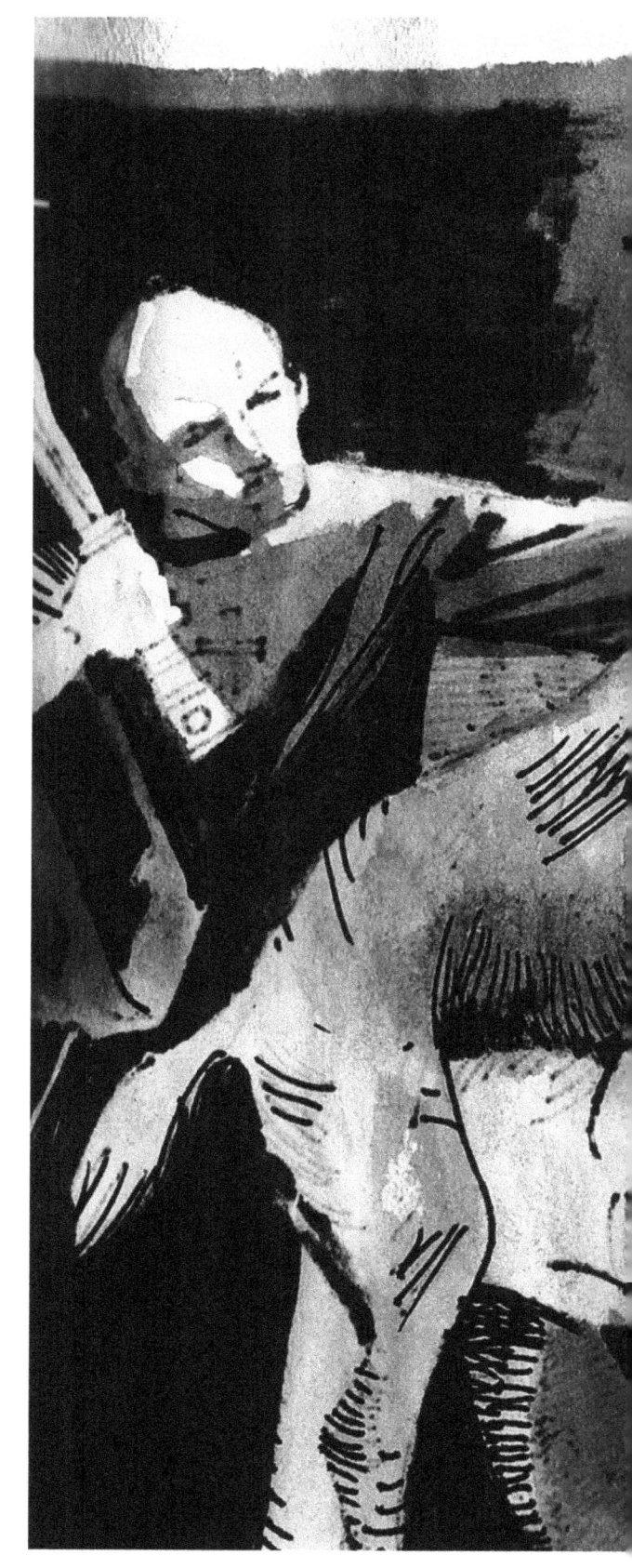

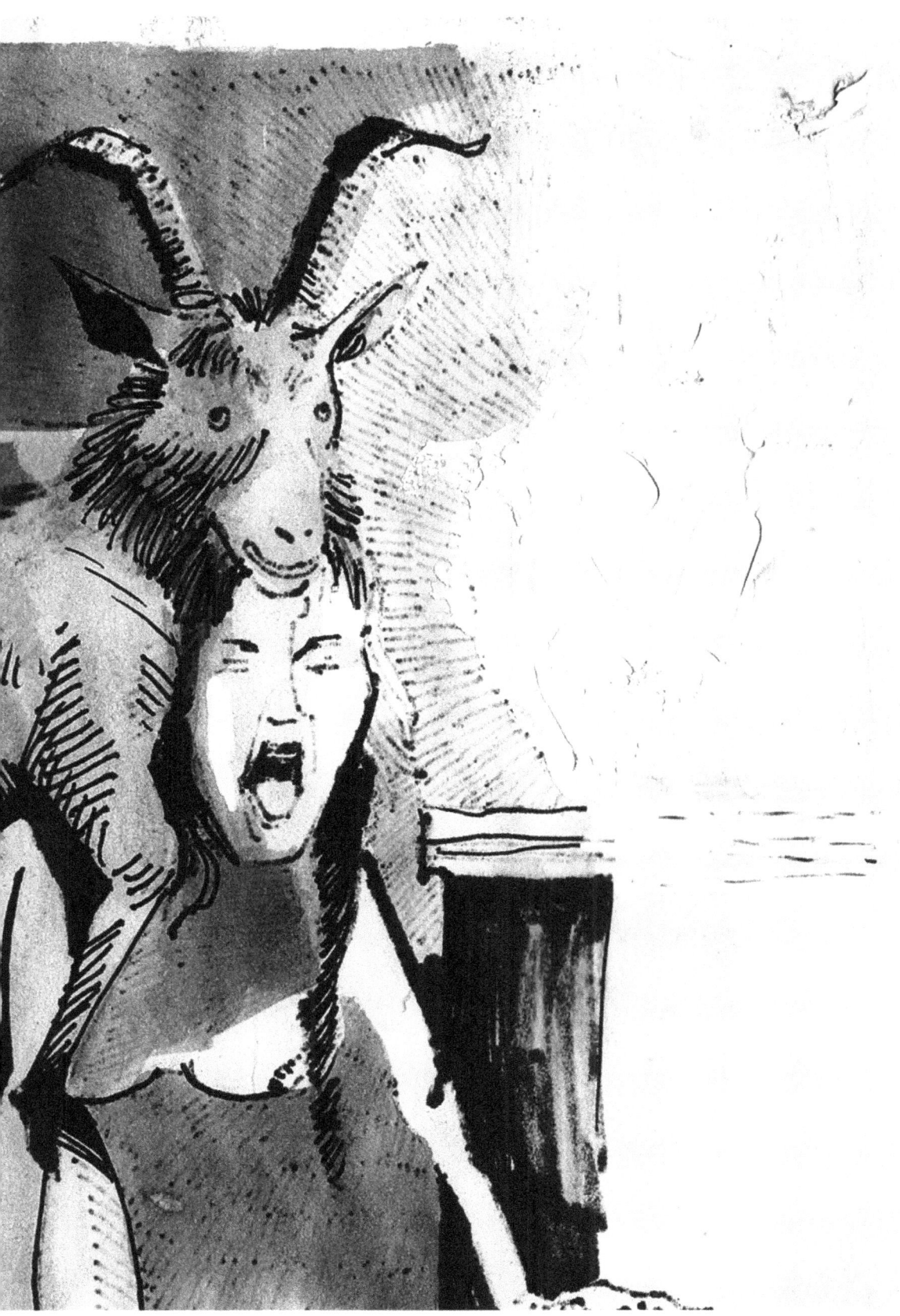

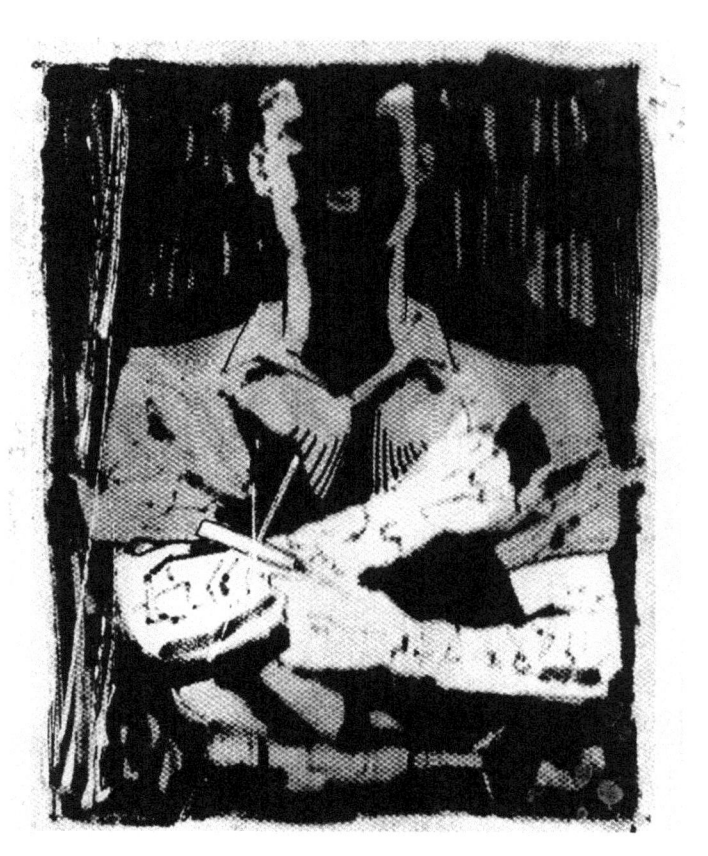

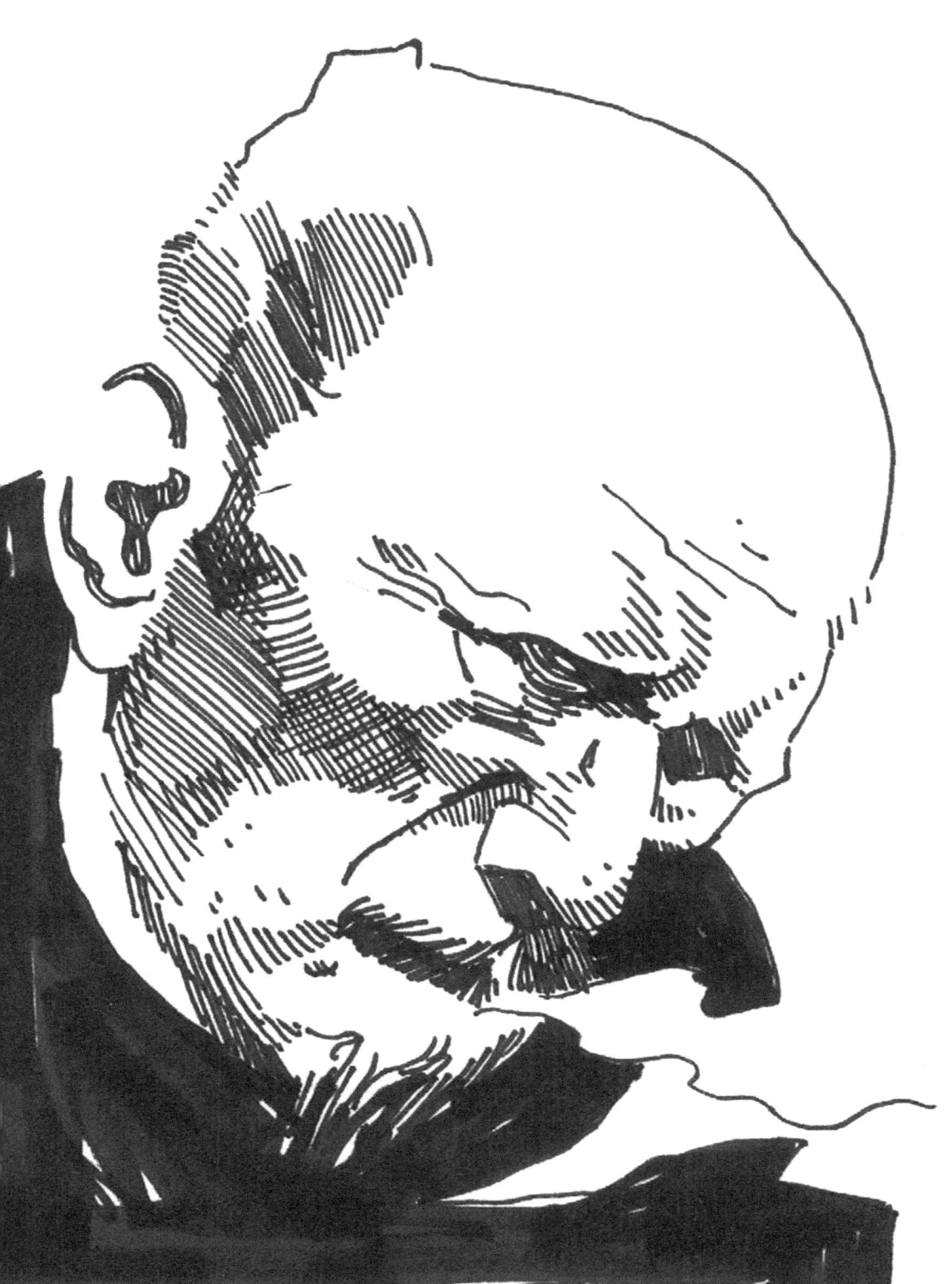

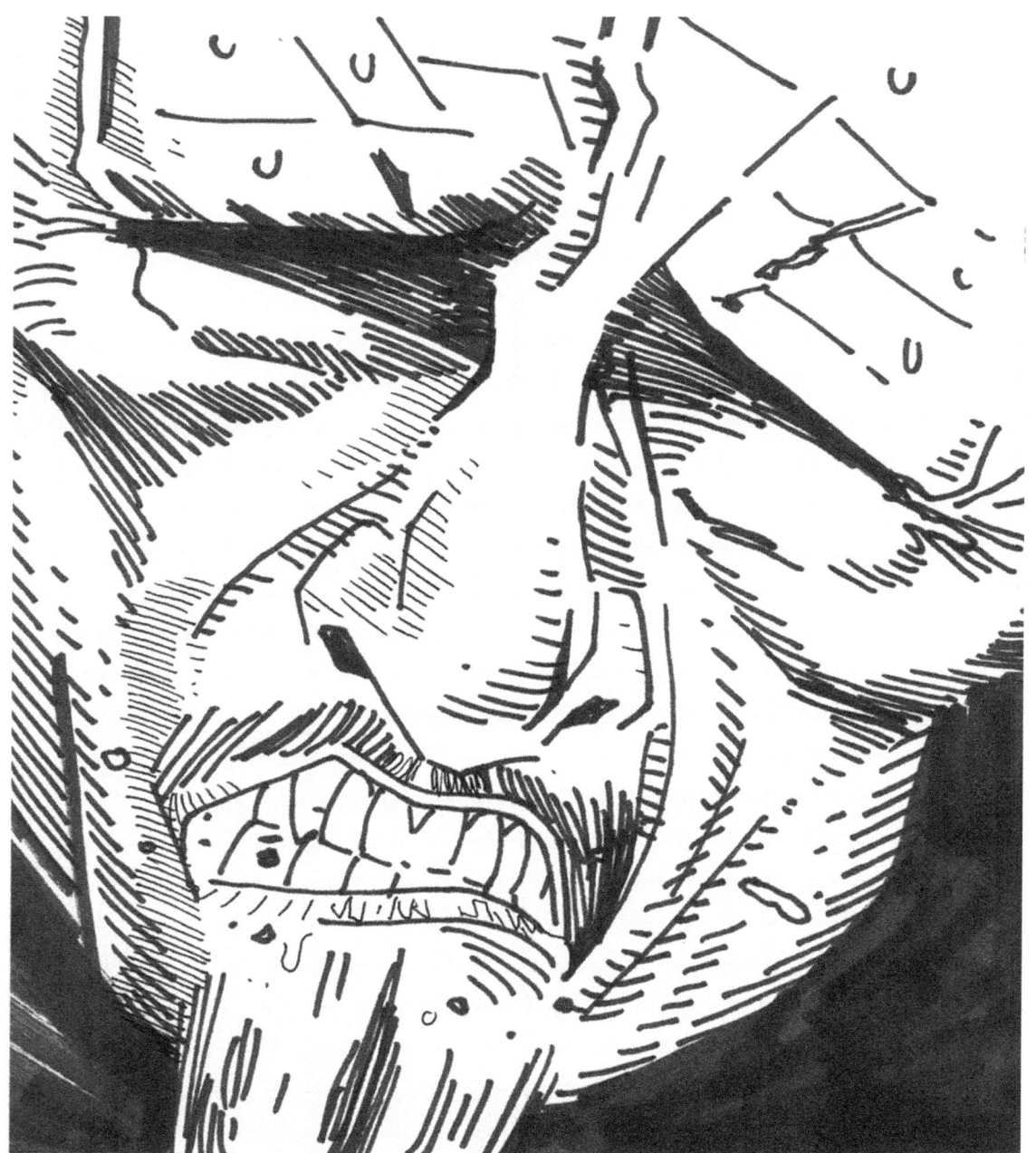

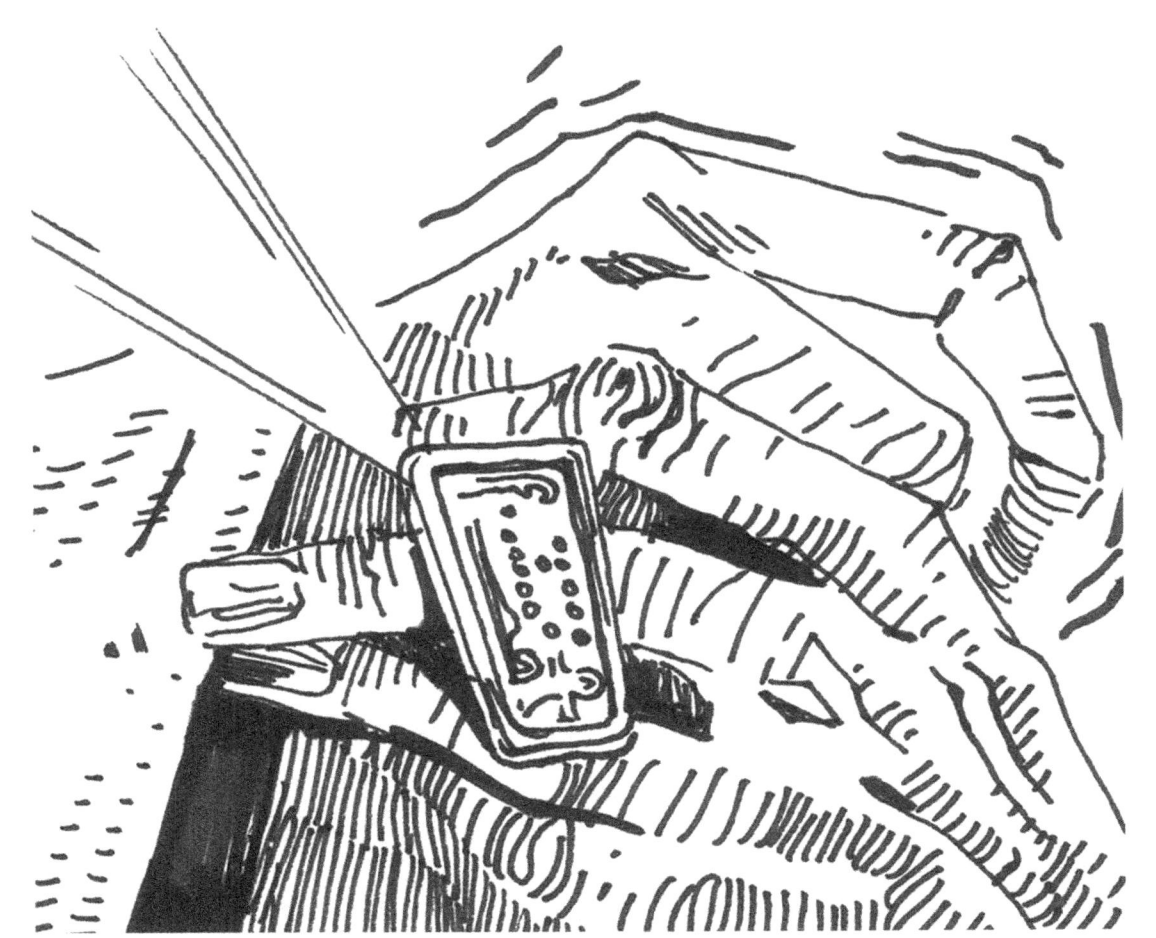

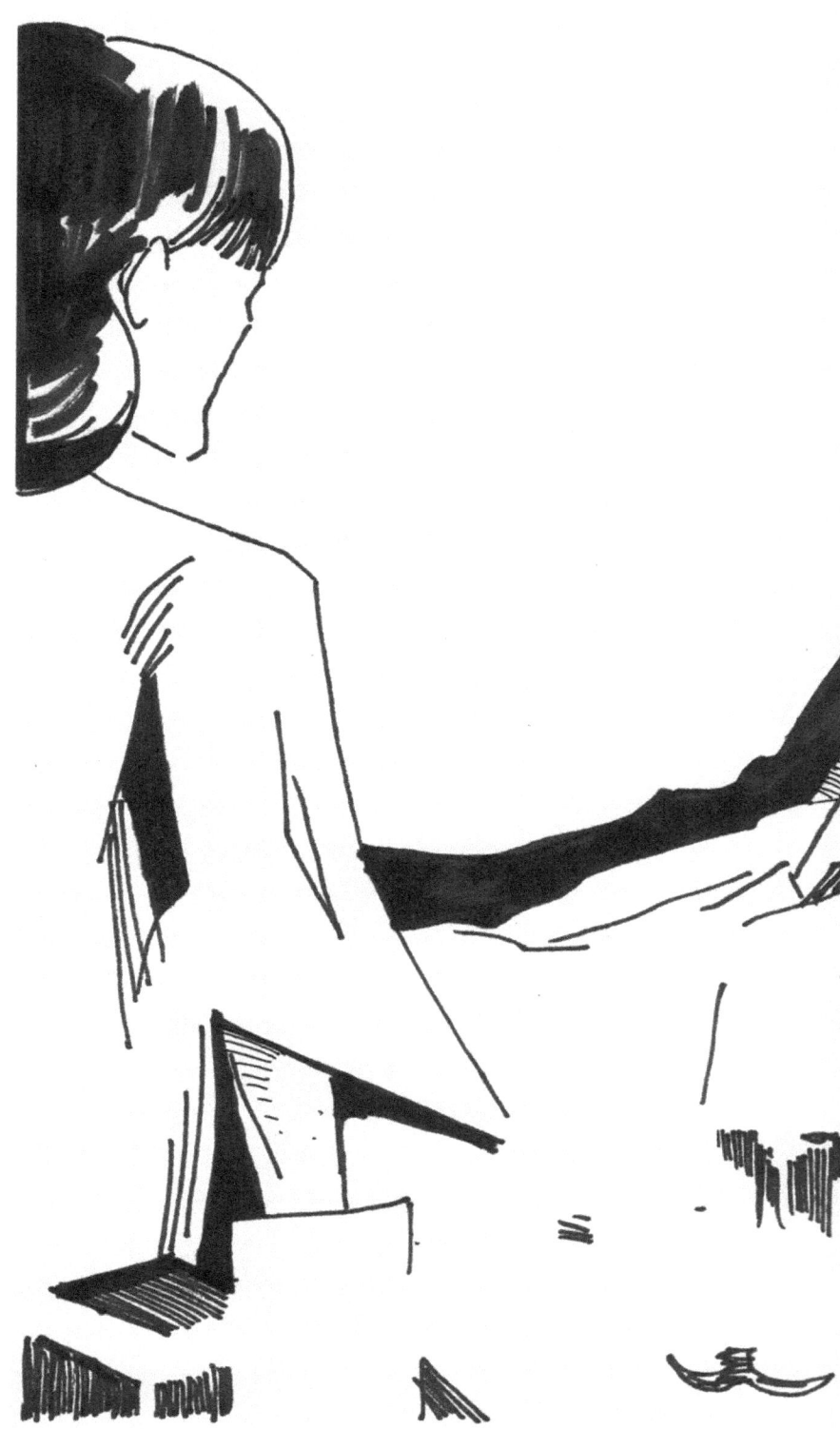

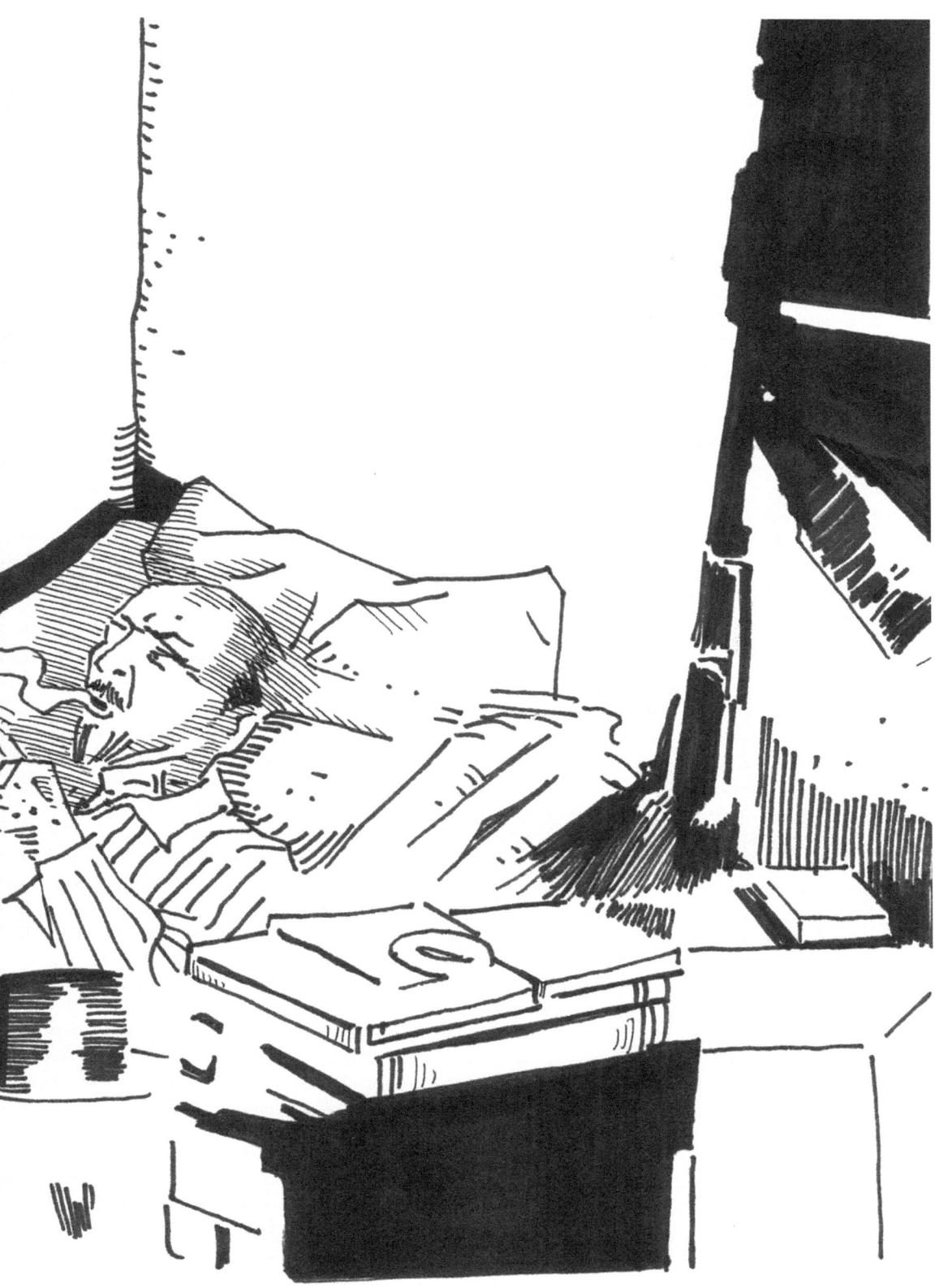

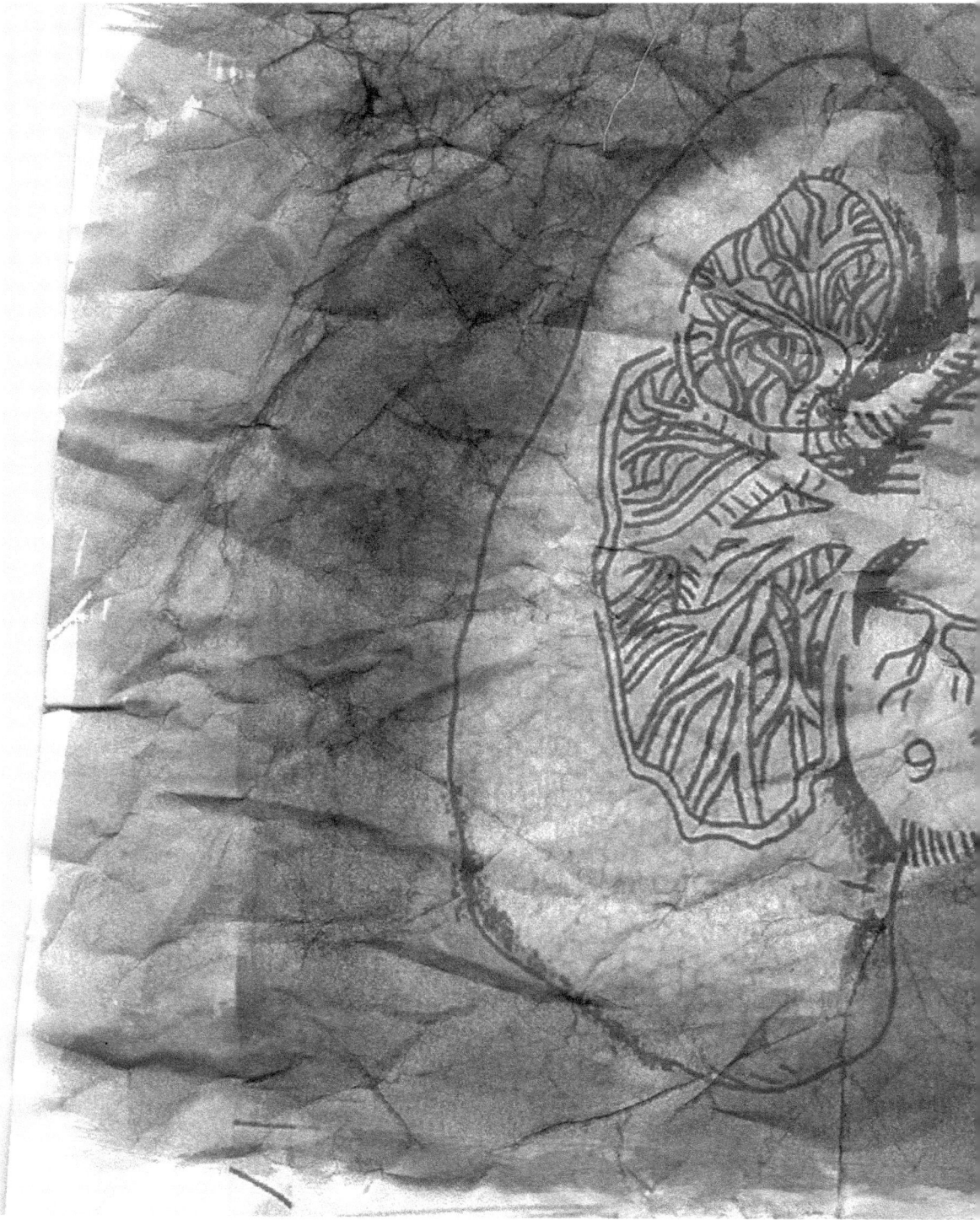

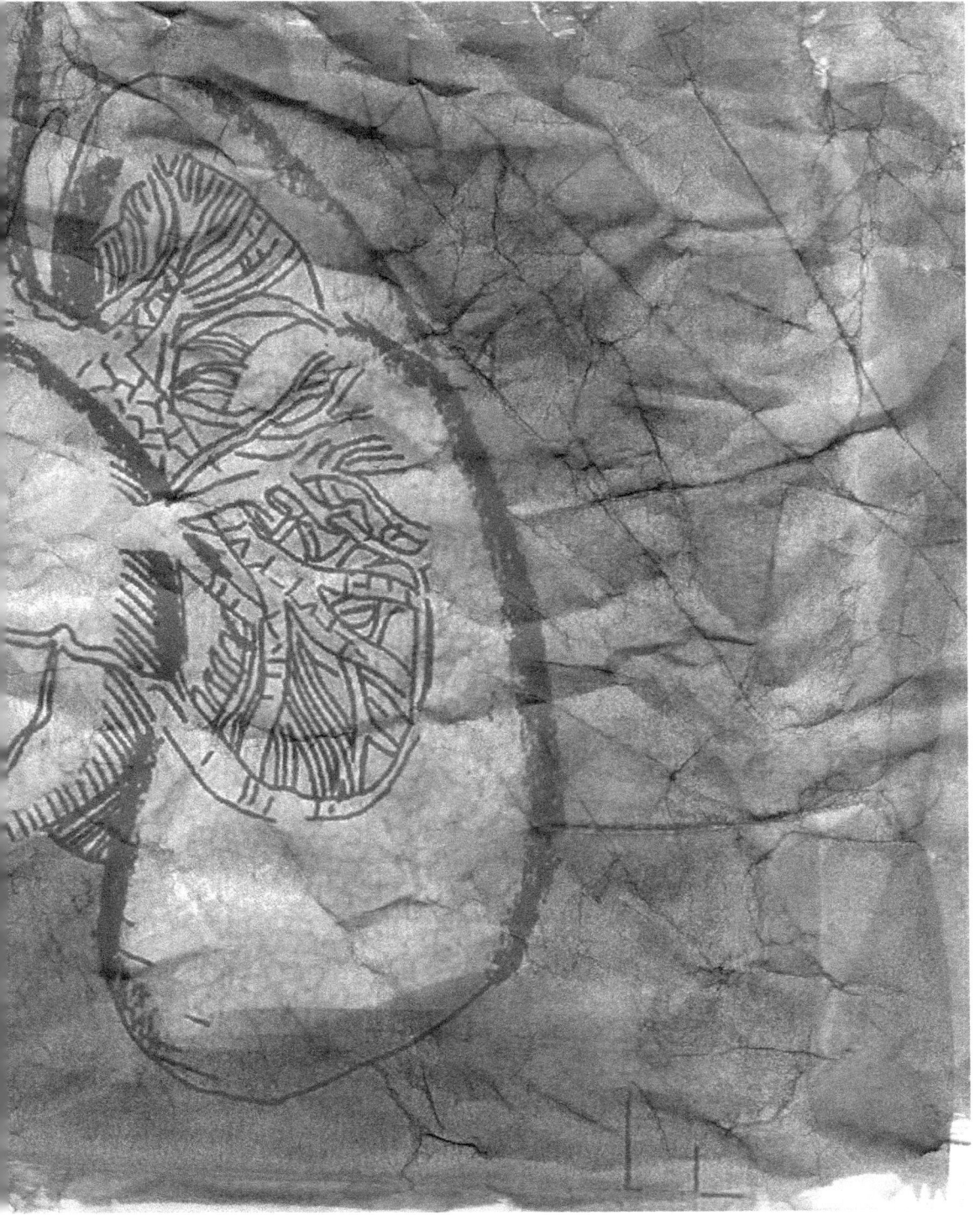

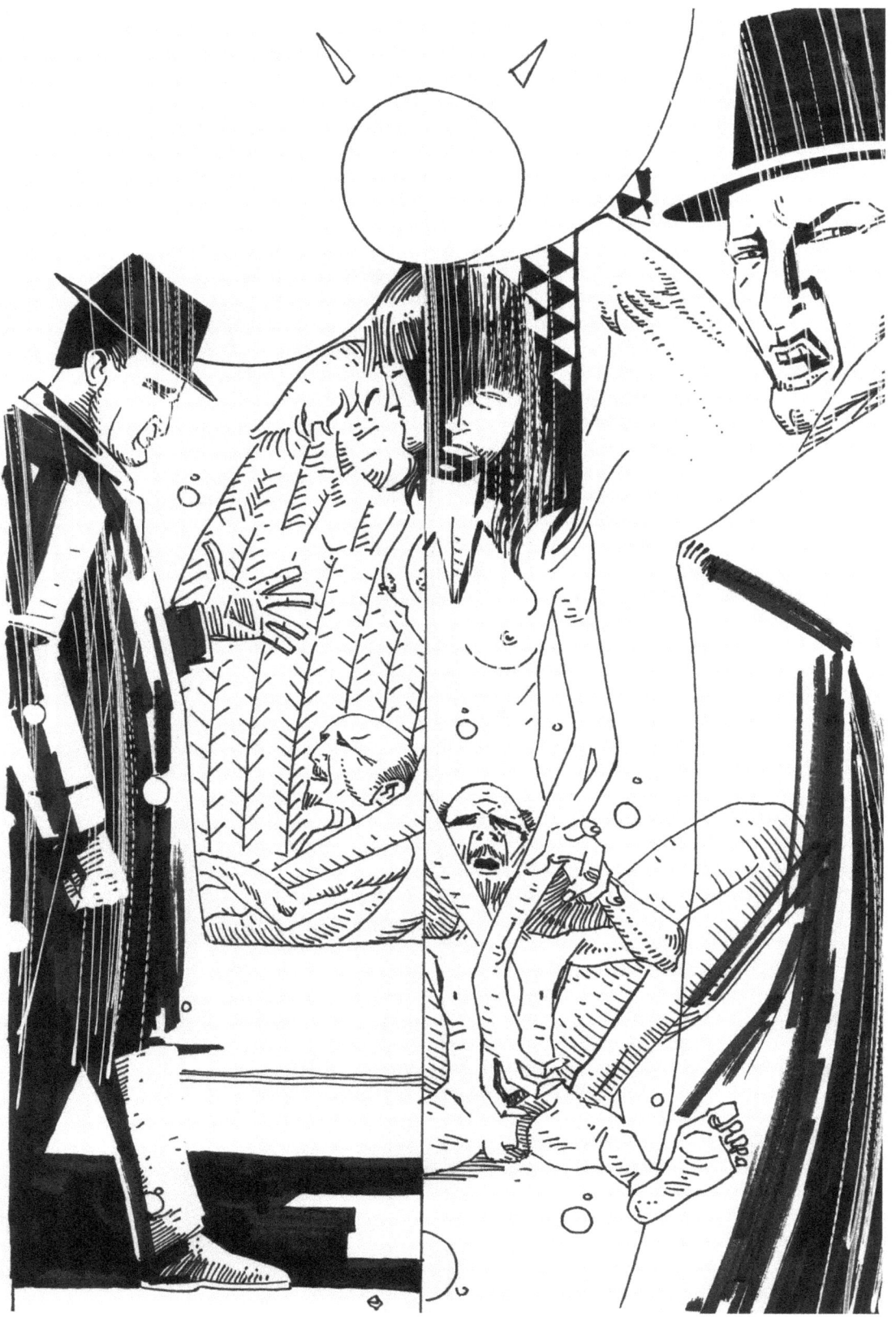

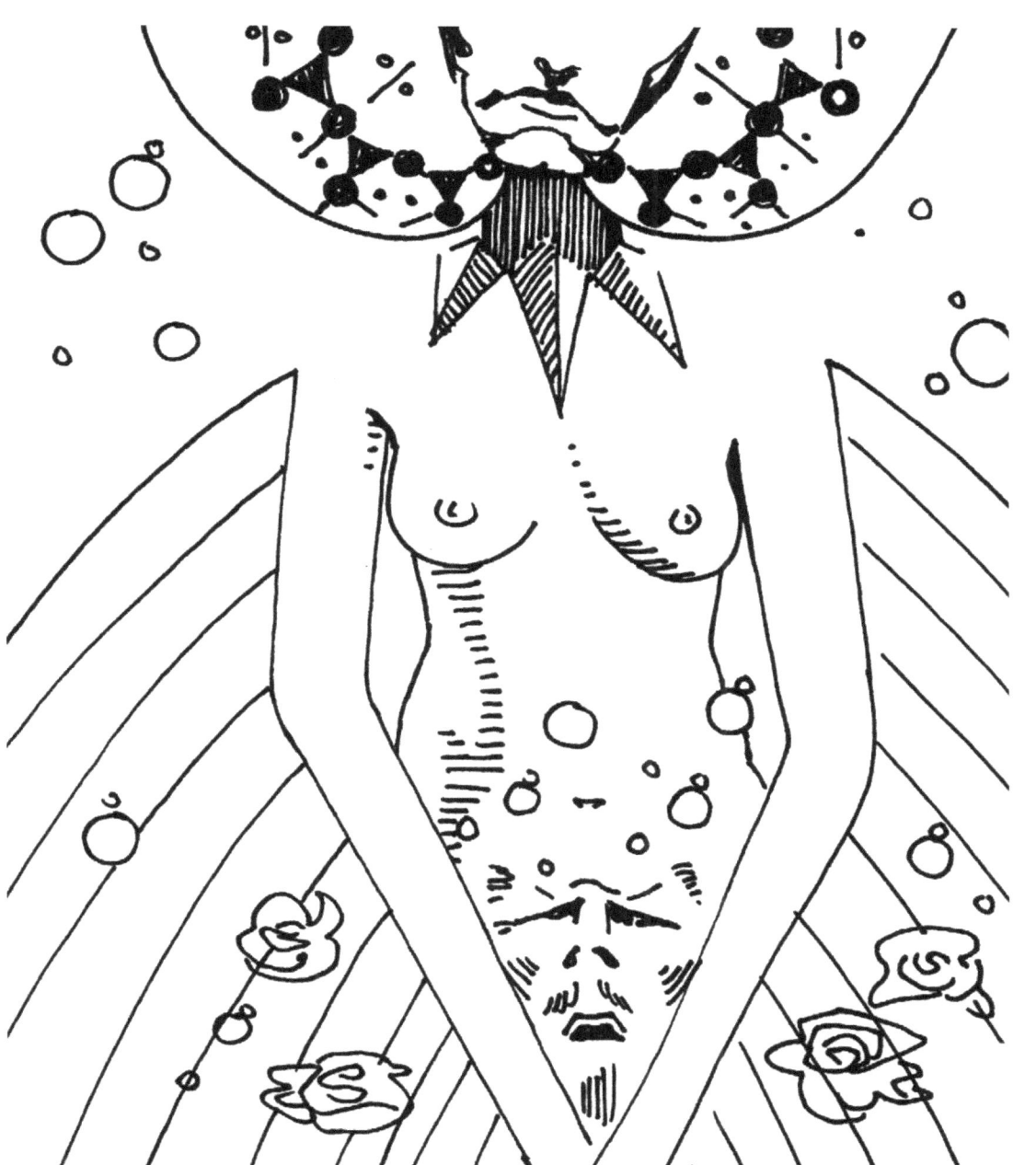

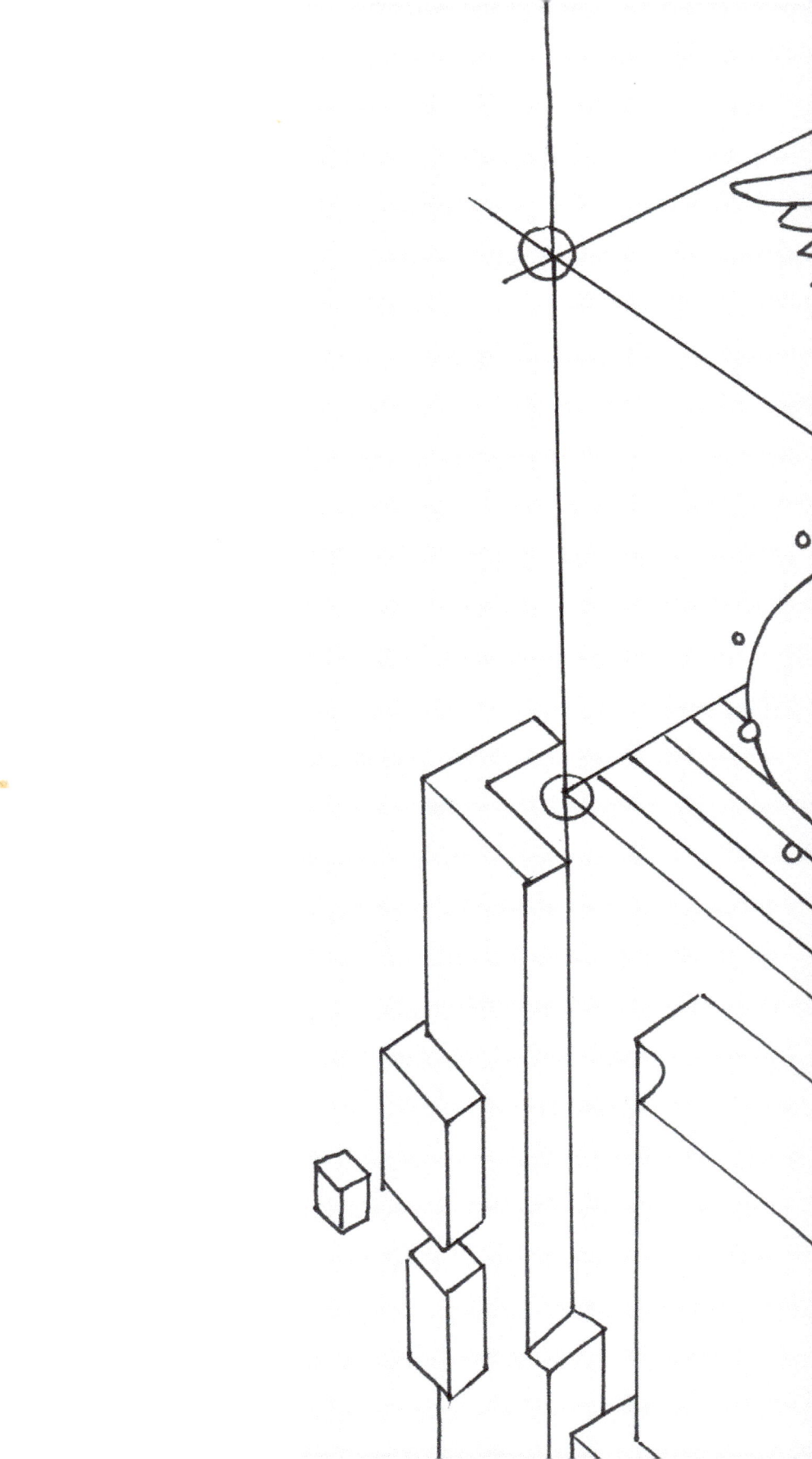

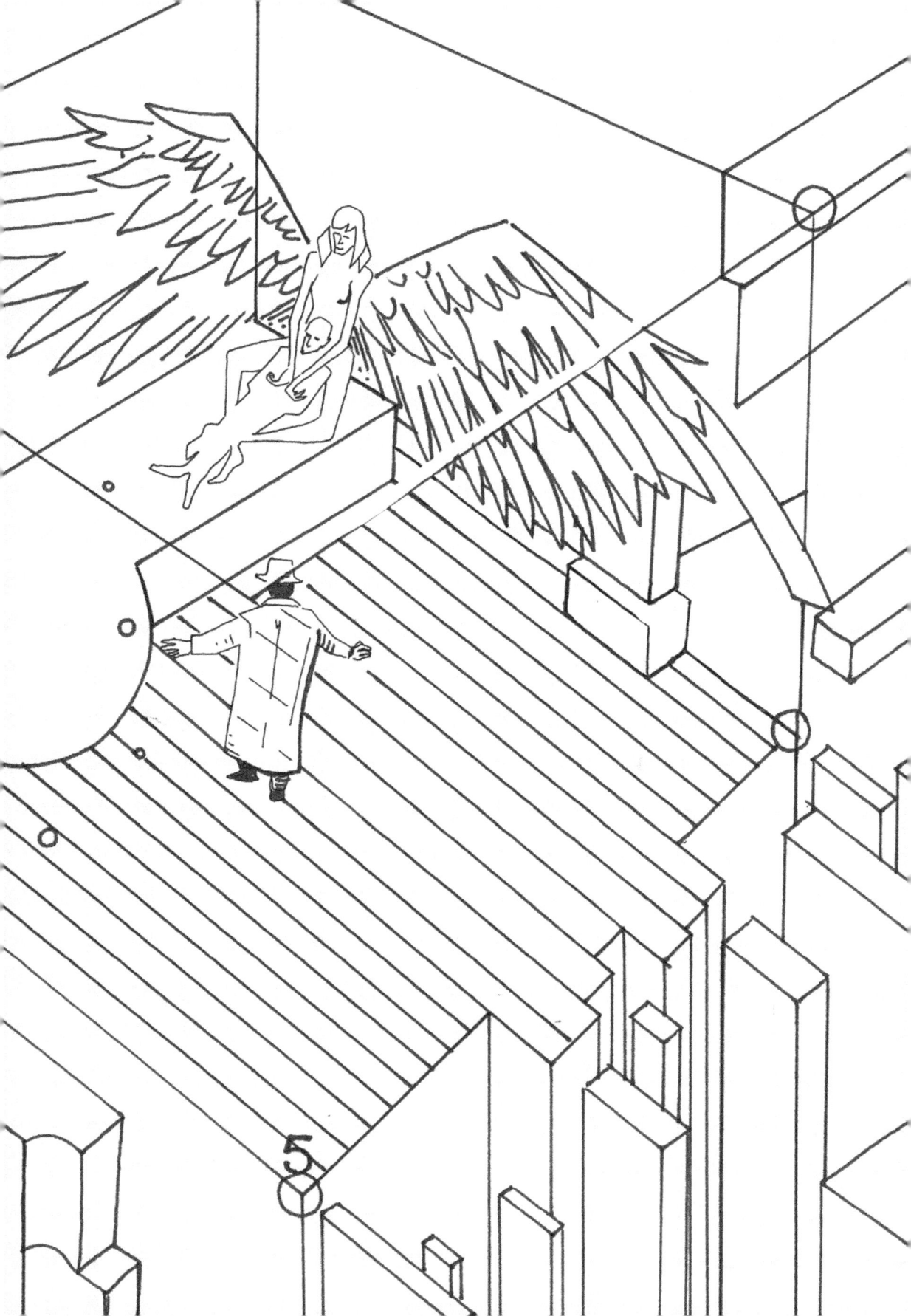

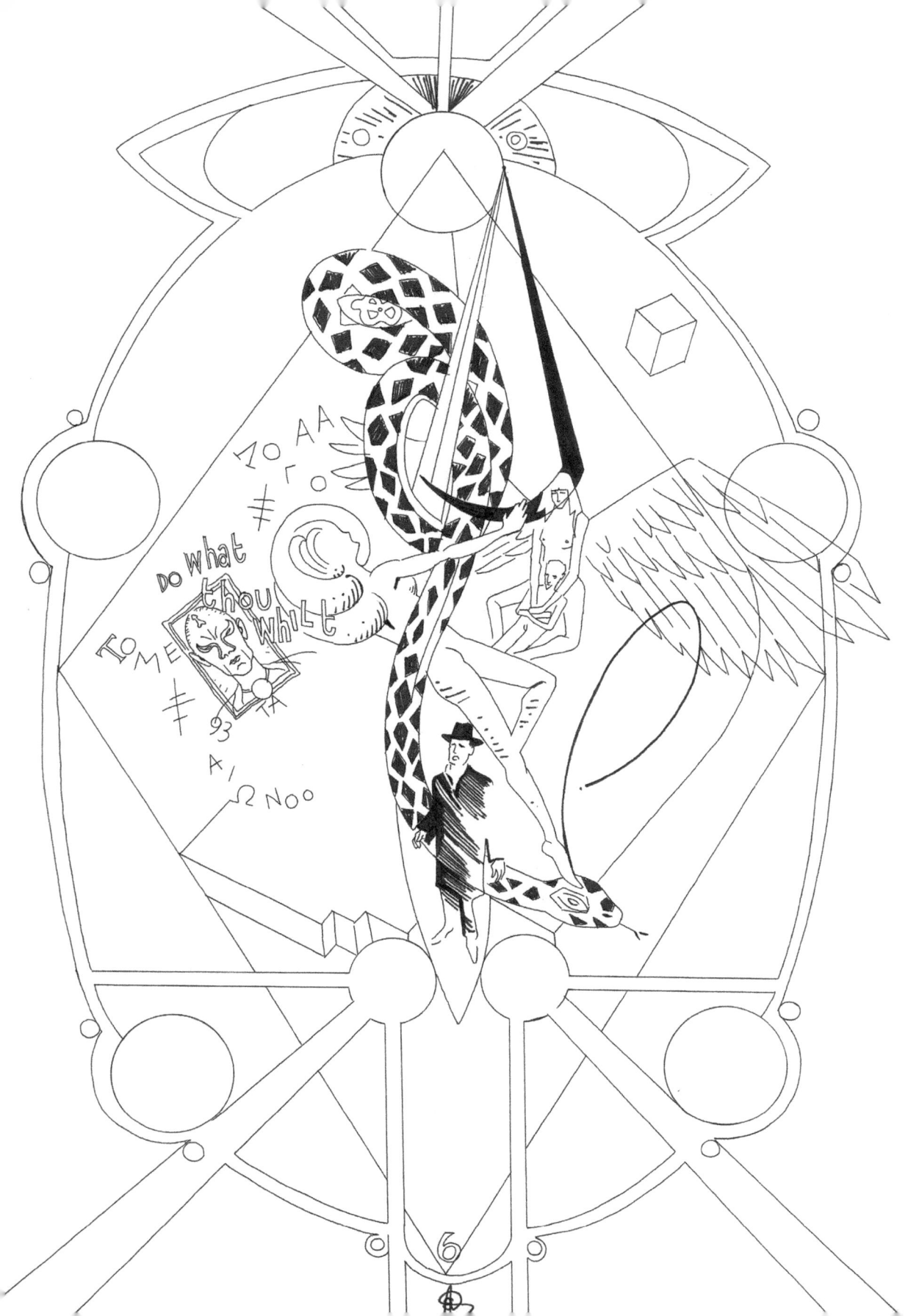

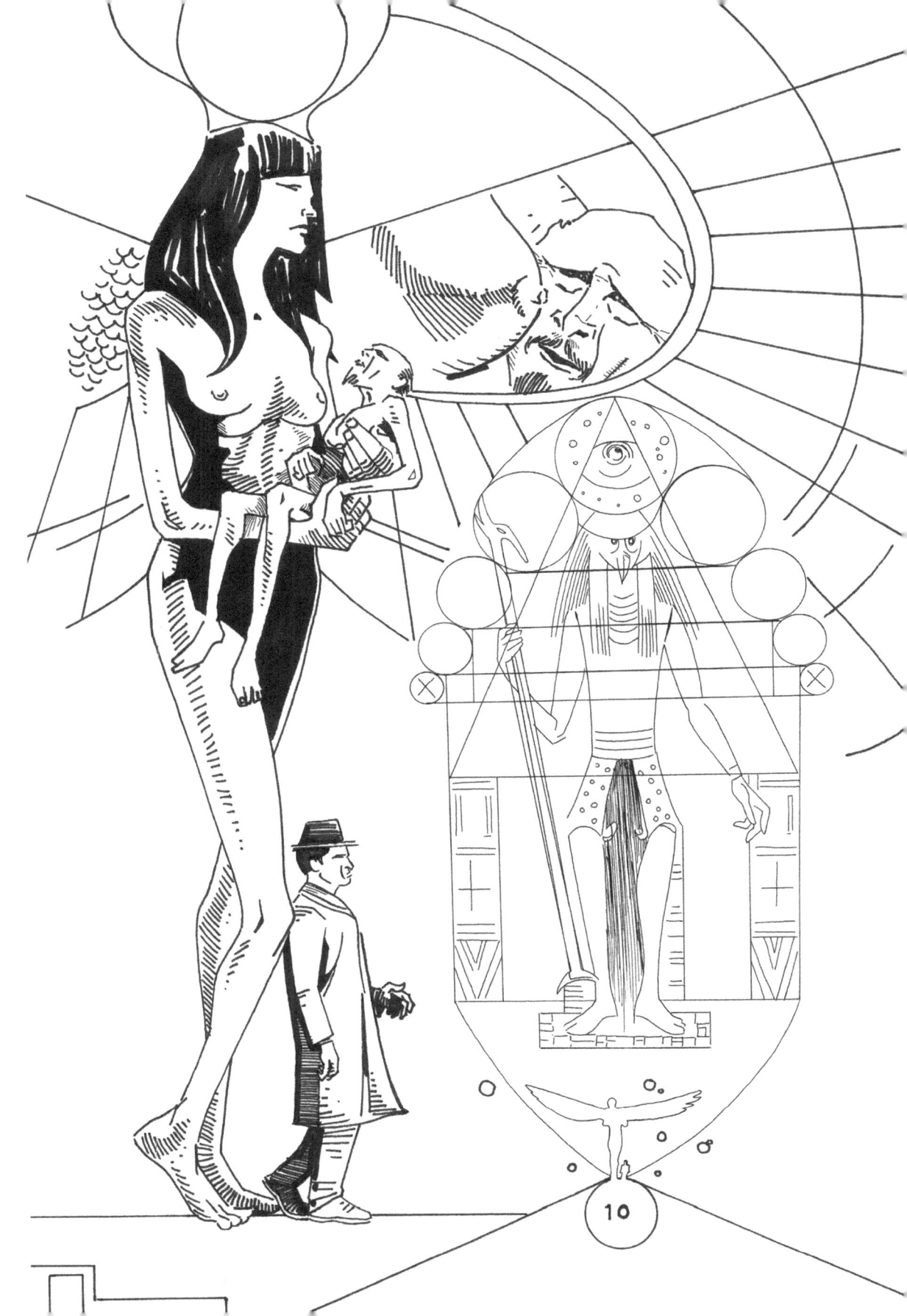

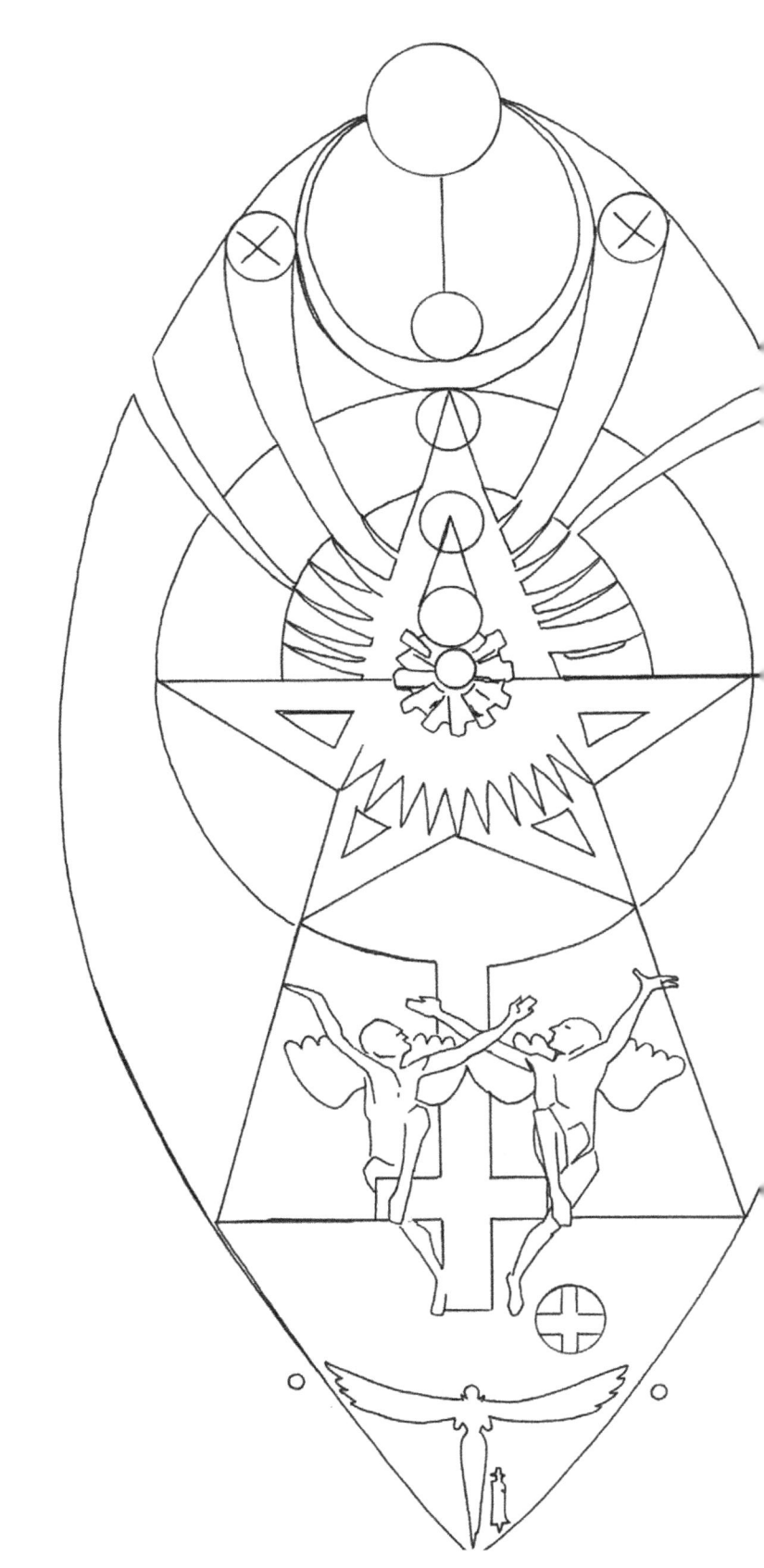

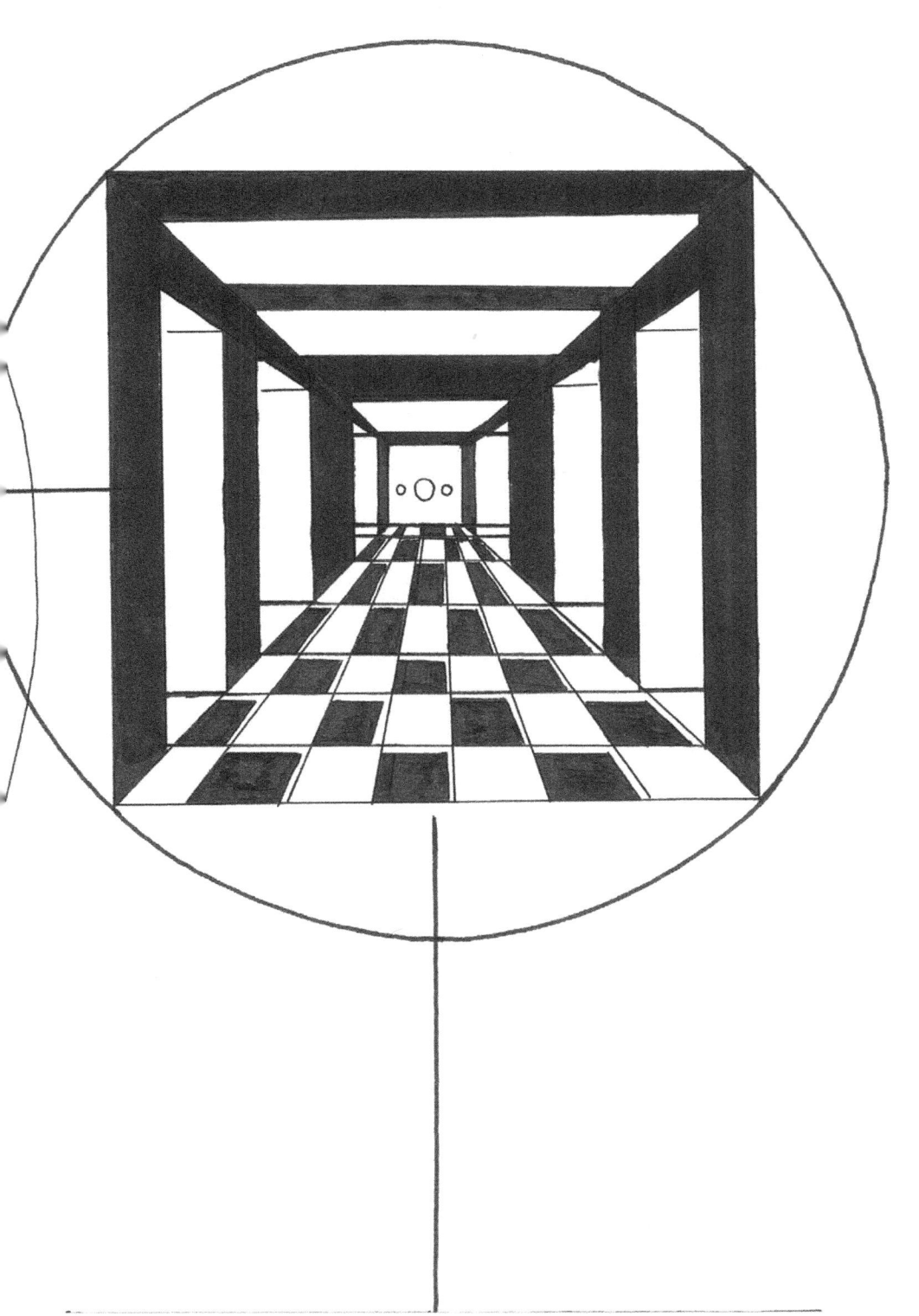

DO WHAT THOU WILT

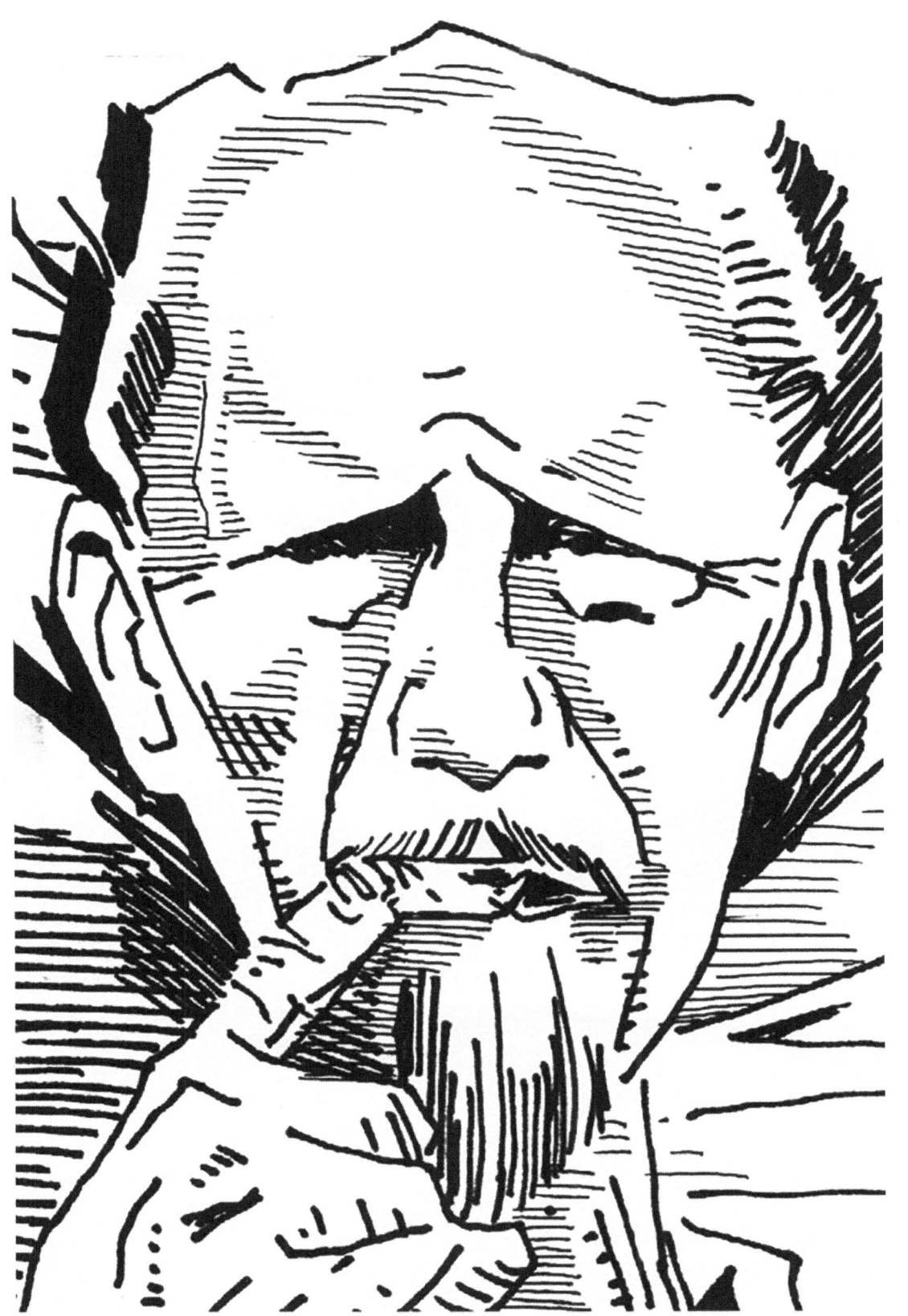

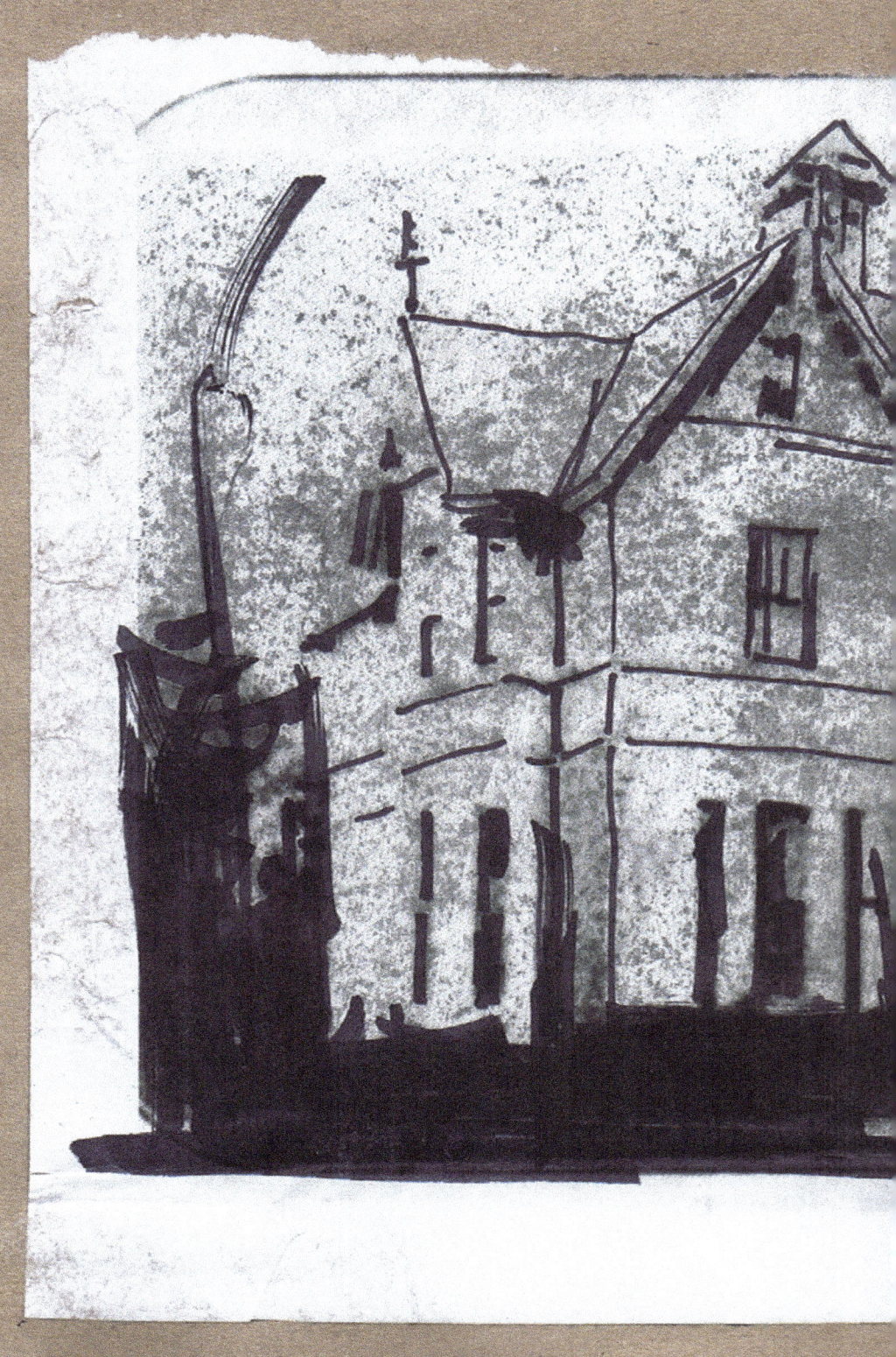

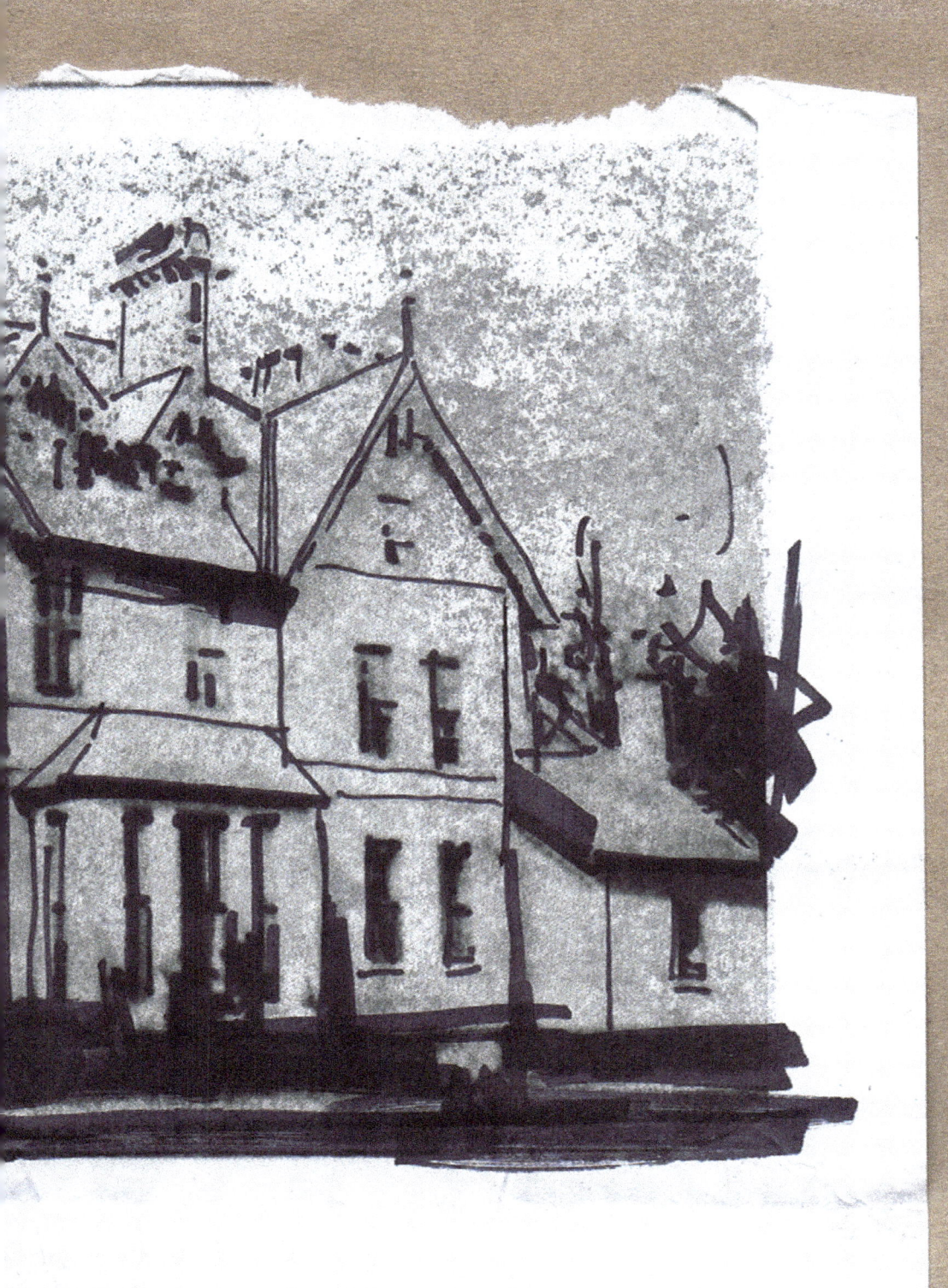

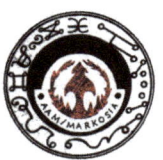